EXAMKRACKERS
1001 Questions
in
MCAT
Physics

OSOTE PUBLISHING

ISBN 1-893858-18-9

2003 Edition

To purchase additional copies of this book, call 1-888-572-2536 or fax orders to 1-201-797-1644.

examkrackers.com

osote.com

Printed and bound in the U.S.A.

Acknowledgements

Although I am the author, the hard work and expertise of many individuals contributed to this book. I would like to thank Dr. Scott Calvin for lending his exceptional science talent and pedagogic skills to this project. I would also like to thank the Examkrackers staff for their comments, suggestions, hard work and dedication to this project. Finally, I wish to thank my wife, Silvia, for her support during the difficult times in the past and those that lie ahead.

How to use this book

This book is specifically designed to improve knowledge and understanding of the physics concepts tested by the MCAT. Because the goal is to understand the physics, I intentionally left out MCAT passages that invariably offer clues that allow for solution of the problem without knowing the science. Although an important part of MCAT success is finding those clues, that part is not taught in this book. This book focuses specifically on understanding the physics. Understanding physics is the FIRST step toward MCAT success. Finding clues in the passage is the SECOND step. After teaching MCAT for 10 years to Columbia University students and others, it is my experience that even the very best students from the very best colleges and universities do not understand the physics concepts as well as they should for the MCAT.

In light of this, I suggest that you study from this book early in your preparation and follow up with MCAT tests from another source, preferably from the real AAMC materials.

1001 questions is likely to be far more than questions than you will attempt. Given that fact, I suggest that you do every 5th question or so, rather than trying to do all 1001 in a row. This way, you will have attempted many questions from all the subjects tested by the MCAT, and you will have questions left over if you need to study weak areas.

The physics taught in this book follows the physics subjects discussed in Examkrackers MCAT Physics. I suggest that you review your physics concepts from Examkrackers MCAT Physics as you use this book. In doing so, you will learn many ways to do the questions in this book much faster than the way you learned to solve them in your physics class. The MCAT is all about solving problems quickly.

Good Luck on your MCAT,

Jonathan Orsay

Table of Contents

Vectors, Scalars, and Triangles

Refer to the following vectors to answer questions 1-9. Assume that they are NOT perpendicular to each other; the angle between them is obtuse (greater than 90°).

1. Which of the following represents the vector sum of vector Q and vector R?

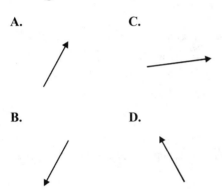

2. The negative of vector R is:

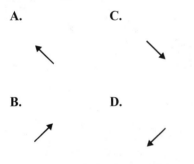

3. Which of the following represents the vector difference $R - Q$:

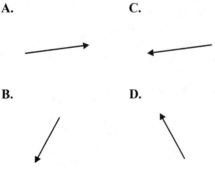

4. If vector R represents the net force F in newtons required to accelerate a 2 kg mass 2 m/s², which of the following vectors represents the force required to accelerate the same 2 kg mass at 1 m/s² in the same direction? (Note: $F = ma$)

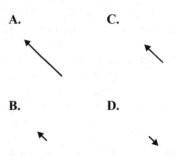

5. All of the following are component vectors for vector Q and obey the Pythagorean theorem EXCEPT:

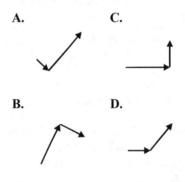

6. Which of the following could not be a pair of component vectors for vector Q?

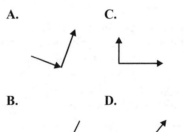

7. Which of the following is true if the product of vectors Q and R is a vector?

   A. The vector product will point in the direction of Q and have a magnitude proportional to the cosine of the angle between Q and R.
   B. The vector product will point in the direction of Q and have a magnitude proportional to the sine of the angle between Q and R.
   C. The vector product will point in a direction perpendicular to both Q and R, and have a magnitude proportional to the cosine of the angle between Q and R.
   D. The vector product will point in a direction perpendicular to both Q and R, and have a magnitude proportional to the sine of the angle between Q and R.

8. Which of the following is true if the product of vectors Q and R is a scalar?

   A. The vector product will have a magnitude proportional to the cosine of the angle between Q and R.
   B. The vector product will have a magnitude proportional to the sine of the angle between Q and R.
   C. The vector product will have a magnitude equal to the product of the magnitudes of Q and R.
   D. This can't happen. The product of two vectors is always a vector.

9. If Q and R were perpendicular, the length of the sum of vectors Q and R would be:

   A. equal to the sum of the magnitudes of Q and R.
   B. greater than the sum of the magnitudes of Q and R.
   C. equal to the sum of the squares of the magnitudes of Q and R.
   D. equal to the square root of the sum of the squares of the magnitudes of Q and R.

_____

Questions 10-16 refer to the triangle shown below:

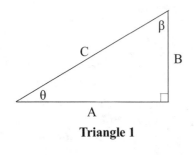

Triangle 1

10. If, in Triangle 1, side A has a length of 16 cm and side C has a length of 20 cm, what is the length of side B?

    A. 9 cm
    B. 10 cm
    C. 12 cm
    D. 16 cm

11. If, in Triangle 1, side B has a length of 3 m, and angle θ is 30°, what is the length of side C?

    A. 4 m
    B. 5 m
    C. 6 m
    D. 9 m

12. If, in Triangle 1, side A is 17 cm and side B is 10 cm, what is the approximate measure of the angle β?

    A. 30°
    B. 45°
    C. 60°
    D. 90°

13. Which of the following represents the length of side A in Triangle 1?

    A. $C\sin\theta$
    B. $C\cos\theta$
    C. $B\sin\theta$
    D. $B\cos\theta$

14. The length of side C is:

    A. $\sqrt{B^2 + C^2}$
    B. $\sqrt{A^2 + B^2}$
    C. $A^2 + C^2$
    D. $A^2 + B^2$

15. If angle θ is 30°, and side C is 25 meters, then:

    A. side A must be 5 meters.
    B. side A must be 12.5 meters.
    C. side B must be 5 meters.
    D. side B must be 12.5 meters.

16. If side C is twice as long as side B, angle θ must be:

    A. 30°
    B. 45°
    C. 60°
    D. 90°

_____

Distance-Displacement, Speed-Velocity, Acceleration

Questions 17-27 refer to the three paths between position 1 and position 2 shown in the diagram below. Path C is a half circle.

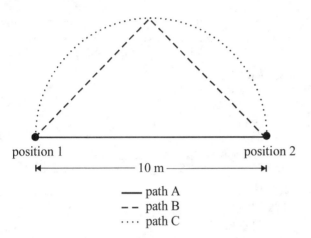

position 1   position 2
|←————————— 10 m —————————→|

—— path A
– – path B
···· path C

17. Which path would result in the greatest displacement for a particle moving from position 1 to position 2?

    A. path A
    B. path B
    C. path C
    D. All paths would result in the same displacement.

18. Three particles move from position 1 to position 2 along separate paths. All three particles require the same amount of time to complete the trip. Which of the following is the same for all three particles?

    A. average speed
    B. average horizontal velocity
    C. instantaneous acceleration
    D. distance traveled.

19. A particle moves from position 1 to position 2 and back in 2 seconds. Its average velocity during the trip is:

    A. 0 m/s
    B. 5 m/s
    C. 10 m/s
    D. 20 m/s

20. If a particle leaves position 1 and moves along path C at a constant speed of 1 m/s, how long will it take to reach position 2?

    A. 5 s
    B. 10 s
    C. 2π s
    D. 5π s

21. A particle moves from position 1 to position 2 traveling along path B. The total trip requires 5 s. Its average vertical velocity during the trip is approximately?

    A. 0 m/s
    B. 2 m/s
    C. 2.8 m/s
    D. 10 m/s

22. A particle moving from position 1 to position 2 moves along path C. It travels at a constant speed of 5π m/s. At exactly half way through the trip its average vertical velocity is:

    A. 0 m/s
    B. 0.5 m/s
    C. 1 m/s
    D. 10 m/s

23. A particle starts at rest and leaves position 1 along path A. It increases its speed at a constant rate. After 2 seconds, it reaches position 2 traveling at 10 m/s. What is the acceleration of the particle during the trip?

    A. 0 m/s^2
    B. 1 m/s^2
    C. 5 m/s^2
    D. 10 m/s^2

24. A particle starts at rest and leaves position 1 along path A. It increases its speed at a constant rate. After 2 seconds, it reaches position 2 traveling at 10 m/s. What is the average horizontal velocity of the particle during the trip?

    A. 1 m/s
    B. 5 m/s
    C. 10 m/s
    D. 20 m/s

25. A particle starts at rest and leaves position 1 along path C. It increases its speed at a constant rate. After 2 seconds, it reaches position 2 traveling at 10 m/s. What is the average velocity of the particle during the trip?

    A. 5 m/s
    B. 2.5π m/s
    C. 10 m/s
    D. 20 m/s

26. A particle moves along path C at a constant speed of 1 m/s. What is the average acceleration of the particle as it moves from position 1 to position 2?

    A. 0 m/s^2
    B. $0.2/\pi$ m/s^2
    C. $0.4/\pi$ m/s^2
    D. 1 m/s^2

27. A particle moves along path C at a constant speed of 1 m/s. What is the magnitude of the average velocity of the particle as it moves from position 1 to position 2?

    A. 0 m/s
    B. $2/\pi$ m/s
    C. $4/\pi$ m/s
    D. 1 m/s

28. Can an object accelerate and have a constant speed at the same time?

    A. No, because acceleration is the rate of change of the speed of an object.
    B. No, because acceleration is a vector and speed is a scalar.
    C. Yes, because a change in direction will result in a change in velocity and may or may not result in a change in speed.
    D. Yes, because the average speed might remain constant over time.

29. All of the following are true statements concerning a particle in motion EXCEPT:

    A. The average velocity must be greater than or equal to the minimum velocity and less than or equal to the maximum velocity.
    B. An object may change its direction of motion without accelerating.
    C. An object may change its velocity without changing its speed.
    D. The distance traveled by an object is always greater than or equal to its displacement.

Uniformly Accelerated Motion and Linear Motion

30. To which of the following situations can the linear motion equations NOT be applied to solve for displacement, velocity, acceleration, and time?

    A. A race car accelerates constantly on a straight track from 0 to 60 mph in 5 seconds.
    B. A cannon ball is fired from a cannon at an angle of $12°$ and an initial velocity of 100 m/s.
    C. Starting from rest, a family travels in their car in a straight line from St. Louis to Chicago (363 miles) in 5½ hours making several stops along the way.
    D. A rock is dropped from a height of 10 m.

31. A constantly accelerating particle increases its velocity from 10 m/s to 20 m/s in 1 s. What is its average velocity during this time?

    A. 10 m/s
    B. 15 m/s
    C. 20 m/s
    D. 30 m/s

32. A constantly accelerating particle increases its velocity from 10 m/s to 20 m/s in 1 s. What is its acceleration during this time?

    A. 5 m/s^2
    B. 10 m/s^2
    C. 15 m/s^2
    D. 20 m/s^2

33. A particle accelerates at 10 m/s^2 for 2 seconds. If its initial velocity was 5 m/s, what is its final velocity?

    A. 15 m/s
    B. 20 m/s
    C. 25 m/s
    D. 50 m/s

34. A particle accelerates at 10 m/s^2 for 2 seconds. If its final velocity is 5 m/s, what was its initial velocity?

    A. -25 m/s
    B. -15 m/s
    C. 25 m/s
    D. 50 m/s

35. A particle accelerates for 2 seconds. If its final velocity is 5 m/s, and its initial velocity was 15 m/s, what was its acceleration?

    A. -2.5 m/s^2
    B. -5 m/s^2
    C. -10 m/s^2
    D. -15 m/s^2

36. A particle starts from rest and accelerates for 4 seconds at 10 m/s^2. What is its final velocity?

    A. 16 m/s
    B. 20 m/s
    C. 30 m/s
    D. 40 m/s

37. A particle starts from rest and accelerates for 4 seconds at 10 m/s^2. What is its displacement from its initial position?

    A. 16 m
    B. 40 m
    C. 80 m
    D. 120 m

38. A particle starts from rest and accelerates at 10 m/s^2. How long does it take for the particle to travel 45 m?

    A. 2 s
    B. 3 s
    C. 4.5 s
    D. 45 s

39. A particle starts from rest and accelerates at 10 m/s^2. How long does it take for the particle to reach a velocity of 45 m/s?

    A. 2 s
    B. 3 s
    C. 4.5 s
    D. 45 s

40. A constantly accelerating particle reaches a velocity of 100 m/s. If its average velocity is 75 m/s, what was its initial velocity?

    A. 0 m/s
    B. 25 m/s
    C. 50 m/s
    D. 75 m/s

41. A constantly accelerating particle starts from rest and travels 50 m. If it reaches a velocity of 100 m/s, how long did the 50 m trip take?

    A. 0.5 s
    B. 1.0 s
    C. 2.0 s
    D. 3.0 s

42. A constantly accelerating particle starts from rest and travels for 4 s. If it reaches a velocity of 100 m/s, how far did the particle travel?

    A. 25 m
    B. 50 m
    C. 100 m
    D. 200 m

43. A constantly accelerating particle travels for 4 s. If it travels 240 m and reaches a velocity of 100 m/s, what was its initial velocity?

    A. 0 m/s
    B. 20 m/s
    C. 25 m/s
    D. 60 m/s

44. A constantly accelerating particle travels for 3 s. If its initial velocity is 10 m/s and it travels 75 m, what is its final velocity?

    A. 20 m/s
    B. 25 m/s
    C. 30 m/s
    D. 40 m/s

45. A constantly accelerating particle travels for 3 s. If its initial velocity is 10 m/s and it travels 75 m, what is its acceleration?

    A. 5 m/s^2
    B. 10 m/s^2
    C. 16.67 m/s^2
    D. 25 m/s^2

46. A particle travels 3.5 m. If its initial velocity is 9 m/s and its final velocity is 16 m/s, what is its acceleration?

    A. 1 m/s^2
    B. 2 m/s^2
    C. 7 m/s^2
    D. 25 m/s^2

47. A particle initially traveling at 30 m/s slows to a stop in just 3 seconds at a constant acceleration. How far does the particle travel?

    A. 10 m
    B. 30 m
    C. 45 m
    D. 80 m

48. A particle initially traveling at 40 m/s slows to 10 m/s in just 3 seconds at a constant acceleration. How far does the particle travel?

    A. 25 m
    B. 30 m
    C. 75 m
    D. 90 m

49. A particle with an initial velocity of 50 m/s slows at a constant acceleration to 20 m/s over a distance of 105 m. How long does it take for the particle to slow down?

    A. 2 s
    B. 3 s
    C. 4 s
    D. 5 s

50. A particle starts from rest and travels in a straight line for 4 s. If the particle is accelerating at a constant rate, which of the following could be the distances traveled by the particle during each consecutive second?

    A. 10 m, 20 m, 30 m, 40 m
    B. 5 m, 15 m, 25 m, 35 m
    C. 5 m, 25 m, 125 m, 625 m
    D. 2 m, 4 m, 8 m, 16 m

51. A particle starts from rest and travels in a straight line for 4 s. If the particle is accelerating at a constant rate, which of the following could be the total distance traveled by the particle at the end of each consecutive second?

    A. 10 m, 20 m, 30 m, 40 m
    B. 5 m, 15 m, 25 m, 35 m
    C. 5 m, 20 m, 45 m, 80 m
    D. 2 m, 4 m, 8 m, 16 m

52. A particle initially traveling at 40 m/s slows to 10 m/s over a distance of 75 m. If the acceleration is constant, what is the average speed of the particle?

    A. 25 m/s
    B. 30 m/s
    C. 50 m/s
    D. 90 m/s

53. How much time is required for a particle to slow from 50 m/s to 20 m/s over a distance of 70 m if the acceleration is constant?

    A. 1 s
    B. 2 s
    C. 2.3 s
    D. 3 s

54. A particle moving at 5 m/s reverses its direction in 1 s to move at 5 m/s in the opposite direction. If its acceleration is constant, what is the magnitude of its acceleration?

    A. 2.5 m/s^2
    B. 5 m/s^2
    C. 10 m/s^2
    D. 20 m/s^2

55. A particle moving at 5 m/s reverses its direction in 1 s to move at 5 m/s in the opposite direction. If its acceleration is constant, what is its displacement from its original position at 1 s?

    A. 0 m
    B. 1.25 m
    C. 2.5 m
    D. 5 m

56. A particle moving at 5 m/s reverses its direction in 1 s to move at 5 m/s in the opposite direction. If its acceleration is constant, what distance does it travel?

    A. 1.25 m
    B. 2.5 m
    C. 5 m
    D. 10 m

57. A particle moving at 5 m/s reverses its direction in 1 s to move at 5 m/s in the opposite direction. If its acceleration is constant, what is its speed at 0.5 s?

    A. 0 m/s
    B. 1.25 m/s
    C. 2.5 m/s
    D. 5 m/s

58. A particle moving at 5 m/s reverses its direction in 1 s to move at 5 m/s in the opposite direction. If its acceleration is constant, what is its displacement at 0.5 seconds?

    A. 0 m
    B. 1.25 m
    C. 2.5 m
    D. 5 m

59. A particle moving at 10 m/s reverses its direction to move at 10 m/s in the opposite direction. If its acceleration is −10 m/s^2, what is the total distance that it travels?

    A. 0 m
    B. 5 m
    C. 10 m
    D. 20 m

60. A particle moving at 10 m/s reverses its direction to move at 10 m/s in the opposite direction. If its acceleration is −10 m/s^2, what is the time required?

    A. 1 s
    B. 2 s
    C. 3 s
    D. 4 s

61. A particle moving at 10 m/s reverses its direction to move at 20 m/s in the opposite direction. If its acceleration is −10 m/s^2, what is the total distance that it travels?

    A. 15 m
    B. 20 m
    C. 25 m
    D. 30 m

62. A particle moving at 10 m/s reverses its direction to move at 20 m/s in the opposite direction. If its acceleration is -10 m/s^2, what is its displacement from its original position?

   A. 10 m
   B. 15 m
   C. 20 m
   D. 30 m

63. A particle moving at 10 m/s reverses its direction to move at 20 m/s in the opposite direction. If its acceleration is -10 m/s^2, what is the time required?

   A. 1 s
   B. 2 s
   C. 3 s
   D. 4 s

Graphs of Linear Motion

Questions 64 through 75 refer to the graphs shown below.

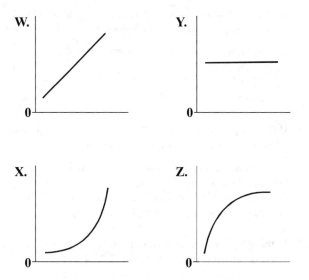

64. If the graphs shown are displacement versus time graphs, which of the graphs could represent a particle with zero acceleration?

   A. W only
   B. Y only
   C. W and Y only
   D. X and Z only

65. If the graphs shown are displacement versus time graphs, which of the graphs could represent a particle with constant non-zero acceleration?

   A. X only
   B. Z only
   C. X and Z only
   D. W, X and Z only

66. If the graphs shown are displacement versus time graphs, the slope of the curve represents:

   A. distance
   B. displacement
   C. velocity
   D. acceleration

67. If the graphs shown are displacement versus time graphs, the area under the curve represents:

   A. displacement
   B. velocity
   C. acceleration
   D. none of these

68. If the graphs shown are displacement versus time graphs, which graph represents a particle with positive acceleration?

   A. W only
   B. X only
   C. Z only
   D. W and X only

69. If the graphs shown are displacement versus time graphs, which graph represents a particle with positive velocity?

   A. W only
   B. X and Z only
   C. W, X, and Z only
   D. all graphs

70. If the graphs shown are velocity versus time graphs, which graph could represent a particle with positive velocity?

   A. W only
   B. X only
   C. W, X and Z only
   D. All graphs

71. If the graphs shown are velocity versus time graphs, the slope of the graphs represents:

   A. distance
   B. displacement
   C. velocity
   D. acceleration

72. The total area between the curve and the zero time axis on any velocity versus time graph represents:

   A. distance
   B. displacement
   C. velocity
   D. acceleration

73. If the graphs shown are velocity versus time graphs, which graph represents constant velocity?

A. W only
B. Y only
C. W and Y only
D. All graphs

74. If graph Y shows acceleration versus time, the particle represented by graph Y has constant:

A. displacement only
B. velocity only
C. acceleration only
D. velocity and acceleration

75. If the graphs shown are acceleration versus time graphs, the area under the curve of the graphs represents:

A. distance
B. displacement
C. change in velocity
D. acceleration

Questions 76 through 84 refer to the graphs below.

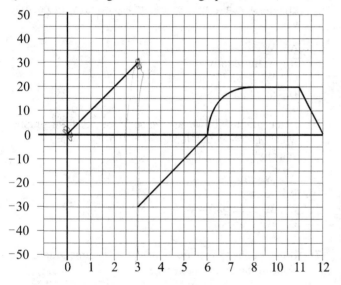

76. If the graph above is a velocity (m/s) vs. time (s) graph, what is the distance traveled in the first 3 s?

A. 30 m
B. 45 m
C. 90 m
D. 180 m

77. If the graph above is a velocity (m/s) vs. time (s) graph, what is the distance traveled in the first 6 s?

A. 0 m
B. 60 m
C. 90 m
D. 180 m

78. If the graph above is a velocity (m/s) vs. time (s) graph, what is the displacement in the first 6 s?

A. 0 m
B. 60 m
C. 90 m
D. 180 m

79. If the graph above is a velocity (m/s) vs. time (s) graph, what is the acceleration in the first 3 s?

A. 3 m/s^2
B. 10 m/s^2
C. 30 m/s^2
D. 45 m/s^2

80. If the graph above is a velocity (m/s) vs. time (s) graph, what is the average velocity in the first 3 s?

A. 0 m/s
B. 15 m/s
C. 30 m/s
D. 60 m/s

81. If the graph above is a velocity (m/s) vs. time (s) graph, what is the average velocity between 2 s and 3 s?

A. 15 m/s
B. 20 m/s
C. 25 m/s
D. 30 m/s

82. If the graph above is a velocity (m/s) vs. time (s) graph, between 6 s and 8 s the motion represented has:

A. positive acceleration and is backwards.
B. positive acceleration and is forwards.
C. negative acceleration and is backwards.
D. negative acceleration and is forwards.

83. If the graph above is a velocity (m) vs. time (s) graph, what is the acceleration between 3.25 s and 5.50 s?

A. 0 m/s^2
B. −5 m/s^2
C. 10 m/s^2
D. −10 m/s^2

84. If the graph above is a velocity (m/s) vs. time (s) graph, at which of the following moments is there negative acceleration?

A. 1 s
B. 4 s
C. 7 s
D. 11.5 s

Projectile Motion

Questions 85 through 97 refer to the diagram of the flight of a projectile near the surface of the earth shown below, where R is the range, v is the initial velocity, h is the maximum height, θ is the angle from the horizontal from which the projectile is launched, and t is the time required for the entire flight. Ignore air resistance.

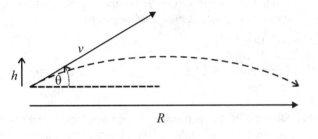

85. Which of the following represents the range R of the projectile?

   A. $vt\sin\theta$
   B. $vt\cos\theta$
   C. vt
   D. $h\sin\theta$

86. Which of the following represents the maximum height h reached by the projectile?

   A. $v^2/2g$
   B. $^1/_8\, gt^2$
   C. vt
   D. $vt\sin\theta$

87. The initial vertical velocity of the projectile is:

   A. $v\sin\theta$
   B. $v\cos\theta$
   C. vt
   D. v

88. The horizontal velocity of the projectile is:

   A. $v\sin\theta$
   B. $v\cos\theta$
   C. vt
   D. v

89. As the angle θ increases from $0°$ to $90°$, the range R:

   A. increases
   B. decreases
   C. increases to a maximum at $45°$ then decreases
   D. increases to a maximum at some angle θ depending upon the velocity v then decreases

90. As the mass of the projectile increases, the range R:

   A. decreases
   B. increases
   C. increases then decreases
   D. remains the same

91. As the mass of the projectile increases, the maximum height h:

   A. decreases
   B. increases
   C. increases then decreases
   D. remains the same

92. In order to maximize the range R, the angle θ should be:

   A. $30°$
   B. $45°$
   C. $60°$
   D. $90°$

93. In order to maximize the height h, the angle θ should be:

   A. $30°$
   B. $45°$
   C. $60°$
   D. $90°$

94. Which two angles θ will result in the same range R?

   A. $30°$ and $45°$
   B. $30°$ and $60°$
   C. $45°$ and $60°$
   D. $45°$ and $90°$

95. When the projectile reaches its maximum height, the vertical velocity is:

   A. 0 m/s
   B. $v\sin\theta$
   C. $v\cos\theta$
   D. v

96. Air resistance would decrease all of the following EXCEPT:

   A. R
   B. h
   C. v
   D. t

97. How are time t and angle θ related?

   A. As θ increases t increases.
   B. As θ increases t decreases.
   C. As θ increases t increases then decreases.
   D. As θ increases t remains the same.

98. Ignoring air resistance, which of the following properties of a projectile remains constant throughout its flight?

    A. vertical velocity
    B. horizontal velocity
    C. speed
    D. displacement

99. A bullet is fired from a high powered rifle at target 20 meters away. The bullet will begin to fall:

    A. the moment it leaves the barrel of the rifle.
    B. the moment it reaches terminal velocity.
    C. the moment its horizontal velocity reaches zero.
    D. The bullet will travel horizontally until it strikes the target.

100. A projectile is launched at a 30° angle over flat ground. Ignoring air resistance, which of the following is NOT true when the projectile reaches its maximum height?

    A. Its vertical velocity is zero.
    B. Its horizontal velocity has not changed.
    C. The time required to reach maximum height is the same as the time required to fall from maximum height.
    D. The instantaneous acceleration is zero.

101. If launched over level ground, which of the following projectiles will remain in the air the least amount of time?

    A. A projectile launched straight up at 10 m/s.
    B. A projectile launched at 30° from the horizontal with a velocity of 20 m/s.
    C. A projectile that remains in the air for 2 seconds.
    D. A projectile that is dropped from 10 meters above the ground.

102. An object is dropped from a height h and strikes the ground with a velocity v. If the object is dropped from a height of $2h$, which of the following represents its velocity when it strikes the ground?

    A. v
    B. $1.4v$
    C. $2v$
    D. $4v$

103. An object is dropped from a height h and strikes the ground in time t. If the object is dropped from a height of $2h$, which of the following represents the time it will take to strike the ground?

    A. t
    B. $1.4t$
    C. $2t$
    D. $4t$

104. An object is dropped from a height h and strikes the ground in time t. In order to double the flight time of the object, it must be dropped from a height of:

    A. h
    B. $1.4h$
    C. $2h$
    D. $4h$

105. An object dropped from a height of 13 m strikes the ground at 16 m/s. In order for the object to strike the ground at 32 m/s, it must be dropped from:

    A. 18 m
    B. 26 m
    C. 39 m
    D. 52 m

106. Object A is dropped from a height of 10 m. Object B is dropped from a height of 10 m, but is given a horizontal velocity of 5 m/s as well. Which of the following statements is false?

    A. Both objects will strike the ground at the same time.
    B. Object B will have a greater velocity when it strikes the ground.
    C. Object B will have a greater acceleration.
    D. Object B will travel a greater distance.

107. A projectile launched straight up at 10 m/s will reach a maximum height of:

    A. 5 m
    B. 10 m
    C. 25 m
    D. 50 m

108. A projectile launched straight up at 10 m/s will strike the ground at:

    A. 5 m/s
    B. 10 m/s
    C. 25 m/s
    D. 50 m/s

109. A projectile launched straight up at 10 m/s will be in the air for:

    A. 1 s
    B. 1.4 s
    C. 2 s
    D. 5 s

110. A projectile launched straight up at 10 m/s will reach a maximum height in:

    A. 1 s
    B. 1.4 s
    C. 2 s
    D. 5 s

111. How far can an animal jump if it can run at 20 m/s and leap from the ground with a vertical velocity of 5 m/s?

    A. 5 m
    B. 10 m
    C. 20 m
    D. 40 m

112. How high can an animal jump if it can run at 20 m/s and leap from the ground with a vertical velocity of 5 m/s?

    A. 1.25 m
    B. 2.5 m
    C. 5 m
    D. 10 m

113. If a basketball player can jump 2 m into the air, with what vertical velocity does he leave the ground?

    A. 5.2 m/s
    B. 6.3 m/s
    C. 7.0 m/s
    D. 8.1 m/s

114. An object is dropped from 80 m. With what velocity does it strike the ground?

    A. 40 m/s
    B. 45 m/s
    C. 80 m/s
    D. 160 m/s

115. If an object strikes the ground with a vertical velocity of 50 m/s, from how high was it dropped?

    A. 25 m
    B. 50 m
    C. 100 m
    D. 125 m

116. An object strikes the ground with a speed of 25 m/s. If it was originally thrown with a horizontal velocity of 15 m/s, and a vertical velocity of zero, from how high was it dropped?

    A. 13 m
    B. 15 m
    C. 20 m
    D. 32 m

117. If a basketball player can jump 2 m into the air, what is his *hang time* (time in the air)?

    A. 0.7 s
    B. 1.3 s
    C. 2.8 s
    D. 4.0 s

118. A projectile is launched at an angle of 30° to the horizontal from a 15 m platform. Its initial velocity is 20 m/s. How far does it travel?

    A. 17 m
    B. 35 m
    C. 52 m
    D. 69 m

119. A projectile is launched from a 25 m platform at an angle of 30° to the horizontal. Its initial velocity is 40 m/s. How long is it in the air?

    A. 2 s
    B. 3 s
    C. 4 s
    D. 5 s

120. A projectile reaches its maximum height in approximately 1.8 seconds. It has a horizontal velocity of 24 m/s. At what speed is it launched?

    A. 17 m/s
    B. 30 m/s
    C. 45 m/s
    D. 52 m/s

121. A projectile launched over level ground reaches its maximum height in 10 seconds. Approximately what was the range of the projectile if it was launched with a speed of 200 m/s?

    A. 1700 m
    B. 2000 m
    C. 3400 m
    D. 4000 m

122. Two objects are dropped from a height of 100 m. If one object is heavier than the other object, which of the following is true? (Note: Ignore air resistance.)

    A. The heavier object will experience *equal force* and accelerate *more slowly*.
    B. The heavier object will experience *more force* and accelerate *more quickly*.
    C. The heavier object will experience *equal force* and accelerate *at the same rate*.
    D. The heavier object will experience *more force* and accelerate *at the same rate*.

123. Two balls with exactly the same size and shape are launched with the same initial velocity from the surface of a perfectly flat plane. When air resistance is considered, the ball with the greater mass will have a:

    A. *longer* flight time and a *greater* maximum height.
    B. *longer* flight time and a *lower* maximum height.
    C. *shorter* flight time and a *greater* maximum height.
    D. *shorter* flight time and a *lower* maximum height.

124. One man drops a rock from a 100 m building. At exactly the same moment, a second man throws a rock from the bottom of the building to the top of the building. At what height do the rocks meet?

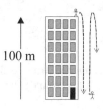

100 m

- **A.** 25 m
- **B.** 50 m
- **C.** 75 m
- **D.** 80 m

125. Air resistance on a smooth ball launched over level ground:

- **A.** *increases* the maximum height and *increases* the range.
- **B.** *increases* the maximum height and *decreases* the range.
- **C.** *decreases* the maximum height and *increases* the range.
- **D.** *decreases* the maximum height and *decreases* the range.

126. All of the following increase the force of air resistance on a projectile EXCEPT:

- **A.** greater mass of the projectile
- **B.** greater surface area of the projectile
- **C.** greater velocity of the projectile
- **D.** greater density of air

127. When air resistance is considered, a spherical projectile will go farther if:

- **A.** the projectile has greater mass.
- **B.** the initial velocity of the projectile is decreased.
- **C.** the projectile has greater surface area.
- **D.** the density of air is increased.

128. A lead ball is dropped from a height of 20 m. When air resistance is considered, approximately how long does it take for the ball to strike the ground?

- **A.** 1.4 s
- **B.** 2 s
- **C.** 3 s
- **D.** 4 s

129. Which of the following would most likely experience the greatest force of air resistance if dropped from an airplane?

- **A.** a feather
- **B.** an elephant
- **C.** a bullet
- **D.** a toaster

The Nature of Force

130. Which of the following is NOT one of the four fundamental forces in nature?

    A. gravitational
    B. electromagnetic
    C. chemical
    D. strong nuclear

131. A weightlifter holds a barbell above his head. What is the fundamental force acting on the barbell to hold it off the ground?

    A. gravitational
    B. electromagnetic
    C. chemical
    D. strong nuclear

Mass and Weight

132. Which of the following has the greatest inertia?

    A. a 5 kg mass at rest
    B. a 5 kg mass moving at 10 m/s
    C. a 5 kg mass accelerating at 10 m/s^2
    D. All have the same inertia

133. An elephant steps on an aluminum can and crushes it. Which of the following physical properties of the elephant crushes the can?

    A. mass
    B. inertia
    C. weight
    D. size

134. A 10 kg ball rolls along the surface of the earth at 5 m/s. If the ball were rolled along the surface of the moon at 5 m/s, which of the following physical properties would be different?

    A. mass
    B. weight
    C. inertia
    D. momentum

135. Two balls of equal size and shape rest on a perfectly smooth surface. One ball is 10 kg; the other is 5 kg. Both balls are spun like tops at the same speed. If equal force is applied to stop each ball, which ball will come to rest first?

    A. The 5 kg ball because it has more inertia.
    B. The 5 kg ball because it has less inertia.
    C. The 10 kg ball because it has more inertia.
    D. The 10 kg ball because it has less inertia.

136. A block slides across a flat surface and slows until it comes to a stop. Which of the following is true?

    A. The block stopped due to its own inertia.
    B. The inertia of the block decreased.
    C. The inertia of the block increased.
    D. The inertia of the block did not change.

137. Ball A and B are the same size and of uniform density. Ball A is twice as massive as Ball B. Both balls are rolled down the same incline. Which of the following is true?

    A. Ball A will accelerate at a greater rate because it has greater rotational inertia.
    B. Ball A will accelerate more slowly because it has greater rotational inertia.
    C. Both balls will accelerate down the plane at the same rate.
    D. Both balls will roll down the plane at a constant velocity.

138. Ball A and B have the same radius and mass. However, Ball A is hollow while Ball B has uniform density. Both balls are rolled down the same incline. Which of the following is true?

    A. Ball A will accelerate at a greater rate because it has greater rotational inertia.
    B. Ball A will accelerate more slowly because it has greater rotational inertia.
    C. Both balls will accelerate down the plane at the same rate.
    D. Both balls will roll down the plane at a constant velocity.

139. Which of the following is NOT true concerning inertia?

    A. Mass is a measure of linear inertia.
    B. Mass is NOT a measure of rotational inertia.
    C. Inertia is the tendency for an object to find a state of rest and remain at rest.
    D. Inertia is the tendency for an object to remain in its present state of motion.

Center of Mass

140. The ring below has a uniform density. Where is its center of mass?

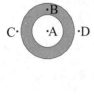

A. A
B. B
C. C
D. D

141. The balls pictured below have a uniform density. The center of gravity of the two ball system is just above which point on the line?

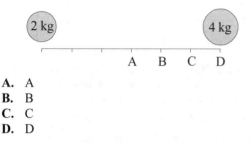

A. A
B. B
C. C
D. D

142. One half of the block shown below is made of lead, the other half from foam. Which point is closest to the center of gravity of the block?

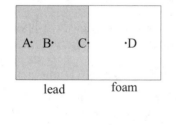

lead   foam

A. A
B. B
C. C
D. D

143. Which of the following is NOT true concerning the center of mass?

A. The center of mass and the center of gravity coincide.
B. There may or may not be mass at the center of mass of a single object.
C. The center of mass is always found at the geometric center of an object.
D. When a net force acts through the center of mass of a rigid object, all parts of the object accelerate equally.

Newton's Laws

1st Law: Objects tend to remain in their present state of motion unless acted upon by a force. (Inertia)
2nd Law: $F = ma$
3rd Law: Every action has an equal and opposite reaction.

144. Which of the following is a violation of Newton's 1st Law? (Note: Ignore air resistance.)

A. The earth perpetually spins at a constant rate in the vacuum of space.
B. A stone rolls down a hill and comes to a stop.
C. A rock slides to a stop along a frictionless, frozen lake.
D. A ball thrown upward from earth, reverses its direction and comes down.

145. A man pushes horizontally on a block at rest. Which of the following is true?

A. Newton's 3rd Law dictates that the block experiences a force equal and opposite to the pushing force.
B. Newton's 1st Law dictates that in the absence of any other forces, the block will remain at rest.
C. Regardless of other forces that may be acting on the block, the acceleration of the block will be inversely proportional to its mass.
D. Newton's 3rd Law dictates that an equal and opposite force will cancel the pushing force and the block will not move.

146. A 5 kg block at rest experiences a net force of 10 N. What is the magnitude of its acceleration?

A. 2 m/s^2
B. 5 m/s^2
C. 10 m/s^2
D. 20 m/s^2

147. A 5 kg block moving at 5 m/s experiences a net force of 10 N in the direction of its motion. What is the magnitude of its acceleration?

A. 2 m/s^2
B. 5 m/s^2
C. 10 m/s^2
D. 20 m/s^2

148. A 5 kg block moving at 5 m/s experiences a net force of 10 N in a direction perpendicular to its motion. What is the magnitude of its acceleration?

   A. 2 m/s^2
   B. 5 m/s^2
   C. 10 m/s^2
   D. 20 m/s^2

149. A 5 kg block moving at 5 m/s experiences a net force of 10 N in a direction opposite to its motion. What is the magnitude of its acceleration?

   A. 2 m/s^2
   B. 5 m/s^2
   C. 10 m/s^2
   D. 20 m/s^2

150. A 25 kg block accelerates at 5 m/s^2, what is the net force acting on the block?

   A. 0 N
   B. 5 N
   C. 125 N
   D. 625 N

151. A block experiencing a net force of 12 N is accelerated at 36 m/s^2. What is the mass of the block?

   A. 1/3 kg
   B. 1 kg
   C. 3 kg
   D. 36 kg

152. A 5 kg block moves at a constant velocity of 10 m/s. What is the net force on the block?

   A. 0 N
   B. ½ N
   C. 2 N
   D. 50 N

153. A 60 kg woman pushes a 20 kg block horizontally with a force of 20 N. If both the woman and the block are on a frictionless surface:

   A. only the block will accelerate because the woman has more inertia.
   B. the acceleration of the block will be greater than the acceleration of the woman and the force on the block will be greater than the force on the woman.
   C. the acceleration of the block will be greater than the acceleration of the woman and the force on the block will be the same as the force on the woman.
   D. the acceleration of the block will be equal to the acceleration of the woman and the force on the block will be the same as the force on the woman.

154. A 100 kg astronaut in space pushes off from his 10,000 kg spaceship with a force of 100 N. If the acceleration of the spaceship is 0.01 m/s^2, what is the acceleration of the astronaut?

   A. 0 m/s^2 because the force is absorbed in accelerating the spaceship.
   B. 100 times greater than the spaceship because he has 100 times less inertia.
   C. 100 times less than the spaceship because he has 100 times less inertia.
   D. The same as the spaceship because their momentums must be equal.

155. A 4 kg block experiences a net force of 80 N in the direction of its movement for 2 seconds. What is its change in velocity?

   A. 10 m/s
   B. 20 m/s
   C. 40 m/s
   D. 80 m/s

156. An 8 kg block experiences a net force of 160 N. Its velocity increases by 40 m/s. For how long did the force act on the block?

   A. 2 s
   B. 5 s
   C. 10 s
   D. 40 s

157. A 9 kg block experiences a net force in the opposite direction of its velocity for 3 seconds. Its velocity decreases by 9 m/s. What is the magnitude of the force?

   A. 1 N
   B. 9 N
   C. 18 N
   D. 27 N

158. A 5 kg block accelerates at 10 m/s^2. What is the magnitude of the net force?

   A. 0.2 N
   B. 0.5 N
   C. 2 N
   D. 50 N

159. A 3 kg box is pushed along the ground at a constant velocity for 10 s. What is the net force acting on the box?

   A. 0 N
   B. 0.3 N
   C. 3.3 N
   D. 30 N

The Law of Universal Gravitation

$$F = G\ \frac{m_1 m_2}{r^2}$$

Newton's Law of Gravitation

Refer to the diagram below to answer questions 160-163. Objects m_1 and m_2 are two objects in space infinitely far from any other mass. ($G = 6.67 \times 10^{-11}$ N m²/kg²)

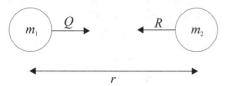

160. A student uses Newton's Law of Universal Gravitation to solve for force in the diagram above. His answer is $F = 10$ N. If m_1 and m_2 have the same mass, which of the following is true?

  A. Objects m_1 and m_2 each experience a force of 5 N.
  B. Objects m_1 and m_2 each experience a force of 10 N.
  C. Objects m_1 and m_2 each experience a force of 20 N.
  D. The forces on objects m_1 and m_2 cancel each other and neither mass experiences a net force.

161. Which of the following is true if m_1 has a mass one thousand times greater than the mass of m_2?

  A. The force on m_1 will be one thousand times greater than the force on m_2.
  B. The force on m_2 will be one thousand times greater than the force on m_1.
  C. The force on m_1 will be equal to the force on m_2 and will not be zero.
  D. The net force on both objects will be zero.

162. Which of the following is true if m_1 has a mass one thousand times greater than the mass of m_2?

  A. m_1 will remain stationary while m_2 accelerates toward m_1.
  B. m_1 and m_2 will accelerate at equal rates.
  C. m_1 will accelerate at a rate one thousand times greater than that of m_2.
  D. m_2 will accelerate at a rate one thousand times greater than that of m_1.

163. $r = 10$ m. m_1 and m_2 each have a mass of 10^9 kg, and a radius of 1.67 m. If they start from rest, the accelerations of the masses will:

  A. remain at zero.
  B. remain constant but not at zero.
  C. increase.
  D. decrease.

164. An object with mass m is dropped near the surface of the earth. The object accelerates at a rate g. If r is the distance between the centers of gravity of the earth and the object, and M is the mass of the earth, which of the following represents the rate at which the earth accelerates due to the gravitational force of the object?

  A. Gm/r^2
  B. GmM/r^2
  C. GM/r^2
  D. g

165. An object with mass m is held near the surface of the earth. If r is the distance between the centers of gravity of the earth and the object, and M is the mass of the earth, which of the following represents the gravitational force on the earth due to the object?

  A. Gm/r^2
  B. GM/r^2
  C. Mg
  D. mg

166. Two planets have the same mass but different radii. Each has a moon with the same orbital radius. Compared to the smaller planet, the larger planet attracts its moon with a gravitational force that is:

  A. greater.
  B. smaller.
  C. the same.
  D. The gravitational force depends upon the masses of the moons.

167. Two planets have the same mass but different radii. Which of the following is true?

  A. A person will have a greater weight when standing on the surface of the larger planet.
  B. A person will have a greater mass when standing on the surface of the larger planet.
  C. A person will have a greater weight when standing on the surface of the smaller planet.
  D. A person will have the same weight when standing on the surface of either planet.

168. Planets A and B have the same mass. Planet A has a radius half as large as Planet B. Compared to an object dropped near the surface of planet B, an object dropped near the surface of Planet A will accelerate at:

  A. four times the rate.
  B. twice the rate.
  C. the same rate.
  D. half the rate.

169. Planets A and B have the same mass. Planet A has a radius half as large as Planet B. Compared to a 100 kg object dropped near the surface of planet B, a 50 kg object dropped near the surface of Planet A will accelerate at:

- **A.** four times the rate.
- **B.** twice the rate.
- **C.** the same rate.
- **D.** half the rate.

170. Planets A and B have the same mass. Planet A has a radius half as large as Planet B. Compared to a 100 kg object dropped near the surface of planet B, a 50 kg object dropped near the surface of Planet A will experience a gravitational force:

- **A.** four times greater.
- **B.** twice as great.
- **C.** of equal magnitude.
- **D.** half as great.

171. Planets A and B have the same mass. Planet A has a radius half as large as Planet B. A rocket in space is the same distance from the centers of both planets. Compared to the gravitational force on the rocket from Planet B, the gravitational force on the rocket from Planet A is:

- **A.** four times as great.
- **B.** twice as great.
- **C.** of equal magnitude.
- **D.** half as great.

172. Planets A and B have the same mass. Planet A has a radius half as large as Planet B. A 5 kg mass is dropped 10 m above the surface of Planet A and at the same time a 5 kg mass is dropped 10 m above the surface of Planet B. If the mass on Planet B strikes the ground in 10 s, the mass on Planet A strikes the ground in:

- **A.** 2.5 s
- **B.** 5 s
- **C.** 10 s
- **D.** 20 s

173. Planet B has twice the mass of Planet A. Planet A has a radius half as large as Planet B. A 5 kg mass is dropped 10 m above the surface of Planet B and at the same time a 10 kg mass is dropped 10 m above the surface of Planet A. If the mass on Planet B strikes the ground in 10 s, the mass on Planet A strikes the ground in approximately:

- **A.** 7 s
- **B.** 10 s
- **C.** 14 s
- **D.** 20 s

Use the diagram below to answer questions 174-176. 40 spheres of equal mass make two rings of 20 spheres each. The ring on the right has a radius twice as large as the ring on the left.

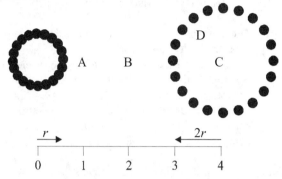

174. At what position could a mass be placed so that the gravitational force that it would experience would be the same from both rings?

- **A.** A
- **B.** B
- **C.** C
- **D.** D

175. At what position could a mass be placed so that the net gravitational force that it would experience would be zero?

- **A.** A
- **B.** B
- **C.** C
- **D.** D

176. If the position of the spheres approximates two uniformly dense rings, which of the following is true concerning a mass placed at position D?

- **A.** The net gravitational force due to the spheres of the larger ring would be zero.
- **B.** The net gravitational force due to the spheres of the smaller ring would be zero.
- **C.** The net gravitational force due to the spheres of both rings would be zero.
- **D.** If the smaller ring were removed, the mass would move toward the center of the larger ring.

177. A 6 kg bowling ball experiences a force due to gravity that is 2,000 times greater than the gravitational force experienced by a 3 g ping-pong ball. Which of the following properties explains why they fall at the same rate?

- **A.** momentum
- **B.** weight
- **C.** inertia
- **D.** size

178. An elephant and a feather are dropped from a height of 10 m in a giant vacuum chamber. Which of the following is correct?

   A. The feather will strike the ground first because it has less inertia.

   B. The elephant will strike the ground first because it experiences less air resistance.

   C. They will strike the ground at the same time because both gravitational force and inertia are proportional to mass.

   D. They will strike the ground at the same time because the greater air resistance on the elephant compensates for its greater mass.

179. Sky Lab with its weightless astronauts orbited the earth 444 km above its surface. The radius of the earth is approximately 6370 km. If $g = 9.8$ m/s^2, what was the correct value for g on Sky Lab?

   A. 0 m/s^2

   B. 8.5 m/s^2

   C. 9.8 m/s^2

   D. 10.4 m/s^2

Inclined Planes

180. An object with mass m sits on a plane inclined from the horizontal at an angle θ. Which of the following represents the force on the object due to gravity?

   A. $mg\sin\theta$

   B. $mg\cos\theta$

   C. mg

   D. $g\sin\theta$

181. An object with mass m sits on a plane inclined from the horizontal at an angle θ. Which of the following represents the normal force on the object due to the inclined plane?

   A. $mg\sin\theta$

   B. $mg\cos\theta$

   C. mg

   D. $g\sin\theta$

182. An object with mass m is placed on a frictionless plane inclined from the horizontal at an angle θ. Which of the following represents the acceleration of the object down the inclined plane?

   A. $g\sin\theta$

   B. $g\cos\theta$

   C. g

   D. ½g

183. An object with mass m is placed on a frictionless plane inclined from the horizontal at an angle θ. Which of the following represents the net force on the object?

   A. $mg\sin\theta$

   B. $mg\cos\theta$

   C. mg

   D. $g\sin\theta$

Questions 184-195 refer to the *frictionless* inclined plane shown below. h is the height of the ramp, d is the total length of the ramp, and θ is the angle the ramp is placed from the horizontal. (Note: the distance x is also frictionless.)

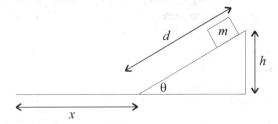

184. If h is 5 m, m is 2 kg, θ is 30°, and the mass starts from rest, how long does it take the mass to move the distance d?

   A. 1 s

   B. 1.4 s

   C. 2 s

   D. 3 s

185. If h is 5 m, m is 5 kg, θ is 30°, and the mass starts from rest, how long does it take the mass to move the distance d?

   A. 1 s

   B. 1.4 s

   C. 2 s

   D. 3 s

186. 2 s is required for the mass to slide the distance d from a resting position. If the height h is increased by a factor of 4, while holding θ at 30°, how long does it take the mass to slide the new distance d from rest?

   A. 4 s

   B. 8 s

   C. 16 s

   D. 32 s

187. If h is 5 m, m is 2 kg, d is 25 m, and the mass starts from rest, how long does it take the mass to move the distance d?

   A. 2 s

   B. 5 s

   C. 10 s

   D. 20 s

188. If h is 5 m and the mass takes 3 s to move the distance d when starting from rest, what is the distance d?

    A. 5 m
    B. 10 m
    C. 15 m
    D. 20 m

189. If θ is 30° m, d is 10 m, and x is 10 m, how long after the mass reaches the bottom of the plane does it require to move the distance x?

    A. 1 s
    B. 2 s
    C. 3 s
    D. 4 s

190. Which of the following would change the acceleration of object m if it were released from the top of the ramp?

    A. changing the shape of the object to a sphere
    B. changing the mass of the object
    C. changing the angle θ
    D. releasing the object from the middle of the ramp

191. Which of the following would increase the velocity of object m at the bottom of the ramp?

    A. changing the shape of the object to a sphere
    B. increasing the mass of the object
    C. increasing the angle θ but not the height h
    D. increasing the height h but not the angle θ

192. Which of the following is true when the object m moves along the distance x?

    A. Acceleration is positive and constant.
    B. Acceleration is negative and constant.
    C. Velocity is constant.
    D. The time required to traverse the distance x does not change when h is changed.

193. As the object m slides down the inclined plane:

    A. the horizontal velocity increases.
    B. the horizontal velocity decreases.
    C. the horizontal acceleration increases.
    D. the horizontal acceleration decreases.

194. If the object m slides down the plane in 3 s, what is the ratio of the distance it travels in the 1st second compared to the distance it travels in the 2nd second?

    A. 1:1
    B. 1:2
    C. 1:3
    D. It depends upon the acceleration of the object m.

195. If the object m slides down the plane in 3 s, what is the ratio of the distance it travels in the 1st second compared to the distance it travels in the 3rd second?

    A. 1:3
    B. 1:4
    C. 1:5
    D. 1:6

Circular Motion and Centripetal Force

196. In order for an object to move in a circle at a constant speed, the object must experience a net force:

    A. toward the center of the circle.
    B. away from the center of the circle.
    C. in the direction of its instantaneous velocity.
    D. No net force is required for an object to move in a circle at constant speed.

197. An object moving at 10 m/s makes a circle with a 2 m radius. The object accelerates at:

    A. 10 m/s^2
    B. 20 m/s^2
    C. 50 m/s^2
    D. 100 m/s^2

198. Acceleration is a vector representing the rate of change of velocity. An object moving in a circle at constant speed:

    A. accelerates without changing its velocity.
    B. has constant acceleration.
    C. changes speed but not velocity.
    D. changes velocity but not speed.

199. An object turns without changing its speed. Which of the following is true?

    A. No net force was necessarily acting on the object.
    B. A net force perpendicular to the object's motion must have been acting on the object.
    C. A net force in the opposite direction of the object's motion must have been acting on the object.
    D. If the turn was not part of a perfect circle, the net force will not be exactly perpendicular to its motion.

200. The centripetal force acting on an object is doubled. The radius of the object's motion is also doubled. The speed of the object:

A. increases by a factor of 4.
B. increases by a factor of 2.
C. decreases by a factor of 2.
D. The change in the object's speed depends upon its mass.

201. A small moon is held in orbit around a planet by gravity. The radius of the orbit is r. If the speed of the moon were reduced by a factor of 2, the new orbital radius of the moon would be:

A. $4r$
B. $2r$
C. r
D. ½ r

202. An object moves at constant speed along the path shown below. Which of the following must be true?

A. There is a constant net force acting on the object. At all times, the force is in a direction perpendicular to the motion of the object.
B. There is a changing net force acting on the object. At all times, the force is in a direction perpendicular to the motion of the object.
C. There is a changing net force acting on the object. The force may or may not act in a direction perpendicular to the motion of the object at any given time.
D. Since the object is not accelerating, there can be no net force on the object.

203. A boy uses a string to swing a 1.5 kg stone around his head. If the string is 1.5 m, and can bear a maximum tension of 1600 N, what is the maximum speed at which the boy can swing the stone without breaking the string?

A. 40 m/s
B. 400 m/s
C. 800 m/s
D. 1600 m/s

204. A man on a unicycle rides in a circular path shown below at a constant speed. Which vector most closely represents the direction of the instantaneous net force on the unicycle due to the friction of the ground?

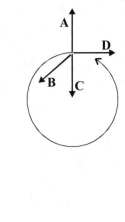

A. A
B. B
C. C
D. D

205. A girl attaches a rock to a string and swings it in a circle around her head. Which of the following would not be affected by the length of the string?

A. the speed of the rock
B. the radius of the rock's motion
C. the force necessary to swing the rock
D. the force on the rock due to gravity

206. A 2 kg object moving at 10 m/s in a circle with a radius of 5 m, is accelerating at:

A. 2 m/s^2
B. 20 m/s^2
C. 40 m/s^2
D. 50 m/s^2

207. The earth has a radius of approximately 6400 km. If an object could orbit the earth just at its surface, how fast would it have to travel?

A. 8 km/s
B. 16 km/s
C. 80 km/s
D. 320 km/s

208. The earth has a radius of approximately 6400 km. If an object could orbit the earth just at its surface, approximately how long would the object take to circle the earth one time?

A. 400π s
B. 800π s
C. 1600π s
D. 6400π s

209. Gravitational force holds a satellite in its orbit. Which of the following would most likely increase the time necessary for a satellite to complete its orbit around a planet?

- **A.** decreasing only the orbital radius
- **B.** increasing only the mass of the satellite
- **C.** decreasing only the mass of the planet
- **D.** decreasing only the radius of the planet

Friction

210. A 2 kg block rests on a plane inclined at 30°. What is the static frictional force on the block?

- **A.** 5 N
- **B.** 10 N
- **C.** 15 N
- **D.** 20 N

211. A 2 kg block rests on an inclined plane with an angle of 30°. A force of 5 N is applied to the block in a direction down the incline plane. If the block doesn't move, what is the static frictional force on the block?

- **A.** 5 N
- **B.** 15 N
- **C.** 20 N
- **D.** 25 N

212. A 2 kg block rests on an inclined plane with an angle of 30°. A steadily increasing force is applied to the block in a direction down the inclined plane until the block begins to move. If the block begins to move when the force reaches 7.3 N, what is the approximate coefficient of static friction between the block and the plane?

- **A.** 0.1
- **B.** 0.6
- **C.** 1
- **D.** 2

213. A 2 kg block rests on a flat board. One end of the board is slowly lifted until the block begins to slide. If the block begins to slide when the board is at an angle of 30° with the horizontal, what is the coefficient of static friction between the block and the board?

- **A.** 0.1
- **B.** 0.6
- **C.** 1
- **D.** 2

214. A block rests on a flat board. One end of the board is slowly lifted until the block begins to slide. If the block begins to slide when the board is at an angle θ with the horizontal, which of the following represents the coefficient of static friction between the block and the board?

- **A.** $\cos\theta/\sin\theta$
- **B.** $\sin\theta/\cos\theta$
- **C.** $\sin\theta/mg\cos\theta$
- **D.** $mg\cos\theta/\sin\theta$

215. The following experiment takes place on the moon. A 2 kg block rests on a flat board. One end of the board is slowly lifted until the block begins to slide. If the block begins to slide when the board is at an angle of 30° with the horizontal, what is the coefficient of static friction between the block and the board?

- **A.** 0.1
- **B.** 0.6
- **C.** 1
- **D.** 2

216. A 156.34 kg block rests on a flat board. One end of the board is slowly lifted until the block begins to slide. If the block begins to slide when the board is at an angle of 30° with the horizontal, what is the coefficient of static friction between the block and the board?

- **A.** 0.1
- **B.** 0.6
- **C.** 1
- **D.** 2

217. Which of the following properties affects the coefficient of static friction between a block and an inclined plane?

- **A.** gravity
- **B.** the mass of the block
- **C.** the amount of surface area of the block making contact with the plane
- **D.** the material of the block and plane

218. A block is at rest on a plane inclined at an angle of θ. Which of the following is a true statement?

- **A.** The static frictional force on the block is greater than the force due to gravity down the inclined plane.
- **B.** The net force on the block is in the upward direction along the inclined plane.
- **C.** The net force on the block is in the downward direction along the inclined plane.
- **D.** There is no net force on the block.

219. A 2 kg object is placed on a plane inclined at an angle of 30°. If the coefficient of static friction is 1, and the coefficient of kinetic friction is 0.1, what is the net force on the block?

A. 0 N
B. 2.7 N
C. 17.3 N
D. 37.3 N

220. A 2 kg object is placed on a plane inclined at an angle of 30°. If the coefficient of static friction is 0.3, and the coefficient of kinetic friction is 0.1, what is the net force on the block?

A. 0 N
B. 8.3 N
C. 10 N
D. 20 N

221. A 4 kg block is placed on a plane inclined at an angle of 30°. If the coefficient of static friction is 0.3 and the coefficient of kinetic friction is 0.2, what is the net force on the block?

A. 0 N
B. 8.3 N
C. 13 N
D. 40 N

222. Which of the following statements is true concerning friction?

A. The frictional force on an object is always in the opposite direction to the motion of that object.
B. A frictional force opposes the motion of the object to which it is applied relative to the motion of the object that applies the force.
C. The force of friction can never be greater than the weight of the object to which it is applied.
D. A frictional force is perpendicular to the surface to which it is applied.

223. A block slides down an inclined plane at constant velocity. Which of the following is true?

A. The plane must be frictionless.
B. The static frictional force on the block is equal to the force down the inclined plane.
C. The kinetic frictional force on the block is equal to the force down the inclined plane.
D. The coefficient of kinetic friction between the block and the plane is greater than the coefficient of static friction.

224. When a car is towed at constant velocity, the frictional force between the road and its tires is:

A. static and in the direction of the motion of the car.
B. static and in the opposite direction to the motion of the car.
C. kinetic and in the direction of the motion of the car.
D. kinetic and in the direction opposite to the motion of the car.

225. When a car moves under its own power at constant velocity, the frictional force between the road and the tires that propel the car is:

A. static and in the direction of the motion of the car.
B. static and in the opposite direction to the motion of the car.
C. kinetic and in the direction of the motion of the car.
D. kinetic and in the direction opposite to the motion of the car.

226. A car moving at 20 m/s brakes and slides to a stop. If the coefficient of kinetic friction between the pavement and the tires of the car is 0.1, how far does the car slide?

A. 50 m
B. 100 m
C. 200 m
D. 400 m

227. A car moving at 20 m/s brakes and slides to a stop. If the coefficient of kinetic friction between the pavement and the tires of the car is 0.1, how much time is needed for the car to come to a complete stop?

A. 1 s
B. 10 s
C. 20 s
D. 40 s

228. Assuming that a vehicle slides to a stop without brake or tire failure, which of the following is NOT true?

A. A heavy truck will require more room to stop than an economy car.
B. The number of wheels on a vehicle does not change the time needed to stop it.
C. Acceleration is constant until the vehicle stops.
D. A greater kinetic coefficient of friction means a shorter stopping time.

229. Three blocks with the same shape and made from the same material, with masses of 1 kg, 2 kg, and 3 kg, respectively, are placed on a board. The board is slowly lifted at one end. Which block will start sliding first?

    A. the 1 kg block
    B. the 2 kg block
    C. the 3 kg block
    D. All three blocks will slide at the same time.

230. Three blocks with the same shape and made from the same material, with masses of 1 kg, 2 kg, and 3 kg, respectively, are placed on a board. The board is slowly lifted at one end. Which block will slide the fastest?

    A. the 1 kg block
    B. the 2 kg block
    C. the 3 kg block
    D. All three blocks will slide at the same speed.

231. Which of the following is true for a ball rolling down an inclined plane?

    A. It experiences no frictional forces due to the plane.
    B. It experiences only static frictional forces due to the plane.
    C. It experiences only kinetic frictional forces due to the plane.
    D. It accelerates at approximately 10 m/s^2.

232. A 5 kg object is dropped from a plane. After a few seconds, it moves at a constant velocity. What is the force of air resistance acting on the object once it has reached a constant velocity?

    A. 0 N
    B. 25 N
    C. 50 N
    D. 100 N

233. A 100 kg object is dropped from a plane. If in the first few seconds, it accelerates at an average of 7 m/s^2, what is the average force of air resistance acting on the object during this time?

    A. 0 N
    B. 300 N
    C. 700 N
    D. 1,000 N

234. A 5 kg object is dropped from a plane. At 3 s, it reaches terminal velocity (Its maximum velocity due to air resistance). What is the object's terminal velocity?

    A. much less than 30 m/s
    B. approximately 30 m/s
    C. much more than 30 m/s
    D. exactly 45 m/s

235. Person A and Person B parachute from a plane. Person A weighs twice as much as Person B. Both move at a constant velocity once their chute is opened. Compared to the force of air resistance on the chute of Person B the force of air resistance on the chute of Person A is:

    A. half as much
    B. the same
    C. twice as much
    D. four times as much

Tension

236. A 1 kg mass hangs from a string. The ceiling pulls upward on the same string with a force of 10 N. What is the tension in the string?

    A. 0 N
    B. 10 N
    C. 20 N
    D. 40 N

237. A professional strongman ties rope A to a building and pulls as hard as he can on the rope. Two other professional strongmen take either end of rope B and pull in opposite directions as hard as they can. If all strongmen possess equal strength, how do the tensions in the ropes compare?

    A. Rope A has half as much tension.
    B. The ropes have the same tension.
    C. Rope A has twice as much tension.
    D. Rope A has four times as much tension.

238. A man dangles a 10 kg mass from the end of a rope. If the man releases the rope, what is the tension in the rope the moment after it is released?

    A. 0 N
    B. 50 N
    C. 100 N
    D. 200 N

239. A man dangles a 10 kg mass from the end of a rope. If he jumps from a plane while still holding the rope, the tension in the rope will be:

A. 0 N
B. 5 N
C. 10 N
D. 20 N

240. A man dangles a 10 kg mass from the end of a rope. If he steps on an elevator while still holding the rope, and the elevator accelerates downward at 3 m/s², the tension in the rope will be:

A. 0 N
B. 30 N
C. 70 N
D. 100 N

241. A 50 kg woman dangles a 50 kg mass from the end of a rope. If she stands on a frictionless surface and hangs the mass over a cliff with a pulley as shown, the tension in the rope will be: (Note: Ignore any frictional forces.)

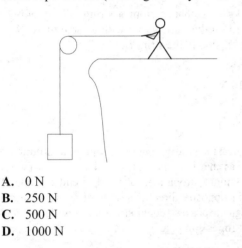

A. 0 N
B. 250 N
C. 500 N
D. 1000 N

242. A 100 kg man dangles a 50 kg mass from the end of a rope. If he stands on a frictionless surface and hangs the mass over a cliff with a pulley as shown in the question above, the tension in the rope will be: (Note: ignore any frictional forces.)

A. 250 N
B. 333 N
C. 500 N
D. 667 N

243. In the question above, as the mass becomes infinitely large, the man's acceleration becomes:

A. 5 m/s²
B. 10 m/s²
C. 20 m/s²
D. infinite

244. The masses below hang across a massless, frictionless pulley. What is the tension in the rope?

A. 0.5 *mg*
B. *mg*
C. 1.33 *mg*
D. 2 *mg*

245. In the question above, as the mass becomes infinitely large, the tension in the rope becomes:

A. 0 N
B. 500 N
C. 1000 N
D. infinite

Hooke's Law

246. A certain object follows Hooke's Law. How much force is necessary to depress the surface of the object a distance *x* if it has spring constant *k*.

A. *k*
B. *kx*
C. *kx²*
D. ½ *kx²*

247. A 10 kg mass hangs from a spring that follows Hooke's Law. If the spring has a spring constant of 200 N/m, how far does the spring distend from its rest position?

A. 0.05 m
B. 0.5 m
C. 20 m
D. 2000 m

248. A 2 kg mass is pushed against a spring ($k = 400$ N/m), compressing the spring 5 cm from its rest position. The mass sits on a frictionless surface. Which of the following accurately describes what will happen after the mass is released, but before the spring reaches its relaxed position?

   A. The velocity and the acceleration of the mass will continually decrease.
   B. The velocity and the acceleration of the mass will continually increase.
   C. The velocity of the mass will continually increase, but the acceleration will continually decrease.
   D. The velocity of the mass will continually decrease, but the acceleration will continually increase.

249. A 2 kg mass is placed on top of a spring ($k = 400$ N/m). How many centimeters is the spring compressed from its relaxed position?

   A. 0.5 cm
   B. 1 cm
   C. 2 cm
   D. 5 cm

250. A 2 kg mass is placed on top of a spring ($k = 400$ N/m) and then pushed downwards with a force of 30 N. How many centimeters is the spring compressed from its relaxed position?

   A. 0.5 cm
   B. 5 cm
   C. 7.5 cm
   D. 12.5 cm

251. A spring ($k = 400$ N/m) is cut in half to make two new springs. What is the spring constant of each of the new springs?

   A. 100 N/m
   B. 200 N/m
   C. 400 N/m
   D. 800 N/m

252. If two springs ($k = 400$ N/m) are placed parallel to each other, what is the spring constant of the two spring system?

   A. 100 N/m
   B. 200 N/m
   C. 400 N/m
   D. 800 N/m

253. A man compresses a 30 cm spring against a wall. If he applies a 100 N force and the wall is rigid, by how much does he shorten the spring? ($k = 1000$ N/m)

   A. 5 cm
   B. 10 cm
   C. 20 cm
   A. 30 cm

254. A man holds one end of a 30 cm spring in each hand. If he applies a 100 N force to each end of the spring, by how much does he shorten the spring? ($k = 1000$ N/m)

   A. 5 cm
   B. 10 cm
   C. 20 cm
   D. 30 cm

255. An object is placed on a spring. The spring is compressed downward and released. From the moment the spring is released until the object leaves the spring, the magnitude of the object's acceleration will:

   A. increase then decrease.
   B. decrease then increase.
   C. increase only.
   D. remain constant.

256. What is the spring constant k for the spring shown below?

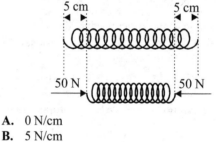

   A. 0 N/cm
   B. 5 N/cm
   C. 10 N/cm
   D. 20 N/cm

Equilibrium

257. Which of the following could NOT be a property of a system in equilibrium?

   A. constant velocity
   B. zero net force
   C. spinning about an axis
   D. acceleration

258. Which of the following properties is always different between a system in static equilibrium and dynamic equilibrium?

   A. velocity
   B. acceleration
   C. net force
   D. the rate of change in the net force

259. Which of the following is always true about a system that is NOT in equilibrium?

   A. The net force is zero.
   B. The instantaneous velocity cannot be zero.
   C. The system is at rest.
   D. The velocity of the system is changing.

260. Which of the following is always true about a system that is NOT in equilibrium?

   A. The motion of the system cannot be linear.
   B. The sum of the forces is proportional to the acceleration of the system.
   C. The velocity of the system is changing at a constant rate.
   D. The acceleration of the system is proportional to its mass.

261. Which of the following objects is in equilibrium?

   A. A car sliding to a stop on a sheet of ice
   B. A flowerpot falling from a 2nd story window
   C. A top spinning in place at a constant velocity
   D. A pendulum swinging in simple harmonic motion

262. Which of the following objects is NOT in equilibrium?

   A. A skydiver falling at terminal velocity
   B. A motionless mass hanging from a string
   C. A garbage can pushed across rough pavement at constant velocity
   D. A projectile near the surface of the earth experiencing no air resistance

263. A 10 kg mass hangs from a rope. A force is applied to the rope so that the mass is accelerated upward at 2 m/s^2. What is the tension in the rope?

   A. 80 N
   B. 100 N
   C. 120 N
   D. 200 N

264. A 25 kg mass is lowered by a rope. If the velocity of the mass is decreasing at a rate of 5 m/s^2, what is the tension in the rope?

   A. 125 N
   B. 250 N
   C. 375 N
   D. 1250 N

265. A 12 kg mass is raised by a rope. If the velocity of the mass is decreasing at a rate of 5 m/s^2, what is the tension in the rope?

   A. 60 N
   B. 120 N
   C. 180 N
   D. 600 N

266. A 32 kg mass is raised by a rope. If the velocity of the mass remains constant at 2 m/s, what is the tension in the rope?

   A. 256 N
   B. 320 N
   C. 384 N
   D. 640 N

267. A 10 kg mass hangs by a rope. If the tension in the rope remains constant at 150 N, which of the following could be true?

   A. The mass is at rest.
   B. The mass has a constant velocity.
   C. The mass is decelerating at 5 m/s^2.
   D. The mass is in dynamic equilibrium.

268. A 25 kg mass hangs by a rope. If the tension in the rope is a constant 200 N and the initial velocity of the mass is 3 m/s upwards, what is the velocity of the mass after 2 seconds?

   A. 1 m/s downward
   B. 1 m/s upward
   C. 7 m/s downward
   D. 7 m/s upward

Questions 269-277 refer to the diagram below.

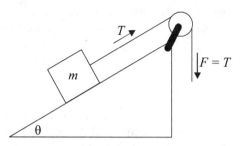

269. The plane above is frictionless and inclined at a 30° angle. The mass *m* is 6 kg. If the mass is lowered at a constant velocity, what is the tension *T* in the rope?

    A. 0 N
    B. 30 N
    C. 60 N
    D. 90 N

270. The plane above is frictionless and inclined at a 30° angle. The mass *m* is 6 kg. If the mass is accelerated up the plane at 2 m/s^2, what is the tension *T* in the rope?

    A. 30 N
    B. 36 N
    C. 42 N
    D. 72 N

271. The plane above is frictionless and inclined at a 30° angle. The mass *m* is 10 kg. If the tension *T* in the rope is a constant 75 N, and the mass starts from rest, what is the velocity of the mass after 2 second?

    A. 5 m/s down the plane
    B. 2.5 m/s up the plane
    C. 5 m/s up the plane
    D. 7.5 m/s up the plane

272. The plane above is inclined at a 30° angle. The coefficient of kinetic friction between the mass and the plane is 0.1. The mass is 100 kg. Once the mass is moving, what is the minimum force *F* necessary to pull the mass up the plane?

    A. 59 N
    B. 413 N
    C. 509 N
    D. 587 N

273. The plane above is inclined at a 30° angle. The coefficient of static friction between the mass and the plane is 0.2. The mass is 100 kg. What is the minimum force *F* necessary to prevent the mass from sliding down the plane?

    A. 0 N
    B. 327 N
    C. 500 N
    D. 673 N

274. The plane above is inclined at a 30° angle. The coefficient of kinetic friction between the mass and the plane is 0.1. The mass is 100 kg. What is the minimum tension required in the rope so that the mass will accelerate down the plane at 2 m/s^2?

    A. 213 N
    B. 387 N
    C. 613 N
    D. 787 N

275. The plane above is inclined at a 30° angle. The coefficient of kinetic friction between the mass and the plane is 0.1. The mass is 100 kg. If the mass is moving up the inclined plane at a velocity of 2 m/s, what tension should be applied to the rope in order to make the mass reverse directions in exactly 1 s?

    A. 213 N
    B. 387 N
    C. 613 N
    D. 787 N

276. The plane above is inclined at a 60° angle. The coefficient of static friction between the mass and the plane is 0.2. The mass is 100 kg. What is the minimum force *F* necessary to prevent the mass from sliding down the plane?

    A. 0 N
    B. 500 N
    C. 766 N
    D. 966 N

277. The plane above is inclined at a 60° angle. The coefficient of static friction between the mass and the plane is 0.2. The mass is 100 kg. What is the minimum force *F* necessary to start the object moving up the plane?

    A. 500 N
    B. 766 N
    C. 866 N
    D. 966 N

Questions 278-281 refer to the diagram below.

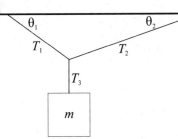

278. Which of the following must be true of magnitudes of the tensions given in the diagram?

    A. $T_1 > T_2$
    B. $T_2 > T_1$
    C. $T_1 = T_2$
    D. $T_3 = T_1 + T_2$

279. If $m = 10$ kg, $\theta_1 = 60°$ and $\theta_2 = 30°$, the tension T_3 is:

    A. 50 N
    B. 100 N
    C. 137 N
    D. 237 N

280. If $m = 10$ kg, $\theta_1 = 60°$ and $\theta_2 = 30°$, the tension T_2 is:

    A. 50 N
    B. 59 N
    C. 100 N
    D. The tension T_2 depends upon the length of T_2.

281. If $m = 100$ kg, $\theta_1 = 30°$ and $\theta_2 = 30°$, the tension T_1 is:

    A. 500 N
    B. 866 N
    C. 1000 N
    D. 1732 N

282. The mass below hangs inside a boxcar of a train. If the train accelerates at 7 m/s^2, what is the approximate tension T in the rope?

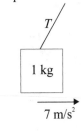

    A. 7 N
    B. 10 N
    C. 12 N
    D. 17 N

283. In the diagram below, tugboat A is towing both tugboats B and C. If the tugboats are moving at a constant velocity, which of the following is true concerning the tension in the ropes between them?

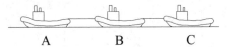

    A. The tension in the ropes is zero.
    B. The tension in the ropes is not zero, but the tension in the rope between A and B is equal to the tension in the rope between B and C.
    C. The tension in the rope between A and B is *greater* than the tension in the rope between B and C.
    D. The tension in the rope between A and B is *less* than the tension in the rope between B and C.

Questions 284-286 refer to the three boxes in the diagram below.

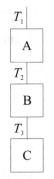

284. Boxes A, B, and C each have a mass of 10 kg. If the boxes are lifted at a constant velocity, what is the tension T_2?

    A. 100 N
    B. 200 N
    C. 250 N
    D. 300 N

285. Boxes A, B, and C each have a mass of 10 kg. If the boxes are accelerated upward at 2 m/s^2, what is the tension T_2?

    A. 110 N
    B. 220 N
    C. 240 N
    D. 360 N

286. Boxes A, B, and C each have a mass of 10 kg. If the rope can withstand a maximum tension of 600 N, how quickly can the boxes be pulled upwards a distance of 20 m starting from rest?

    A. 1 s
    B. 2 s
    C. 3 s
    D. 4 s

Questions 287-293 refer to the elevator shown below. The mass of the elevator and everything in it is 1000 kg. The man in the elevator has a mass of 90 kg. The box that he holds has a mass of 10 kg. The floors of the building in which the elevator operates are separated by 5 m. The elevator accelerates and decelerates at 1 m/s², and moves at a maximum velocity of 5 m/s. The scale reads in newtons.

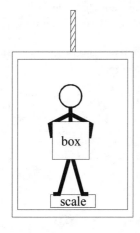

287. What is the maximum reading on the scale during a trip from the 5th floor to the 11th floor?

  A. 900 N
  B. 1000 N
  C. 1090 N
  D. 1100 N

288. What is the minimum reading on the scale during a trip from the 11th floor to the 2nd floor?

  A. 0 N
  B. 900 N
  C. 1000 N
  D. 1100 N

289. What is the maximum tension achieved by the elevator cable during a trip from the 1st floor to the 10th floor?

  A. 9,000 N
  B. 10,000 N
  C. 11,000 N
  D. 11,200 N

290. What is the maximum apparent weight of the box during a trip from the 3rd floor to the 1st floor?

  A. 80 N
  B. 90 N
  C. 100 N
  D. 110 N

291. If the man drops the box while the elevator is accelerating downward, at what rate will the box accelerate?

  A. 9 m/s²
  B. 9.5 m/s²
  C. 10 m/s²
  D. 11 m/s²

292. How much time is required for the elevator to leave the 1st floor and stop on the 10th floor?

  A. 14 s
  B. 20 s
  C. 24 s
  D. 25 s

293. On a trip from the 1st to the 6th floor, the man wondered if he could throw the box into the air the moment the elevator leaves the 1st floor, and catch it the moment the elevator arrives at the 6th floor. What would the initial vertical velocity of the box have to be in order for this to work?

  A. 5 m/s
  B. 10 m/s
  C. 37 m/s
  D. 55 m/s

Questions 294-296 refer to the 5 kg block in the diagram below.

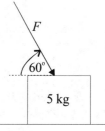

294. If the force F is 120 N, and the surface upon which the block rests is frictionless, at what rate does the block accelerate?

  A. 10 m/s²
  B. 12 m/s²
  C. 24 m/s²
  D. 30 m/s²

295. The coefficient of kinetic friction between the block and the surface upon which it rests is 0.1. The force F is 100 N. At approximately what rate does the block accelerate?

  A. 1 m/s²
  B. 4.5 m/s²
  C. 6 m/s²
  D. 7.3 m/s²

296. A 5×10^3 kg airplane moves horizontally through the sky at 30 m/s. If there is 8.7×10^4 N of air resistance against the forward motion of the plane, what force must be applied to the airplane in order to continue its motion?

   A. 0 N
   B. 10^5 N at a $30°$ angle upward
   C. 10^5 N at a $60°$ angle upward
   D. 10^5 N straight up

Torque

297. If F equals 10 N, which of the following wrenches applies the most torque?

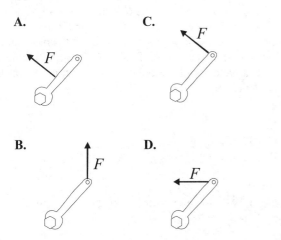

   A.

   C.

   B.

   D.

298. If the net torque acting upon a system is zero, which of the following is true?

   A. The system can have no translational motion.
   B. The system can have no rotational motion.
   C. The system may be rotating if and only if it is rotating at a constant speed about its center of gravity.
   D. The system may be rotating about any point if and only if it is rotating at a constant speed.

299. Which of the following systems is not in rotational equilibrium?

   A. A top spinning in place at a constant speed about its center of gravity
   B. A seesaw balanced motionless by two children
   C. A figure skater spinning faster and faster on ice
   D. A ball spinning in place at a constant angular velocity

300. Which of the following is true for any system in rotational equilibrium?

   A. Only the torque about the center of gravity must be zero.
   B. Only the torque about any part of the object must be zero.
   C. The torque about any point on the object or any point in space must be zero.
   D. The object must not be spinning.

301. If F equals 10 N, which of the following wrenches applies the most torque?

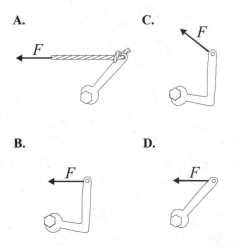

   A.   C.

   B.   D.

302. A one meter board with a mass of 12 kg hangs by a rope as shown. A block is hung from the left end of the board. If the board is to be balanced level to the ground, what must be the mass of the block?

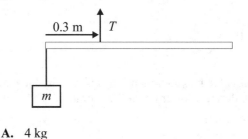

   A. 4 kg
   B. 6 kg
   C. 8 kg
   D. 12 kg

303. A one meter board with a mass of 3 kg sits on the point of a block. Blocks are hung from the board as shown. If the board is to be balanced level to the ground, what must be the mass of the block hanging from the right side?

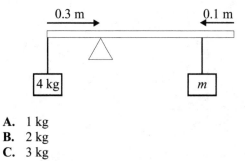

- **A.** 1 kg
- **B.** 2 kg
- **C.** 3 kg
- **D.** 4 kg

304. A 10 m board with a mass of 15 kg rests on a large stationary block as shown. A 75 kg box is positioned so that its center of gravity is one meter from the right end of the board. What distance x could a 60 kg woman walk from the right end of the board before it falls?

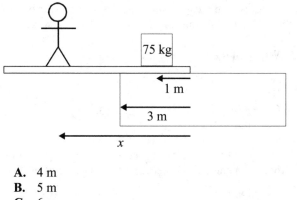

- **A.** 4 m
- **B.** 5 m
- **C.** 6 m
- **D.** 8 m

305. A one meter board with a mass of 16 kg hangs by a rope as shown. A 4 kg mass is hung from the left end of the board. If the board is to be balanced level to the ground, what is the distance x from the left end that the rope with the tension T must be attached?

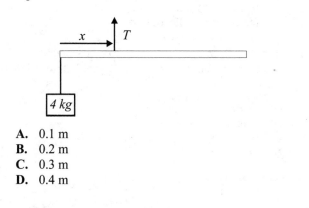

- **A.** 0.1 m
- **B.** 0.2 m
- **C.** 0.3 m
- **D.** 0.4 m

306. Mary and Tim balance on a 10 m board as shown. The board has a mass of 20 kg. If Mary and Tim have a combined mass of 180 kg, what is Mary's mass?

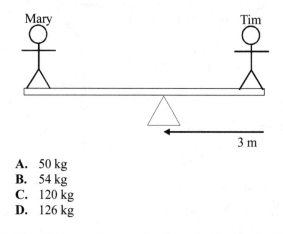

- **A.** 50 kg
- **B.** 54 kg
- **C.** 120 kg
- **D.** 126 kg

307. What is the net force on the dipole inside the capacitor?

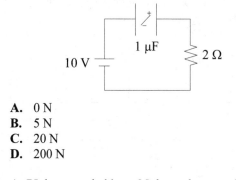

- **A.** 0 N
- **B.** 5 N
- **C.** 20 N
- **D.** 200 N

308. A 75 kg man holds a 25 kg pole at a 60° angle as shown. He leans backward at a 60° angle so that his center of gravity is 0.5 m to the right of his feet. How long is the pole?

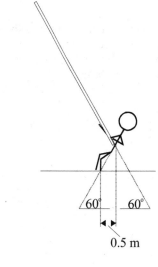

- **A.** 4 m
- **B.** 6 m
- **C.** 7 m
- **D.** 8 m

309. The crane shown below has mass of 4,000 kg and a base of 3.4 m. The arm of the crane is 22 m and attaches to the center of the crane. If the arm is placed at an angle of 30°, what is the largest mass that the crane can hold off the ground without tipping?

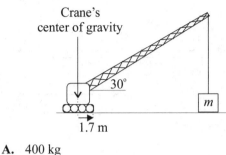

A. 400 kg
B. 440 kg
C. 4,000 kg
D. 40,000 kg

310. A 10 m board with a weight hangs by two ropes as shown below. If the board has a mass of 20 kg, what is the tension T_2?

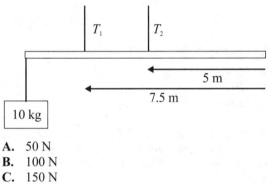

A. 50 N
B. 100 N
C. 150 N
D. 200 N

311. A 1 m board weighted at one end hangs by two ropes as shown below. If the board has a mass of 8 kg, what is the distance x at which T_1 must act in order to balance the board in static equilibrium?

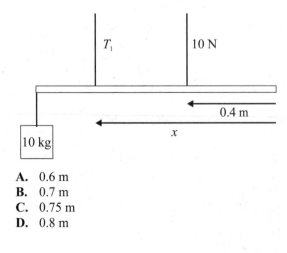

A. 0.6 m
B. 0.7 m
C. 0.75 m
D. 0.8 m

312. A 0.8 m long sign extends from a wall supported by a rope as shown. If the sign has uniform density, what is the minimum coefficient of friction between the sign and the wall?

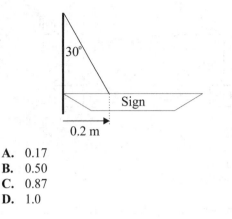

A. 0.17
B. 0.50
C. 0.87
D. 1.0

Energy

Unless otherwise stated, for all questions on energy, assume g is the free-fall acceleration near the surface of the earth, r is the radius of the earth, m_e is the mass of the earth, and G is the gravitational constant ($G = 6.67 \times 10^{-11}$ N m^2/kg^2).

313. Which of the following is not a unit of energy?

A. J
B. eV
C. kg m/s^2
D. kg m^2/s^2

314. Which of the following represents the gravitational potential energy of object m_0 at the surface of the earth?

A. Gm_em_0/r^2
B. Gm_0/r
C. Gm_e/r
D. m_0gr

315. If a moving object doubles its speed, its kinetic energy:

A. decreases by a factor of 2.
B. remains the same.
C. increases by a factor of 2.
D. increases by a factor of 4.

316. A ball with mass m is dropped from a height h. How much kinetic energy does it have just before it hits the ground?

A. ½ mg/h^2
B. ½ mg^2
C. mgh
D. gh

317. A 4 kg ball is thrown straight into the air at 6 m/s. How high does it travel?

   A. 1.0 m
   B. 1.6 m
   C. 1.8 m
   D. 2.0 m

318. A 4 kg projectile has 1400 J of kinetic energy when it leaves the ground. If it has 120 J of kinetic energy at its highest point, how high did it travel?

   A. 3 m
   B. 30 m
   C. 32 m
   D. 35 m

319. A 2 kg projectile is launched from the ground at an angle of $60°$ and a velocity of 40 m/s. Which of the following is true concerning the projectile when it reaches its highest point?

   A. The projectile will have equal amounts of kinetic and potential energy.
   B. The gravitational potential energy of the projectile will be 1200 J.
   C. The kinetic energy of the projectile will be zero.
   D. If a 1 kg projectile were used instead, the potential energy at the highest point would remain the same.

320. The spring on a jack-in-the-box has a spring constant of 400 N/m. The spring is compressed by 20 cm when the box is closed. If the jack-in-the-box has a mass of 1 kg, what will be its speed when it is opened and the spring reaches its rest length? (Note: Ignore gravity.)

   A. 2 m/s
   B. 4 m/s
   C. 6 m/s
   D. 8 m/s

321. A 2 kg block is dropped from 45 cm above a spring. If the spring compresses 5 cm when struck by the block, what is its spring constant?

   A. 8×10^{-5} N/m
   B. 4×10^{3} N/m
   C. 8×10^{3} N/m
   D. 1.6×10^{4} N/m

322. Which of the following is equal to g for an object with mass m_o?

   A. $Gm_e m_o/r^2$
   B. $Gm_e m_o/r$
   C. Gm_o/r^2
   D. Gm_e/r^2

323. A 2 kg ball and a 4 kg ball are dropped from a height of 40 m. At what height will the 2 kg ball be, when the kinetic energy of the balls are equal?

   A. 10 m
   B. 20 m
   C. 30 m
   D. 40 m

324. A 2 kg ball and a 4 kg ball are thrown upwards each with a speed of 20 m/s. At what height will the 2 kg ball be, when the kinetic energy of the balls are equal?

   A. 5 m
   B. 10 m
   C. 15 m
   D. 20 m

325. A 2 kg ball is thrown upwards with a speed of 40 m/s. At what height will the ball be, when its kinetic energy is equal its potential energy?

   A. 20 m
   B. 40 m
   C. 60 m
   D. 80 m

326. A 2 kg ball and an 8 kg ball are placed on separate springs, each with the same spring constant. The springs are compressed by the same distance and released. Which of the following is true about the maximum heights reached by the balls?

   A. The 2 kg ball will go four times as high.
   B. The 2 kg ball will go twice as high.
   C. The balls will reach equal maximum heights.
   D. The 8 kg ball will go four times as high.

327. A 2 kg ball and an 8 kg ball are placed on separate springs, each with the same spring constant. The springs are compressed by the same a distance and released. Which of the following is true about the velocities of the balls upon leaving the springs?

   A. The 2 kg ball has a velocity four times greater.
   B. The 2 kg ball has a velocity two times greater.
   C. Their velocities are equal
   D. The 8 kg ball has a velocity four times greater.

328. A 2 kg ball and an 8 kg ball are placed on the same spring at the same time. The spring is compressed and released. Which of the following is true about the maximum heights reached by the balls?

   A. The 2 kg ball will go four times as high.
   B. The 2 kg ball will go twice as high.
   C. The balls will reach equal maximum heights.
   D. The 8 kg ball will go four times as high.

329. A 2 kg ball and an 8 kg ball are placed on the same spring at the same time. The spring is compressed and released. Which of the following is true about the velocities of the balls upon leaving the spring?

   A. The 2 kg ball has velocity four times greater.
   B. The 2 kg ball has velocity two times greater.
   C. Their velocities are equal
   D. The 8 kg ball has velocity four times greater.

330. A man puts springs on the bottoms of his shoes and jumps off a 10 m cliff. Assuming the springs follow Hooke's law, from the moment the springs touch the ground to when they are fully compressed, the magnitude of the man's acceleration will:

   A. decrease then increase.
   B. increase then decrease.
   C. remain constant at 10 m/s^2.
   D. remain constant at zero.

Work

331. In which of the following examples is work done?

   A. A man rubs his hands together and they get warm.
   B. A 50 kg girl leans against a wall at a 30° angle.
   C. A pot of water sits over a fire until it boils.
   D. The moon orbits the earth.

Questions 332-336 refer to the diagram below.

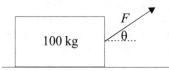

332. θ is 60°, and F is 50 N. If the block is moved along the surface for 20 m, and the surface is frictionless, how much work is done on the block?

   A. 500 J
   B. 1000 J
   C. 50,000 J
   D. 100,000 J

333. θ is 60°, and F is 50 N. If the block is moved from rest along the surface for 20 m, and the surface is frictionless, what is the kinetic energy of the block?

   A. 250 J
   B. 500 J
   C. 25,000 J
   D. 50,000 J

334. If the block is initially moving at 5 m/s to the right, and force F is applied over a distance d, which of the following would NOT change the amount of work done on the block?

   A. changing the angle θ
   B. changing the mass of the block
   C. changing the force F
   D. changing the distance d

335. Assume the force F acts for a time t. Assume the block has an initial velocity v. Initial velocity in which direction would result in the greatest amount of work done on the block?

   A. initial velocity to the right
   B. initial velocity to the left
   C. Initial velocity in either direction would result in the same amount of work done because the time t is constant.
   D. Initial velocity in either direction would result in the same amount of work done because the distances traveled would be the same.

336. θ is 60°, and F is 50 N. If the block is moved from rest along the surface for 200 m, and the surface is frictionless, what is final velocity of the block?

   A. 5 m/s
   B. 10 m/s
   C. 20 m/s
   D. 40 m/s

Questions 337-339 refer to the diagram below. Assume no friction unless otherwise stated.

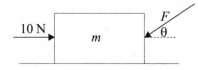

337. Force F is 20 N, m is 100 kg, and θ is 60°. If both forces are applied for 1 second, how much work is done on the block?

   A. 0 J
   B. 8.7 J
   C. 20 J
   D. 30 J

338. Force F is 200 N, m is 100 kg, and θ is 60°. If the block moves 10 m to the left, how much work is done on the block?

   A. 900 J
   B. 1000 J
   C. 1100 J
   D. 2100 J

339. Force F is 100 N, m is 10 kg, and θ is 30°. The coefficient of friction between the block and the surface is 0.1. If the block starts from rest, and is pushed for 5 m, what is the approximate final velocity of the block?

A. 0 m/s
B. 4.5 m/s
C. 5.8 m/s
D. 7.9 m/s

Questions 340-345 refer to the diagram below. Assume no friction unless otherwise stated.

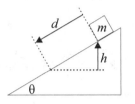

340. If the mass m, starting from rest, slides a distance d in time t, accelerating to a velocity v, which of the following does NOT represent the work done by gravity?

A. mgh
B. $mgd(\sin\theta)$
C. $\frac{1}{2}mv^2$
D. $vtmg$

341. The mass m slides a distance d. Which of the following would NOT change the work done on the mass?

A. a change in the angle θ
B. a change in the distance d
C. a change in the mass m
D. All of the above would change the work done on the mass.

342. A mass m slides a distance d. Which of the following is altered by changing m?

A. the work done on the mass
B. the velocity of the mass
C. the acceleration of the mass
D. the time required for the mass to move distance d

343. If θ is 30°, and m is 2.5 kg, how much work is done on the block if it slides 20 cm?

A. 2.5 J
B. 5.0 J
C. 25 J
D. 50 J

344. If θ is 30°, h is 10 cm, and m is 4 kg, how much work is done on the block if it slides a distance d?

A. 2 J
B. 4 J
C. 6 J
D. 8 J

345. If θ is 60°, h is 10 cm, and m is 4 kg, how much work is done on the block if it slides a distance d?

A. 2 J
B. 4 J
C. 6 J
D. 8 J

Conservative and Nonconservative Forces

346. A man puts springs on the bottoms of his shoes and jumps off a 10 m cliff. If the springs follow Hooke's Law, the man should bounce to a height of:

A. 5 m
B. 7.5 m
C. 10 m
D. 20 m

347. Molecules within a gas are attracted to one another by electrostatic forces. If the volume of a gas were allowed to increase, and no energy were allowed to enter or leave the gas, as the molecules moved farther apart, the kinetic energy of the molecules would:

A. increase
B. decrease
C. increase then decrease
D. remain the same

348. In which of the following examples is a nonconservative force acting?

A. A feather falls to earth in a vacuum.
B. A bonding pair of Electrons are attracted to the nuclei of the bonding atoms.
C. A spring returns to its original shape after being compressed.
D. An astronaut on the moon picks up a rock.

349. If the only energy transfer is work, and only conservative forces act on a large object, which of the following properties of that object can NOT be changed?

A. kinetic energy
B. potential energy
C. temperature
D. velocity

350. Which of the following is a true statement?

    A. Conservative forces conserve potential energy.
    B. Conservative forces conserve kinetic energy.
    C. When only conservative forces are acting, the sum of the change in mechanical energies is zero.
    D. Nonconservative forces do not follow the Law of Conservation of Energy.

351. Gravity is the only force acting on a 2 kg mass. The potential energy of the mass increases by 144 J. What is the change in velocity of the mass?

    A. an increase of 12 m/s
    B. a decrease of 12 m/s
    C. The change in velocity depends upon the initial amount of potential energy.
    D. The change in velocity depends upon the initial velocity.

Work and Friction

352. Which of the following statements is true?

    A. No work is done on an object if that object remains stationary.
    B. Work can only change the velocity or position of an object and not its temperature.
    C. Energy is conserved when frictional forces are applied to an object.
    D. Energy transfer as heat always accompanies friction.

353. A block slides to a stop along a table top. Which of the following statements is NOT true?

    A. The change in the mechanical energy of the block is equal to the force of friction times the distance that the block slid.
    B. The temperature of the block increased.
    C. The temperature of the table increased.
    D. The temperature change of the table is equal to the temperature change of the block.

354. A block slides to a stop along a table top. Which of the following statements is true?

    A. The work done by friction is equal to the force of friction times the distance that the block slid.
    B. The work done on the block is equal to the force of friction times the distance that the block slid.
    C. The work done on the table is equal to the force of friction times the distance that the block slid.
    D. The work done on the block is equal to the sum of its changes in kinetic and internal energies.

355. A boy swings a ball attached to a string in a circle parallel to the ground at a constant velocity. Which of the following is true? (Assume no air resistance.)

    A. The tension in the string does work on the ball.
    B. No work is done on the ball while it swings.
    C. The mechanical energy of the ball changes.
    D. Gravity does work on the ball.

356. A 4 kg block moving 10 m/s slides to a stop over 5 m. What was the force of friction on the block?

    A. 10 N
    B. 20 N
    C. 30 N
    D. 40 N

357. A 2 kg block requires 2 m to slide to a stop. If the force of friction was 18 N, what was the initial velocity of the ball?

    A. 2 m/s
    B. 4 m/s
    C. 6 m/s
    D. 8 m/s

Questions 358-359 refer to the diagram below. h represents the vertical distance from the bottom of the curve to the center of mass of the block. The curved portion of the ramp is frictionless.

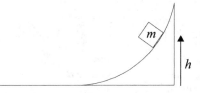

358. The block has a mass of 500 g and h is 4 cm. The block starts from rest, and slides down the curve. If the coefficient of kinetic friction between the block and the flat portion of the ramp is 0.2, how far does the block travel along the flat portion of the ramp?

    A. 10 cm
    B. 20 cm
    C. 30 cm
    D. 40 cm

359. The block has a mass of 50 g and h is 20 cm. The block has an initial velocity of 2 m/s, and slides down the curve. If the coefficient of kinetic friction between the block and the flat portion of the ramp is 0.2, how far does the block travel along the flat portion of the ramp?

    A. 0.5 m
    B. 1 m
    C. 2 m
    D. 5 m

Examples of Work

Questions 360-364 refer to the diagram below.

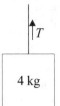

T

4 kg

360. The block is lowered by a rope as shown. The tension T in the rope is 35 N. If the block is lowered 10 m, how much work is done on the block by the rope?

   A. −50 J
   B. −175 J
   C. −350 J
   D. −400 J

361. The block is lowered by a rope as shown. The tension T in the rope is 35 N. If the block is lowered 10 m, how much work is done by the weight of the block?

   A. 50 J
   B. 175 J
   C. 350 J
   D. 400 J

362. The block is lowered by a rope as shown. The tension T in the rope is 35 N. If the block is lowered 10 m, what is the change in kinetic energy of the block?

   A. 50 J
   B. 175 J
   C. 350 J
   D. 400 J

363. The block is lowered by a rope as shown. The tension T in the rope is 35 N. If the block begins at rest and is lowered 10 m, what is the approximate change in velocity of the block?

   A. 5 m/s
   B. 7 m/s
   C. 10 m/s
   D. 12 m/s

364. The block is lowered by a rope as shown. The tension T in the rope is 35 N. If the block begins at 5 m/s downward and is lowered 10 m, what is the approximate final velocity of the block?

   A. 5 m/s
   B. 7 m/s
   C. 10 m/s
   D. 12 m/s

365. A car moving at 35 m/s on dry pavement, skids to a stop in 7 seconds. What is the coefficient of friction between the car's tires and the pavement?

   A. 0.2
   B. 0.5
   C. 1
   D. 2

366. A car moving at 35 m/s on dry pavement, skids to a stop over 175 m. What is the coefficient of friction between the car's tires and the pavement?

   A. 0.25
   B. 0.35
   C. 0.45
   D. 0.50

367. In 0.5 s, a hammer drives a 30 cm nail into a piece of wood. If the frictional force between the nail and the wood is 200 N, approximately how much work is done by the hammer?

   A. 30 J
   B. 60 J
   C. 120 J
   D. 600 J

Power

368. In 0.5 s, a hammer drives a 30 cm nail into a piece of wood. If the frictional force between the nail and the wood is 200 N, how much power is dissipated by the friction?

   A. 30 W
   B. 60 W
   C. 120 W
   D. 600 W

369. In 50 minutes a forklift lifts twenty-five 60 kg boxes from the floor onto a shelf 2 m high. What is the minimum power of the forklift?

   A. 2 W
   B. 10 W
   C. 100 W
   D. 6000 W

370. A 5,000 kg rocket moves straight up at 30 m/s near the earth's surface. What is the minimum power of the rocket's engines?

   A. 6×10^{-4} W
   B. 1.5×10^{6} W
   C. 1.5×10^{6} W
   D. 3.0×10^{6} W

371. A 100 W light bulb is left on for 2 days. How many 20 cm steps must a 60 kg women climb to burn the same amount of energy?

- **A.** 1,440
- **B.** 14,400
- **C.** 144,000
- **D.** 1,440,000

372. Which of the following requires the most power?

- **A.** lifting 1,000 kg 2 m in 2 s
- **B.** lifting 1,500 kg 1.5 m in 2 s
- **C.** lifting 2,000 kg 1 m in 2 s
- **D.** lifting 2,000 kg 2 m in 4 s

373. A rocket leaves the earth's atmosphere heading for the moon. Once in space, as the rocket moves farther from the earth, the power required to maintain its velocity:

- **A.** decreases with time because the force of gravity decreases.
- **B.** decreases with time because the force of gravity increases.
- **C.** increases with time because the force of gravity decreases.
- **D.** increases with time because the force of gravity increases.

374. Assuming constant gravity and no air resistance, as an object falls to the ground near the surface of the earth, the rate at which potential energy becomes kinetic energy:

- **A.** decreases because the same force is applied over a shorter distance in the same amount of time.
- **B.** increases because the same force is applied over a shorter distance in a shorter amount of time.
- **C.** decreases because the same force is applied over a greater distance in a shorter amount of time.
- **D.** increases because the same force is applied over a greater distance in a shorter amount of time.

375. A 10,000 kg locomotive speeds toward Lois Lane at 10 m/s, and will hit her in 10 s if Superman doesn't try to stop it. If Superman applies a constant force, what average power does he need in order to stop the train?

- **A.** 2.5×10^4 W
- **B.** 5.0×10^4 W
- **C.** 2.5×10^5 W
- **D.** 5.0×10^5 W

376. A stationary 10 kg box is lifted and placed at rest on top of a 10 m shelf. The move takes 2 s. A student argues that the minimum average power is greater than 500 W. The student is:

- **A.** right because the box must have a change in kinetic energy in addition to the change in potential energy.
- **B.** right because the box had to be accelerated which requires a force greater than mg.
- **C.** wrong because the box can be moved at an infinitely slow constant velocity, and thus the work done is equal to the weight times the distance.
- **D.** wrong because the force on the box could be twice the weight for the first half of the trip, and zero for the second half of the trip.

377. A forklift holds a 500 kg box 4 m in the air for 100 s. What is the minimum power required by the forklift?

- **A.** 0 W
- **B.** 2×10^2 W
- **C.** 2×10^4 W
- **D.** 2×10^6 W

378. A forklift lifts a 500 kg box 4 m in the air in 100 s. What is the minimum power required by the forklift?

- **A.** 0 W
- **B.** 2×10^2 W
- **C.** 2×10^4 W
- **D.** 2×10^6 W

379. A forklift moves a 500 kg box from one 4 m shelf to a second 4 m shelf in 100 s. What is the minimum power required by the forklift?

- **A.** 0 W
- **B.** 2×10^2 W
- **C.** 2×10^4 W
- **D.** 2×10^6 W

380. A car moving at a constant velocity of 20 m/s applies a net frictional force to the road of 1,000 N in order to maintain its velocity. What is the minimum power of the engine?

- **A.** 1,000 W
- **B.** 2,000 W
- **C.** 10,000 W
- **D.** 20,000 W

Momentum

381. Which of the following has the greatest momentum?

    A. a 5 kg ball moving at 9 m/s
    B. a 7 kg ball moving at 7 m/s
    C. a 10 kg ball moving at 5 m/s
    D. a 12 kg ball moving at 4 m/s

382. Which of the following has the greatest kinetic energy?

    A. a 5 kg ball moving at 9 m/s
    B. a 7 kg ball moving at 7 m/s
    C. a 10 kg ball moving at 5 m/s
    D. a 12 kg ball moving at 4 m/s

383. Which of the following has the greatest inertia?

    A. a 5 kg ball moving at 9 m/s
    B. a 7 kg ball moving at 7 m/s
    C. a 10 kg ball moving at 5 m/s
    D. a 12 kg ball moving at 4 m/s

384. Which of the following would require the greatest force to stop in just one second?

    A. a 5 kg ball moving at 9 m/s
    B. a 7 kg ball moving at 7 m/s
    C. a 10 kg ball moving at 5 m/s
    D. a 12 kg ball moving at 4 m/s

385. Which of the following would require the greatest force in order to change its velocity by 1 m/s in one second?

    A. a 5 kg ball moving at 9 m/s
    B. a 7 kg ball moving at 7 m/s
    C. a 10 kg ball moving at 5 m/s
    D. a 12 kg ball moving at 4 m/s

386. A boy on a sled slides over a frozen lake at 10 m/s. The boy has a mass of 40 kg; the sled has a mass of 10 kg. If the boy rolls off the sled, the sled will most likely continue to move at:

    A. 2 m/s
    B. 8 m/s
    C. 10 m/s
    D. 50 m/s

387. A 2 kg block moves 12 m/s. What is its momentum?

    A. 6 kg m/s
    B. 12 m/s
    C. 24 kg m/s
    D. 144 kg m/s

388. A bucket full of water is slid across a sheet of ice in the rain. As the bucket fills, what happens to its velocity and its momentum? (Assume no friction)

    A. both decrease
    B. both remain constant
    C. velocity remains constant; momentum increases
    D. velocity decreases; momentum remains constant

389. A bucket full of water is slid across a sheet of ice. If the bucket has a slow leak, what happens to its velocity and its momentum? (Assume no friction)

    A. both decrease
    B. both remain constant
    C. both increase
    D. velocity remains constant; momentum decreases

Collisions

390. A 1 kg lump of clay moving through space at 2 m/s collides with a second 1 kg lump of clay at rest. If the lumps stick together what is their final velocity?

    A. 0.5 m/s
    B. 1 m/s
    C. 2 m/s
    D. 4 m/s

391. A 1 kg lump of clay moving through space at 2 m/s collides with a second 1 kg lump of clay at rest. If the lumps stick together what portion of the original kinetic energy is lost to internal energy?

    A. 25%
    B. 50%
    C. 75%
    D. 100 %

Questions 392-396 refer to the diagram below. Two masses in space move toward each other and collide. Assume no rotational motion occurs before or after the collision.

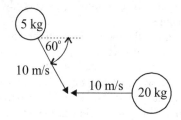

392. If the two masses stick together after colliding, what is the final horizontal velocity of the masses?

    A. 0 m/s
    B. 5 m/s to the left
    C. 7 m/s to the left
    D. 9 m/s to the left

393. If the two masses make an elastic collision, which of the following will NOT be conserved?

A. momentum
B. kinetic energy
C. total energy
D. velocity of the 5 kg mass

394. Which of the following properties of colliding objects will remain constant before, during, and after both an inelastic and an elastic collision?

I. velocity
II. momentum
III. kinetic energy

A. II only
B. III only
C. I, II, and III
D. None

395. If the masses collide and stick together, what will be their approximate final velocity after the collision?

A. 7.2 m/s down and to the left
B. 8.3 m/s directly downward
C. 10 m/s directly to the left
D. 12.2 m/s down and to the right

396. If the masses make an elastic collision, what will be the sum of their horizontal momentums after the collision?

A. 150 kg m/s
B. 175 kg m/s
C. 200 kg m/s
D. 225 kg m/s

---

397. Which of the following is NOT true concerning elastic collisions?

A. Only conservative forces are involved in elastic collisions.
B. The sum of the kinetic energies of the colliding objects is always conserved.
C. The speed of all colliding objects always remains unchanged.
D. The sum of the momentums of the colliding objects is always conserved.

398. A 2 kg ball moving at 4 m/s collides elastically with a 6 kg ball that is stationary. If the 2 kg ball bounces off with a speed of 2 m/s, what is the speed of the 6 kg ball?

A. $^1/_3$ m/s
B. $^2/_3$ m/s
C. 2 m/s
D. 3 m/s

399. A ball falls from a height of 10 M. If it makes a perfectly elastic collision with the level ground, how high will it bounce? (Assume that the ground is infinitely heavier than the ball)

A. 0 m
B. 5 m
C. 10 m
D. infinitely high

400. A small object moving at 10 m/s to the right collides with a heavier object that is initially stationary. Which of the following is a possible velocity of the smaller object after the collision?

A. 10 m/s to the right
B. 5 m/s to the right
C. 5 m/s to the left
D. 12 m/s to the left

401. A small object moving at 10 m/s to the right collides with a heavier object that is initially stationary. Which of the following is NOT a possible velocity of the smaller object after the collision?

A. 1 m/s to the right
B. 5 m/s to the right
C. 1 m/s to the left
D. 5 m/s to the left

402. A large object moving at 10 m/s to the right collides with a lighter object that is initially stationary. Which of the following is a possible velocity of the lighter object after the collision?

A. 1 m/s to the right
B. 5 m/s to the right
C. 18 m/s to the right
D. 25 m/s to the right

Questions 403-409 refer to the diagram below. Bob m_1 is swung from a height h and allowed to collide with bob m_2, which is at rest. The bobs are the same size but may have different masses. The velocity of m_1 just before striking m_2 is v.

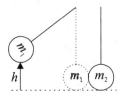

403. If the bobs collide elastically, and m_1 is heavier than m_2, which of the following is true?

    A. m_1 and m_2 will both move to the right at the same speed.

    B. m_1 and m_2 will both move to the right, but m_1 will move more slowly.

    C. m_2 will move to the right, and m_1 will move to the left.

    D. m_2 will move to the right, and m_1 will stop.

404. If the bobs collide elastically, and m_1 and m_2 have the same mass, which of the following is true?

    A. m_1 and m_2 will both move to the right at the same speed.

    B. m_1 and m_2 will both move to the right, but m_1 will move more slowly.

    C. m_2 will move to the right, and m_1 will move to the left.

    D. m_2 will move to the right, and m_1 will stop.

405. If the bobs collide elastically, and m_2 is heavier than m_1, which of the following is true?

    A. m_1 and m_2 will both move to the right at the same speed.

    B. m_1 and m_2 will both move to the right, but m_1 will move more slowly.

    C. m_2 will move to the right, and m_1 will move to the left.

    D. m_2 will move to the right, and m_1 will stop.

406. As the mass of m_1 becomes much greater than m_2, what is the maximum velocity that can be reached by m_1 after the collision? (Note: Assume a completely elastic collision.)

    A. 0 m/s

    B. v

    C. $2v$

    D. The maximum velocity is infinite.

407. As the mass of m_1 becomes much greater than m_2, what is the maximum velocity that can be reached by m_2? (Note: Assume a completely elastic collision.)

    A. 0 m/s

    B. v

    C. $2v$

    D. The maximum velocity is infinite.

408. If m_2 is three times greater than m_1, what is the velocity of m_2 after the collision? (Note: Assume a completely elastic collision.)

    A. v

    B. $^1/_2\,v$

    C. $^1/_3\,v$

    D. $^1/_4\,v$

409. If the collision of the bobs is completely inelastic, and m_1 and m_2 have the same mass, which of the following is true?

    A. m_1 and m_2 will move to the right with a velocity $^1/_2\,v$.

    B. m_1 and m_2 will move to the right with a velocity v.

    C. m_1 and m_2 will move to the right with a velocity $2v$.

    D. m_1 and m_2 will collide and stop.

Questions 410-411 refer to the diagram below. Bob m_1 and m_2 are swung from a heights h_1 and h_2 respectively, so that they collide as shown. The heights h_1 and h_2 are not necessarily equal. The bobs are the same size but may have different masses. The velocities of the bobs just before striking are v_1 and v_2 respectively.

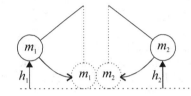

410. If the bobs collide elastically, and m_1 and m_2 have the same mass, and are dropped from the same height, which of the following is true?

    A. m_1 and m_2 will stop.

    B. m_1 will stop, and m_2 will bounce to a height h_2.

    C. m_1 and m_2 will bounce to their original heights.

    D. m_1 and m_2 will bounce to twice their original heights.

411. Assume the bobs collide elastically, and m_1 and m_2 have the same mass. If $h_1 = 2h_2$, which of the following is the most likely result?

    A. m_1 will stop and m_2 will bounce to a height of $3h_2$.

    B. m_1 will bounce to a height of h_1 and m_2 will bounce to a height of h_2, and they will bounce in opposite directions.

    C. m_1 will bounce to a height of h_2 and m_2 will bounce to a height of h_1, and they will bounce in opposite directions.

    D. m_1 will move to a height of h_2 and m_2 will bounce to a height of h_1, and they will both move to the right.

Reverse Collisions

Questions 412-16 refer to the diagram below. A man and a block rest on a frictionless frozen lake. The man has a mass of 50 kg.

412. The man pushes off from the block and slides away at a speed of 30 m/s. The speed of the box is:

   A. 10 m/s
   B. 15 m/s
   C. 30 m/s
   D. 90 m/s

413. The man pushes off from the block and slides away at a speed of 30 m/s. After the push, the sum of the momenta of the man and the block is:

   A. 0 kg m/s
   B. 1500 kg m/s
   C. 3000 kg m/s
   D. 6000 m/s

414. Which of the following could the man accomplish by himself?

   I.   move only the box to the shore
   II. move only himself to the shore
  III. move both the box and himself to the shore

   A. I only
   B. II only
   C. I and II only
   D. I, II, and III

415. If the man climbs on top of the box, the box will:

   A. shift to the right and stop
   B. shift to the left and stop
   C. slide to the right with some constant velocity
   D. slide to the left with some constant velocity

416. The man attaches himself to the box with a long rope, and pushes off from the box giving himself a leftward velocity. What will happen when the rope runs out?

   A. The man and box will move to the right because the box has greater inertia.
   B. The man and box will stop because they have equal and opposite momentums.
   C. The man and box will move to the left because the man has greater kinetic energy.
   D. The man cannot give himself a leftward velocity because the surface is frictionless and the box will not move under any force.

Questions 417-419 refer to the diagram below. A 50 kg woman stands on a massless board. The board rests on a frictionless frozen lake 45 m from a rock. Ten 5 kg blocks are stacked on the board next to the woman. (Diagram not drawn to scale)

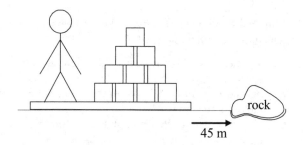

417. Which of the following will move the woman to the rock in exactly 3 s?

   A. All at once, the woman slides all the blocks to the left at 15 m/s.
   B. All at once, the woman slides all the blocks to the left at 45 m/s.
   C. All at once, the woman slides all the blocks to the right at 15 m/s.
   D. All at once, the woman slides all the blocks to the right at 30 m/s.

418. The woman slides 5 blocks to the right at 6 m/s, and 2 s later slides the remaining 5 blocks to the left at 6 m/s. At $t = 2$ s she is:

   A. 49 m from the rock and stationary.
   B. 57 m from the rock and stationary.
   C. 57 m from the rock and moving at 1 m/s to the right.
   D. 57 m from the rock and moving at 2 m/s to the right.

419. The woman slides 1 block to the left. Which of the following is true after she releases the block?

   A. She is stationary.
   B. She is accelerating to the right.
   C. She is moving to the right with a constant velocity.
   D. She has increased her inertia.

---

420. Which of the following is true concerning a rocket in space starting from rest and accelerating to 100 m/s?

   A. The magnitude of the velocity of the gas expelled from the back of the rocket is equal to the magnitude of the velocity of the rocket.
   B. The magnitude of the momentum of the gas expelled from the back of the rocket is equal to the magnitude of the momentum of the rocket.
   C. The kinetic energy of the gas expelled from the back of the rocket is equal to the kinetic energy of the rocket.
   D. The magnitude of the acceleration of the gas expelled from the back of the rocket is equal to the magnitude of the acceleration of the rocket.

Impulse

421. If the same force were applied to each of the following, the change in velocity would be the greatest for:

   A. a 5 kg ball moving at 9 m/s
   B. a 7 kg ball moving at 7 m/s
   C. a 10 kg ball moving at 5 m/s
   D. The change in velocity would be the same for all three.

422. If the same force were applied to each of the following, the change in momentum would be the greatest for:

   A. a 5 kg ball moving at 9 m/s
   B. a 7 kg ball moving at 7 m/s
   C. a 10 kg ball moving at 5 m/s
   D. The change in momentum would be the same for all three.

423. Which of the following would require the greatest average force?

   A. stopping a 5 kg ball moving at 9 m/s in one second
   B. stopping a 7 kg ball moving at 7 m/s in one second
   C. stopping a 10 kg ball moving at 5 m/s in one second
   D. stopping a 12 kg ball moving at 4 m/s in one second

424. Which of the following could be accomplished with the least average force?

   A. accelerating a 2 kg ball from 0 m/s to 9 m/s in half a second
   B. accelerating a 6 kg ball from 0 m/s to 6 m/s in one second
   C. accelerating a 9 kg ball from 0 m/s to 8 m/s in two seconds
   D. accelerating a 10 kg ball from 0 m/s to 7 m/s in two seconds

425. Which of the following requires the greatest average force?

   A. accelerating a 7 kg ball from 30 m/s to 39 m/s in one second
   B. accelerating a 16 kg ball from 12 m/s to 20 m/s in two seconds
   C. decelerating a 9 kg ball from 21 m/s to 14 m/s in one second
   D. decelerating a 20 kg ball from 10 m/s to 4 m/s in two seconds

Questions 426-429 refer to the graph shown below. The graph below shows the net force F applied through the center of gravity of a 200 g mass as a function of time t.

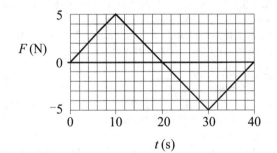

426. What is the change in momentum of the mass in the first 20 seconds?

   A. 0 kg m/s
   B. 10 kg m/s
   C. 50 kg m/s
   D. 250 kg m/s

427. What is the average force on the mass in the first 20 seconds?

   A. 2.5 N
   B. 5 N
   C. 25 N
   D. 100 N

428. How fast is the particle moving at t = 20 s?

   A. 0 m/s
   B. 50 m/s
   C. 100 m/s
   D. 250 m/s

429. Which of the following statements is true if the mass is at rest at $t = 0$?

A. The velocity of the mass is decreasing between 10 and 20 seconds.
B. The acceleration of the mass is constant between 0 and 10 seconds.
C. At 40 seconds, the mass is stationary.
D. The distance traveled by the mass between 0 and 10 seconds is equal to the distance traveled by the mass between 10 and 20 seconds.

430. Two 1 kg lumps of clay sit in some mud. A boy picks up one lump of clay and drops it onto the second lump from a height of 1 m. The lumps stick together when they collide. If the second lump is driven into the mud a distance of 1 cm, what is the average force exerted on the mud?

A. 500 N
B. 520 N
C. 1,000 N
D. 1,020 N

431. In a karate demonstration, a heavy anvil is placed on the chest of a karate master, who is lying on his back on the floor. A second master strikes the anvil with a sledgehammer making an inelastic collision. The first master is unharmed because the block protects the first master from the sledgehammer's:

A. momentum
B. impulse
C. kinetic energy
D. kinetic energy and momentum

432. In the karate demonstration of the previous question, during the collision between the sledgehammer and the anvil:

A. the sledgehammer experiences a greater change in momentum than the anvil.
B. the sledgehammer experiences a smaller change in velocity than the anvil.
C. the sledgehammer experiences a smaller impulse than the anvil.
D. the center of mass of the sledgehammer experiences a greater displacement than the center of mass of the anvil.

433. In the karate demonstration of the previous question, if we know the masses of the sledgehammer and anvil, and the speed of the sledgehammer just before it strikes the anvil, which of the following can be calculated?

A. length of time of the collision
B. distance over which the collision took place
C. average force on the anvil
D. the change in velocity of the sledgehammer

Machines

434. A mass m is lifted to a height h. If a machine working under *ideal* conditions uses a mechanical advantage to lift the mass, the machine:

A. does less work only.
B. uses less force only.
C. does less work and uses less force.
D. does more work but uses less force.

435. A mass m is lifted to a height h. If a machine working under *real* conditions uses a mechanical advantage to lift the mass, the machine:

A. does less work only.
B. uses less force only.
C. does less work and uses less force.
D. does more work but uses less force.

436. An engineer designs a machine that lifts a 5 kg object to a height h. If the force required is 10 N, what is the minimum distance over which this force must be applied?

A. $h/2$
B. h
C. $2h$
D. $5h$

Questions 437-441 refer to the diagram below. An engineer with a mass of 100 kg has designed an ideal mechanical advantage machine shown below. Platforms 1 and 2 are attached to the machine. When he steps on platform 1, platform 2 rises straight up. The maximum weight that he can lift using his machine in this manner is twice his own. The mechanical advantage of the machine cannot be adjusted. Platform 1 can be lowered a maximum of 10 m.

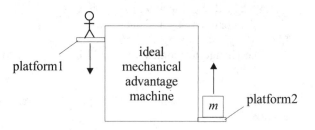

437. What is the maximum height to which platform 2 will rise?

A. 4 m
B. 5 m
C. 10 m
D. 20 m

438. If a 50 kg mass is placed on platform 2, when the engineer steps on platform 1 he will:

A. be lowered at a constant velocity.
B. accelerate downward at less than 10 m/s^2.
C. accelerate downward at 10 m/s^2.
D. accelerate downward at greater than 10 m/s^2.

439. Assume mass m is twice the mass of the engineer and the engineer gives himself a push downwards to get moving. Including the push, the work done on the mass as platform 2 rises to its top height of 5 m will be equal to:

A. the original potential energy of the engineer.
B. the final kinetic energy of the engineer.
C. the original potential energy of the engineer plus half of the final kinetic energy of the engineer.
D. the original potential energy of the engineer minus the final kinetic energy of the engineer.

440. If mass m is less than twice the mass of the engineer, the work done on the mass when platform 2 has risen to its top height of 5 m will be equal to:

A. the original potential energy of the engineer.
B. the final kinetic energy of the engineer.
C. the original potential energy of the engineer plus the final kinetic energy of the engineer.
D. the original potential energy of the engineer minus the final kinetic energy of the engineer.

441. If a very small mass were placed on platform 2 while on the floor, and a very large mass were placed on platform 1 while raised, to what maximum height above the floor could the small mass be thrown when platform 2 stops abruptly?

A. The mass will not be thrown from platform 2.
B. 7.5 m
C. 10 m
D. There is no limit to which the small mass could be thrown.

The Ramp

442. A ramp is to be constructed so that the force necessary to push a wheelchair to the top of a 1.5 m step is reduced to 1/10 the weight of the wheelchair and its occupant. How long must the ramp be?

A. 3 m
B. 10 m
C. 15 m
D. 30 m

443. An engineer wishes to design a ramp so that a ball rolled down the ramp will reach a velocity of 10 m/s. How long must the ramp be?

A. 5 m
B. 10 m
C. 20 m
D. Only the height and not the length of the ramp will affect the velocity of the ball.

444. A 10 kg box accelerates down a frictionless ramp at 5 m/s^2. If the block reaches a velocity of 10 m/s at the bottom of the ramp, what is the mechanical advantage of the ramp?

A. 1:1
B. 2:1
C. 5:1
D. 10:1

445. A 5 kg box is pushed 4 m up a frictionless ramp. Its height is increased by 1 m and its velocity is increased from 2 m/s to 4 m/s. How much work is done on the box?

A. 50 J
B. 55 J
C. 70 J
D. 90 J

446. A winding path leads to the top of a 100 m tall mountain. The path is 1.2 km long and at a constant incline. How much work is done on a 24 kg backpack of a hiker that walks up the mountain along this path?

A. 2,000 J
B. 12,000 J
C. 24,000 J
D. 48,000 J

447. A frictionless ramp is 7 m high and 21 m long. How much force is required to push a 150 kg box up the ramp?

A. 100 N
B. 300 N
C. 500 N
D. 1500 N

448. A farmer has a 200 kg barrel that he must pull up a ramp to a height of 5 m. His old horse can apply a maximum force of only 1,000 N and only for 4 s. What is the shortest distance that the farmer can make the ramp if the barrel starts from rest?

A. 5 m
B. 10 m
C. 20 m
D. 40 m

449. A frictionless ramp is 4 m high and 36 m long. How much force is required to push a 180 kg box up the ramp?

    A. 200 N
    B. 300 N
    C. 600 N
    D. 900 N

The Lever

Questions 450-458 refer to the three types of levers shown below: Each lever stick is one meter long and massless. The triangle beneath each lever represents the fulcrum. The circle represents the point 25 cm from the right end of the lever stick.

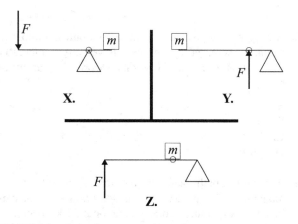

X.   **Y.**

Z.

450. Which of the levers require a force greater than mg in order to lift the mass?

    A. X only
    B. Y only
    C. Z only
    D. X and Y only

451. Which of the levers require the *least* force in order to lift the mass?

    A. X only
    B. Y only
    C. Z only
    D. X and Y only

452. If mass m is 12 kg, what is the minimum force F required to lift the mass with lever Z?

    A. 30 N
    B. 40 N
    C. 120 N
    D. 480 N

453. If mass m is 12 kg, what is the minimum force F required to lift the mass with lever X?

    A. 30 N
    B. 40 N
    C. 120 N
    D. 480 N

454. If mass m is 12 kg, what is the minimum force F required to lift the mass with lever Y?

    A. 30 N
    B. 40 N
    C. 120 N
    D. 480 N

455. If mass m is lifted 10 cm by each lever, which lever does the most work?

    A. X only
    B. Y only
    C. Z only
    D. All do the same amount of work.

456. If the same force F is applied through 10 cm by each lever, which lever does the most work?

    A. X only
    B. Y only
    C. Z only
    D. All do the same amount of work.

457. If the same force F is applied through 10 cm by each lever, which lever lifts the mass to the greatest height?

    A. X only
    B. Y only
    C. Z only
    D. All do the same amount of work.

458. If same force F is applied through 10 cm by each lever, which lever gives the mass the greatest final velocity?

    A. X only
    B. Y only
    C. Z only
    D. All do the same amount of work.

459. A very strong man stands on a table as shown and pulls up on the edge. Which of the following is true if the table does not break?

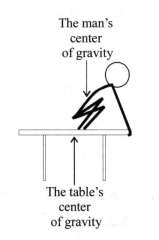

The man's center of gravity

The table's center of gravity

A. If the man pulls hard enough, the end of the table on which he is pulling will rise.
B. The man's center of gravity must be on the other side of the table's center of gravity. Then, if he pulls hard enough, the end of the table on which he is pulling will rise.
C. The man's center of gravity must be on the other side of the left table leg. Then, if he pulls hard enough, the end of the table on which he is pulling will rise.
D. No matter how hard the man pulls, the table will remain motionless as long as his weight pushes down on the table.

460. The crane below uses a steel cable to lift one end of a 1,000 kg iron sheet as shown. If the sheet is 10 m long and of uniform density, what is the minimum tension in the cable?

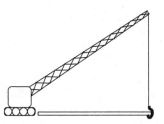

A. 5,000 N
B. 10,000 N
C. 20,000 N
D. 50,000 N

461. The crane below uses a steel cable to lift one end of a 1,000 kg iron sheet as shown. A 100 kg box sits on the sheet 2 m from its left end. If the sheet is 10 m long and of uniform density, what is the minimum tension in the cable?

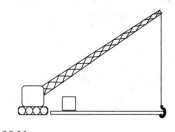

A. 5,200 N
B. 5,500 N
C. 5,800 N
D. 11,000 N

462. The crane below uses a steel cable to lift one end of a 10 m, 1,000 kg iron sheet of uniform density. A 100 kg box sits on the sheet 2 m from its right end. What is the minimum tension in the cable?

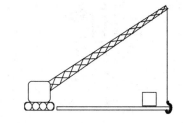

A. 5,200 N
B. 5,500 N
C. 5,800 N
D. 11,000 N

463. The crane below uses a steel cable to lift one end of a 1,000 kg iron sheet as shown. The crane has a mass of 4,000 kg and sits 1 m from the left end of the sheet. If the sheet is 10 m long and of uniform density, what is the minimum tension in the cable?

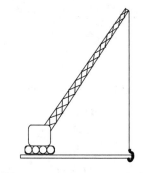

A. 5,200 N
B. 5,500 N
C. 6,000 N
D. As shown in the diagram, the crane could not move the iron sheet.

The Pulley

464. The center of each pulley in the pulley system below remains stationary. The pulleys are massless and frictionless. What minimum force F is required to lift the mass?

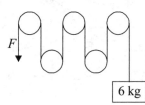

A. 10 N
B. 20 N
C. 30 N
D. 60 N

465. What minimum force F is required to lift the mass?

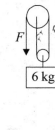

A. 15 N
B. 20 N
C. 30 N
D. 60 N

466. What minimum force F is required to lift the mass?

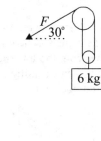

A. 15 N
B. 20 N
C. 30 N
D. 60 N

467. What minimum force F is required to lift the mass?

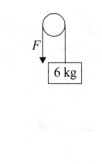

A. 15 N
B. 20 N
C. 30 N
D. 60 N

468. What minimum force F is required to lift the mass?

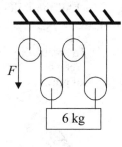

A. 12 N
B. 15 N
C. 20 N
D. 30 N

469. What minimum force F is required to lift the mass?

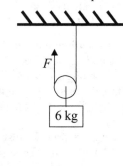

A. 20 N
B. 30 N
C. 60 N
D. 120 N

470. What minimum force F is required to lift the mass?

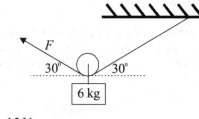

A. 15 N
B. 30 N
C. 60 N
D. 120 N

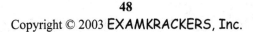

471. What is the tension T in the rope?

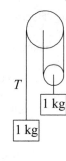

A. 5 N
B. 6 N
C. 10 N
D. 12 N

Questions 472-474 refer to the diagram below. An engineer with a mass of 100 kg has designed an ideal mechanical advantage machine shown below. Platforms 1 and 2 are attached to the machine. When he steps on platform 1, platform 2 rises straight up. The maximum weight that he can lift using his machine in this manner is twice his own. The mechanical advantage of the machine cannot be adjusted. Platform 1 can be lowered a maximum of 10 m.

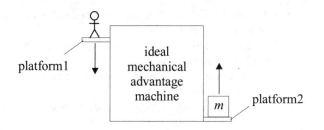

472. If the mass m is 100 kg, what are the forces upward on the engineer and the mass m, respectively?

A. 500 N, 1000 N
B. 600 N, 1200 N
C. 1000 N, 500 N
D. 1200 N, 600 N

473. If the mass m is 100 kg, what are the magnitudes of the acceleration of the engineer and mass m, respectively?

A. 1.33 m/s^2, 0.33 m/s^2
B. 4.00 m/s^2, 2.00 m/s^2
C. 10.0 m/s^2, 5.00 m/s^2
D. 20.0 m/s^2, 10.0 m/s^2

474. Assume the mass m is 100 kg. After 2 seconds, how far has platform 1 fallen and platform 2 risen, respectively?

A. 2 m, 4 m
B. 4 m, 8 m
C. 8 m, 4 m
D. 16 m, 8 m

Radioactive Decay

475. Which of the following is true concerning the ratio of neutrons to protons in stable atoms?

A. The ratio for all stable atoms is 1:1.
B. The ratio for small stable atoms is 1:1, and the ratio for large stable atoms is greater than 1:1.
C. The ratio for large stable atoms is 1:1, and the ratio for small stable atoms is greater than 1:1.
D. There is no correlation between the stability of an atom and its neutron to proton ratio.

476. Which of the following most accurately describes radioactive decay?

A. Molecules spontaneously break apart to produce energy.
B. Atoms spontaneously break apart to produce energy.
C. Protons and neutrons spontaneously break apart to produce energy.
D. Electrons spontaneously break apart to produce energy.

477. Which of the following is an electron?

A. neutrino
B. gamma particle
C. photon
D. beta particle

Half-Life

478. A half-life is:

A. the time required for half the amount of a substance to decay.
B. half the time required for half the amount of a substance to decay.
C. the time required for all of a substance to decay.
D. half the time required for all of a substance to decay.

479. After 2 half-lives:

A. all of a sample substance should have decayed.
B. half of a sample substance should have decayed.
C. three quarters of a sample substance should have decayed.
D. the log base 10 of a sample substance should have decayed.

480. Substance X has a half-life of 30 min. If 10 g remain after 2 hours, what was the original amount?

A. 20 g
B. 40 g
C. 80 g
D. 160 g

481. Substance X has a half-life of 12 hours. How much of a 400 g sample remains after 2 days?

A. 25 g
B. 50 g
C. 100 g
D. 200 g

482. If 30 g of substance X remain from an original sample of 240 g after 300 days, what is the half-life of substance X?

A. 50 days
B. 100 days
C. 150 days
D. 200 days

483. If 12 g of substance X remain from an original sample of 384 g, and substance X has a half-life of 10 hours, how much time has passed?

A. 20 hours
B. 50 hours
C. 100 hours
D. 320 hours

484. Polonium-218 undergoes alpha decay with a half life of 3.1 minutes. Approximately how much lead-214 would be formed from a sample of 109 g of Polonium-218 after 15.5 minutes?

A. 0
B. 3.3 g
C. 21.8 g
D. 103.7 g

Types of Radioactive Decay

485. Uranium-238 undergoes alpha decay to form:

A. Thorium-234
B. Thorium-238
C. Protactinium-234
D. Uranium-234

486. Which of the following is true concerning beta decay?

A. A proton and an electron are created while a neutron is destroyed.
B. A proton and a neutron are created while an electron is destroyed.
C. An electron and a neutron are created while a proton is destroyed.
D. A proton and an electron are destroyed while a neutron is created.

487. Which of the following is true concerning positron emission?

A. A proton and a positron are created while a neutron is destroyed.
B. A proton and a neutron are created while a positron is destroyed.
C. A positron and a neutron are created while a proton is destroyed.
D. A proton and a positron are destroyed while a neutron is created.

488. Which of the following is true concerning electron capture?

A. A proton and an electron are created while a neutron is destroyed.
B. A proton and a neutron are created while an electron is destroyed.
C. An electron and a neutron are created while a proton is destroyed.
D. A proton and an electron are destroyed while a neutron is created.

489. ^{218}Po undergoes one alpha decay and two beta decays to make:

A. ^{214}Po
B. ^{214}Pb
C. ^{214}Bi
D. ^{210}Pb

490. ^{222}Rn decays once to form ^{218}Po. What type of particle is emitted?

A. a gamma particle
B. an alpha particle
C. a beta particle
D. a positron

491. ^{238}U undergoes seven alpha decays and six beta decays to make:

A. ^{210}Po
B. ^{210}Pb
C. ^{210}Bi
D. ^{206}Pb

492. In 1940 neutron bombardment of ^{238}U resulted in ^{239}U, which spontaneously underwent beta decay to produce the new element:

A. ^{239}Np
B. ^{238}Np
C. ^{239}Pa
D. ^{238}Pa

493. Scientists are able to date certain objects based upon the ratio of ^{14}C to ^{12}C within those objects. ^{14}C decays via β-particle production to form:

A. ^{13}B
B. ^{14}B
C. ^{13}N
D. ^{14}N

494. ^{222}Rn decays via α-particle production to form:

A. ^{218}Po
B. ^{220}Th
C. ^{222}At
D. ^{226}Ra

495. ^{11}C produces a positron to form:

A. ^{10}B
B. ^{11}B
C. ^{12}C
D. ^{11}N

496. ^{201}Hg undergoes electron capture to form:

A. ^{200}Au
B. ^{201}Au
C. ^{201}Tl
D. ^{202}Tl

497. When ^{238}U undergoes α-particle decay an α-particle and 2 γ rays are produced to form:

A. ^{234}Ra
B. ^{234}Th
C. ^{236}Th
D. ^{242}Pu

498. *Annihilation* occurs during a matter-antimatter collision changing mass to pure energy. Which of the following is produced during annihilation?

A. γ rays
B. α-particle
C. positron
D. β-particle

499. Molybdenum-99 has a half-life of 67.0 h. If a 1.000 mg sample is left for 335 hours, how much molybdenum remains?

A. 0.031 mg
B. 0.062 mg
C. 0.124 mg
D. 0.248 mg

500. Technetium-99 has a half-life of 6.00 hours. A 4 g sample is placed in a 1.00 g container. The expected mass of the container and sample after 24.0 hours is approximately:

A. 0.25 g
B. 1.25 g
C. 1.50 g
D. 5.00 g

Mass Defect

501. Which of the following is true concerning the mass of a lithium atom compared to the sum of the masses of three protons, three neutrons, and three electrons?

A. The mass of the complete atom is greater.
B. The mass of the complete atom is less.
C. The mass of the complete atom is the same.
D. More information is required in order to predict the difference in mass.

502. The difference between the mass of a complete atom and the sum of the masses of its individual parts is called:

A. The specific mass
B. The binding mass
C. The critical mass
D. The mass defect

503. The difference between the mass of one oxygen atom and the sum of the masses of its parts is approximately 2.27×10^{-28} kg. What is the binding energy that holds an oxygen atom together? (Note: the charge on one electron is 1.6×10^{-19} C)

A. 1.9×10^{-14} eV
B. 1.9×10^{-11} eV
C. 1.2×10^5 eV
D. 1.2×10^8 eV

Fission and Fusion

504. As the mass number increases, the binding energy per nucleon generally:

  A. increases
  B. decreases
  C. increases then decreases
  D. decreases then increases

505. Which of the following is likely to have the most stable nucleus?

  A. ^{2}H
  B. ^{4}He
  C. ^{56}Fe
  D. ^{235}U

506. Which of the following is most likely to undergo fission?

  A. ^{2}H
  B. ^{4}He
  C. ^{56}Fe
  D. ^{235}U

507. Which of the following is most likely to release energy when undergoing fusion with another nuclei?

  A. ^{2}H
  B. ^{56}Fe
  C. ^{235}U
  D. ^{238}U

508. The sun consists of 73% hydrogen, 26% helium, and 1% other elements. The sun most likely produces heat via:

  A. nuclear fission
  B. nuclear fusion
  C. alpha decay
  D. beta decay

509. Based upon the constant energy production of the sun, the mass of the sun is most likely:

  A. increasing
  B. decreasing
  C. not changing
  D. fluctuating

Fluids

510. Which of the following phases contains molecules that are held together by intermolecular bonds?

   I. solid
  II. liquid
 III. gas

   A. I only
   B. II only
   C. I and II only
   D. I, II, and III

511. Which of the following phases contains molecules that are held together by intermolecular bonds that continually break and reform?

   I. solid
  II. liquid
 III. gas

   A. I only
   B. II only
   C. I and II only
   D. I, II, and III

512. Which of the following phases is capable of permanently withstanding a force perpendicular to its surface?

   I. solid
  II. liquid
 III. gas

   A. I only
   B. II only
   C. III only
   D. I, II, and III

513. Which of the following phases is capable of permanently withstanding a force that is NOT perpendicular to its surface?

   I. solid
  II. liquid
 III. gas

   A. I only
   B. II only
   C. III only
   D. I, II, and III

514. The ocean is able to permanently support a battleship because:

   A. the ocean is heavier than the battleship.
   B. the metal of the battleship is less dense than ocean water.
   C. at the point of contact the forces exerted by the battleship are perpendicular to the surface of the water.
   D. The volume of water displaced by the battleship is equal to the volume of the battleship resting below the surface.

515. A man pushes a motorboat away from its dock. Which of the following is true?

   A. The boat will move in the direction of the force regardless of the magnitude of the force.
   B. The boat will not move until the force is great enough to overcome the resistance of the water.
   C. The acceleration of the boat will be directly proportional to the pushing force.
   D. The water will provide no resistance against the force.

516. Which of the following statements is true concerning a gas?

   A. Gas molecules are too small to be affected by gravity.
   B. Gravity causes a gas to form to the shape of its container.
   C. Gas molecules generally move so fast and for such short distances that the change in their velocities due to gravity has a negligible effect on their behavior.
   D. Because electrostatic forces are so great, gravity has no affect on a gas.

517. Two rooms are connected by a closed door. A scientist finds the mass, density, energy, and pressure of the gas in each room to be identical. The door is opened. The scientist measures the mass, density, energy, and pressure in the two rooms combined. Which values changed in the second measurement?

   I. mass
  II. density
 III. energy
 IV. pressure

   A. I and III only
   B. II and IV only
   C. I, II, and III only
   D. I, II, III and IV

Density

518. Which of the following phases typically exhibits large changes in density?

   I.   solid
  II.   liquid
 III.   gas

  A. I only
  B. II only
  C. III only
  D. II, and III only

519. A mass is placed on the moveable piston of each of the cylinders shown. Which phase(s) will experience a significant change in volume?

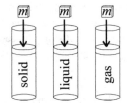

   I.   solid
  II.   liquid
 III.   gas

  A. III only
  B. II and III only
  C. I, II, and III
  D. None of the volumes will change significantly.

520. A mass is placed on the moveable piston of each of the cylinders shown. Which phase(s) will experience a significant change in density?

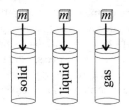

   I.   solid
  II.   liquid
 III.   gas

  A. III only
  B. II and III only
  C. I, II, and III
  D. None of the volumes will change significantly.

521. Which of the following phases experiences the greatest change in density due to gravity?

  A. solid
  B. liquid
  C. gas
  D. All experience the same change in density.

522. Seawater has a specific gravity of 1.25. If a chemist empties a glass of seawater, it will fall through the air:

  A. 1.25 times faster than fresh water.
  B. 1.25 times more slowly than fresh water.
  C. at the same rate as freshwater.
  D. 2.5 times more slowly than fresh water.

523. A forklift has a maximum power of 4×10^3 W. If, when operating at maximum power, it is capable of lifting 100 waterjugs to a height of 1 meter in 10 seconds. How long will it require to lift 100 of the same size jugs filled with alcohol? (Note: Alcohol has a specific gravity of 0.8.)

  A. 8 s
  B. 10 s
  C. 11.25 s
  D. 12 s

524. If the volume of a gas is decreased by a factor of 2, what is the change in its density?

  A. Density remains the same.
  B. Density decreases by a factor of 2.
  C. Density increases by a factor of 2.
  D. Density increases by a factor of 4.

525. A rigid container holds air (density 1.3 kg/m^3) at 0 °C. If the temperature is increased to 273 °C, what is the new density of the air?

  A. 0.65 kg/m^3
  B. 1.3 kg/m^3
  C. 2.6 kg/m^3
  D. 3.9 kg/m^3

526. A rigid container holds air (density 1.3 kg/m^3) at 1 atm. If the pressure is increased to 2 atm by adding more air, what is the density of the air?

  A. 0.65 kg/m^3
  B. 1.3 kg/m^3
  C. 2.6 kg/m^3
  D. 3.9 kg/m^3

527. An ice cube sits in a container that is exactly the same size as the cube. Which of the following is true, if the ice is allowed to melt? (Note: Ice has a specific gravity of 0.9.)

    A. The water level will be exactly even with the top of the container and no water will spill over the sides.
    B. 10% of the water will spill over the sides of the container.
    C. The water will occupy only 90% of the container.
    D. The water will occupy only 91% of the container.

528. A container is filled to the brim with water. Which of the following is true, if the water is allowed to freeze? (Note: ice has a specific gravity of 0.9.)

    A. The ice will fill the container exactly.
    B. 10% of the ice will freeze outside of the container.
    C. The ice will occupy only 10% of the container.
    D. The ice will occupy only 90% of the container.

529. What is the weight of 1 liter of water?

    A. 1 kg
    B. 10 kg
    C. 100 kg
    D. 1000 kg

530. 12 grams of water occupies:

    A. 1 cm^3
    B. 1.2 cm^3
    C. 12 cm^3
    D. 120 cm^3

531. Mercury has a specific gravity of 13.6. 13.6 grams of mercury occupies a volume of:

    A. 1 cm^3
    B. 13.6 cm^3
    C. 136 cm^3
    D. 185 cm^3

532. Lead has a density of $11.3 \times 10^3 \text{ kg/m}^3$. What is the specific gravity of lead?

    A. 1.13
    B. 11.3
    C. 1.13×10^3
    D. 11.3×10^3

533. A block of wood measuring 5 cm x 3 cm x 10 cm has a mass of 90 grams. What is the density of the wood?

    A. $1.6 \times 10^2 \text{ kg/m}^3$
    B. $6.0 \times 10^2 \text{ kg/m}^3$
    C. $1.6 \times 10^3 \text{ kg/m}^3$
    D. $6.0 \times 10^3 \text{ kg/m}^3$

534. A block of a certain substance measures 4 cm x 3 cm x 10 cm and weighs 60 grams. A second block of the same substance measures 40 cm x 30 cm x 100 cm. What is the density of the second block?

    A. $5.0 \times 10^2 \text{ kg/m}^3$
    B. $1.0 \times 10^3 \text{ kg/m}^3$
    C. $2.0 \times 10^3 \text{ kg/m}^3$
    D. $5.0 \times 10^3 \text{ kg/m}^3$

535. A block of a certain substance measures 4 cm x 3 cm x 10 cm and weighs 60 grams. A second block of the same substance measures 40 cm x 30 cm x 100 cm. What is the specific gravity of the second block?

    A. 0.5
    B. 2.0
    C. 5.0
    D. 5.0×10^2

Pressure

536. All of the following approximately equal atmospheric pressure at sea level EXCEPT:

    A. 1 atm
    B. 10^5 Pa
    C. 760 torr
    D. 500 mm Hg

537. Which of the following is the lowest pressure?

    A. 1 atm
    B. 1 Pa
    C. 1 torr
    D. 1 mm Hg

538. Which of the following is pressure?

    A. F/A
    B. FA
    C. FV
    D. A/V

539. A small object is submerged in a fluid. The fluid pressure is measured based upon the change in momentum of the molecules that collide with the object. When the object is removed, the fluid pressure:

    A. is zero because the molecules no longer collide with the object.
    B. is zero because the space occupied by the object becomes a vacuum which must be filled.
    C. remains the same because the kinetic energy per unit volume of the molecules has not changed.
    D. remains the same because the volume of the fluid has increased.

540. A diver swims in a pool that is 30 m deep. The diver swims 20 m above the bottom. What is the gauge pressure?

  A. 10^5 Pa
  B. 10^5 atm
  C. 10^5 torr
  D. $2x10^5$ Pa

541. A diver swims in a pool that is 30 m deep. The diver swims 20 m above the bottom. If the diver descends to 10 m above the bottom, what is the gauge pressure?

  A. $1x10^4$ Pa
  B. $2x10^5$ Pa
  C. $4x10^5$ Pa
  D. $6.6x10^5$ Pa

542. A diver swims in a pool that is 30 m deep. The diver swims 20 m above the bottom. What is the Absolute pressure?

  A. $1x10^4$ Pa
  B. $1x10^5$ Pa
  C. $2x10^5$ Pa
  D. $4x10^5$ Pa

543. Which of the following could be the absolute pressure inside the chest cavity of a person who is inhaling?

  A. −0.2 atm
  B. 0.9 atm
  C. 1.0 atm
  D. 1.1 atm

544. What depth of water creates 1 atm of pressure?

  A. 1 m
  B. 5 m
  C. 10 m
  D. 20 m

545. Imagine that a cylinder were constructed with a cross-sectional area of 1 m^2 and spanning from the ground to the top of the atmosphere. Now imagine that the air inside that cylinder were weighed and the mass calculated. What would be the mass? (Note: Assume the acceleration of gravity is 10 m/s^2.)

  A. 101 kg
  B. 1,010 kg
  C. 10,100 kg
  D. 101,000 kg

Questions 546 through 550 refer to the diagram below. Four fluids with different densities are held in an open container. Each fluid has a depth of 10 m. p_1, p_2, and p_3 are points in the container.

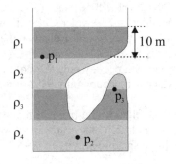

546. What is the correct order of densities from highest to lowest?

  A. $\rho_1 > \rho_2 > \rho_3 > \rho_4$
  B. $\rho_2 > \rho_3 > \rho_4 > \rho_1$
  C. $\rho_4 > \rho_3 > \rho_2 > \rho_1$
  D. The densities are all the same.

547. Where is the fluid pressure the greatest?

  A. p_1
  B. p_2
  C. p_3
  D. The pressure is the same everywhere in the container.

548. If the values of ρ_1, ρ_2, ρ_3, and ρ_4 are 500 kg/m^3, 1000 kg/m^3, 2000 kg/m^3, and 4000 kg/m^3, respectively, then what is the approximate pressure at p_3?

  A. 0.5 atm
  B. 1.5 atm
  C. 2.5 atm
  D. 8.5 atm

549. If the values of ρ_1, ρ_2, ρ_3, and ρ_4 are 500 kg/m^3, 1000 kg/m^3, 2000 kg/m^3, and 4000 kg/m^3, respectively, then what is the approximate pressure at p_2?

  A. 5.5 atm
  B. 6.5 atm
  C. 7.5 atm
  D. 8.5 atm

550. An object completely submerged in a fluid with a specific gravity of 3 has an apparent loss of weight of 40 N. If the mass of the object is 12 kg, what is its specific gravity?

  A. 3
  B. 6
  C. 9
  D. 12

551. A ball has a volume of 1 L and a mass of 0.75 kg. If the ball is floating in water, what portion of the ball will float above the surface?

 A. 0
 B. ¼
 C. ½
 D. ¾

552. Using the ideal gas equation, $PV = nRT$, if M is the molecular weight of a gas, what is its density?

 A. *PM/RT*
 B. *PV/nRTM*
 C. *PM/nRT*
 D. *nMRT/PV*

553. At atmospheric pressure, air is approximately seven times heavier than helium. A sealed helium balloon rises into the atmosphere. If the helium remains in thermal equilibrium with its surroundings, the balloon will rise:

 A. until the pressure inside the balloon is equal to the pressure of the surrounding atmosphere.
 B. until the pressure inside the balloon is seven times greater than the pressure of the surrounding atmosphere.
 C. until the pressure inside the balloon is seven times less than the pressure of the surrounding atmosphere.
 D. The balloon will not rise if the temperature of the helium is equal to the temperature of its surroundings.

554. As a hot air balloon rises into the atmosphere its volume does not change. It is opened at the bottom to allow air exchange with the atmosphere. Ignoring the weight of the balloon and the undercarriage, which of the following will stop a hot air balloon from rising?

 A. the pressure inside the balloon is equal to the pressure of the surrounding atmosphere
 B. the volume inside the balloon is equal to the volume of the surrounding atmosphere displaced by the balloon
 C. the temperature inside the balloon is equal to the temperature of the surrounding atmosphere
 D. the number of moles of air inside the balloon is equal to the number of moles of air in the surrounding atmosphere

555. Ice has a specific gravity of 0.9. What percentage of an iceberg is above the water?

 A. 10%
 B. 45%
 C. 90%
 D. 100%

556. An experiment is performed with a brick and a bucket of water. In which of the following cases does the brick displace the most water?

 A. The brick is allowed to sink to the bottom of a bucket.
 B. The brick is floated on a piece of massless styrofoam.
 C. The brick is held just beneath the surface of the water.
 D. In all cases the same amount of water is displaced.

557. Can a battleship float in a swimming pool? (Note: assume that the pool has a shape similar to the hull of the battleship.)

 A. Yes, but only if the weight of the water remaining in the pool is as great as the weight of the battleship.
 B. Yes, but only if the pool is capable of holding a mass of water as great as the mass of the battleship when the ship is not in the pool.
 C. No, because the volume of water remaining in the pool must be at least as great as the volume of the battleship.
 D. No, because the battleship requires a minimum depth of water beneath it in order to float.

558. A 25 kg object has an apparent weight of 200 N when placed in a fluid with a specific gravity of 0.6. What is the specific gravity of the object?

 A. 1.2
 B. 2.0
 C. 3.0
 D. 12

Questions 559-562 refer to the diagram below. A siphon is used to draw water from a water tower.

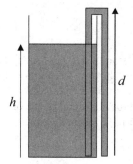

559. What is the approximate maximum height d at which the siphon will be capable of draining the water tower nearly completely?

 A. 1 m
 B. 10 m
 C. 100 m
 D. There is no maximum height.

560. What is the maximum difference in height between d and h?

A. 1 m
B. 10 m
C. 100 m
D. There is no maximum height.

561. If h is 5 m and d is 10 m, and the siphon is closed at the end that is not submerged, what is the absolute pressure at the top of the siphon?

A. −0.5 atm
B. 0 atm
C. 0.5 atm
D. 1.0 atm

562. If h is 5 m and d is 10 m, and the siphon is closed at the end that is not submerged, what is the absolute pressure at the bottom of the tower?

A. −0.5 atm
B. 0.5 atm
C. 1.0 atm
D. 1.5 atm

563. A cylindrical vacuum pump with a cross-sectional area of 1 cm^2 is used to lift the mass as shown. What is the greatest mass that the vacuum can lift?

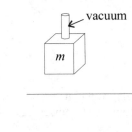

A. 1 g
B. 10 g
C. 1 kg
D. 10 kg

564. A 75 kg man stands on a 10 m long block which floats on the water as shown. The block is half metal and half massless styrofoam. If the mass of the block is 100 kg, how far from the right end of the block should the man stand in order to keep the block level?

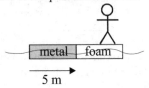

A. 1.0 m
B. 1.7 m
C. 2.5 m
D. 3.3 m

565. The manometer below contains a gas and a liquid (shaded region). The density of the gas is 1.29 kg/m^3, and the density of the fluid is 0.800x10^3 kg/m^3. If height h is 20.0 cm, what is the pressure of the gas?

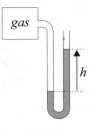

A. 0.800x10^3 Pa
B. 1.600x10^3 Pa
C. 9.840x10^4 Pa
D. 1.026x10^5 Pa

566. The mass below has a specific gravity less than 1 and is held under water by a string as shown. If the entire container is accelerated upward, the tension in the string will:

A. *decrease* and the buoyant force will *decrease*.
B. *decrease* and the buoyant force will *increase*.
C. *increase* and the buoyant force will *decrease*.
D. *increase* and the buoyant force will *increase*.

567. As a fully submerged solid sinks deeper into water, the buoyant force on the object:

A. increases.
B. decreases.
C. remains the same.
D. decreases to zero then increases.

Fluids in Motion

568. When comparing two points of fluid flowing through the same horizontal pipe, if the fluid velocity is greater, then:

A. the random translational motion of the molecules is less.
B. the random translational motion of the molecules is greater.
C. the random translational motion of the molecules is unchanged.
D. the uniform translational motion of the molecules is less.

569. When comparing two points of fluid flowing through the same horizontal pipe, if the fluid velocity is greater, then:

A. the temperature is less.
B. the temperature greater.
C. the temperature is unchanged.
D. the pressure is greater.

570. A decrease in which of the following fluid characteristics would increase the pressure at any given point in a moving ideal fluid?

A. temperature
B. density
C. cross-sectional area of pipe
D. velocity

571. Which of the following describes fluid pressure against a flat surface?

A. The pressure is equal to the change of *momentum* of the fluid molecules as they collide with the surface of the object divided by the *time* and the surface *area*.
B. The pressure is equal to the change in *kinetic energy* of the fluid molecules as they collide with the surface of the object divided by the *time* and the surface *area*.
C. The pressure is equal to the change in *momentum* of the fluid molecules as they collide with the surface of the object divided by the *number* of molecules and the surface *area*.
D. The pressure is equal to the *temperature* of the fluid molecules divided by the *time* and surface *area*.

Ideal Fluids

572. An ideal fluid flows through a horizontal pipe. Which of the following is NOT true at the points where fluid velocity increases?

A. the temperature decreases.
B. the cross-sectional area of the pipe decreases.
C. the volume flow rate increases.
D. the pressure decreases.

573. All of the following are characteristics of an ideal fluid EXCEPT:

A. volume flow rate remains constant.
B. molecules of an ideal fluid have no volume.
C. an ideal fluid has no viscosity.
D. an ideal fluid is incompressible.

574. In ideal fluid flow, velocity is inversely proportional to:

A. pressure.
B. the cross-sectional area of the conduit.
C. the volume flow rate.
D. viscosity.

575. Which of the following descriptions is inaccurate for ideal fluid flow?

A. Fluid always flows from high pressure to low pressure.
B. Mass flow rate remains constant.
C. Volume flow rate remains constant.
D. Density remains constant.

576. An ideal fluid flows through a pipe. If the length of the pipe is doubled while the radius is decreased by a factor of 2, the volume of fluid passing any point in a given second will:

A. decrease by a factor of 4.
B. decrease by a factor of 2.
C. remain the same.
D. increase by a factor of 4.

Questions 577-582 refer to the diagram below. An ideal fluid with a specific gravity of 1.0 flows through the pipe in the direction from *c* to *a*. The pipe has the same diameter at *a* and *c*. The vertical pipes are vacuum sealed at the top. The height of the fluid at h_1, h_2, and h_3 are measured from the center of the pipe, and are not drawn to scale.

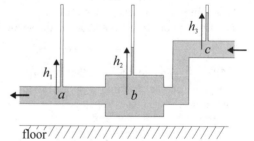

Heights h_1, h_2, and h_3 not drawn to scale.

577. Measuring from the floor, which of the following gives the height of the fluid in each vertical column from highest to lowest?

A. $a > b > c$
B. $c > b > c$
C. $b > a > c$
D. $b > a = c$

578. Which of the following represents the relative velocities at *a*, *b*, and *c*?

A. $a > b > c$
B. $c > b > a$
C. $b > a = c$
D. $a = c > b$

579. Which of the following represents the volume flow rate at a, b, and c?

    A. $a > b > c$
    B. $a = c > b$
    C. $b > a = c$
    D. $a = b = c$

580. If a second ideal fluid with a specific gravity of 2.0 were passed through the pipe at the same volume flow rate the pressure at any point in the pipe would:

    A. decrease by a factor of 2.
    B. remain the same.
    C. increase by a factor of 2.
    D. More information is required to predict the change in pressure.

581. If a second ideal fluid with a specific gravity of 2.0 were passed through the pipe at the same volume flow rate, the height h_1 would:

    A. decrease by a factor of 2.
    B. remain the same.
    C. increase by a factor of 2.
    D. More information is required to predict the change in h_1.

582. What would happen if the small vertical pipes were opened at the top?

    A. h_1, h_2, and h_3 would decrease.
    B. h_1, h_2, and h_3 would increase.
    C. h_1, h_2, and h_3 would remain the same.
    D. The fluid would flow up and out of the small pipes.

Questions 583-591 refer to the diagram below. An open container of fluid begins draining a spigot at time $t = 0$. Assume ideal fluid flow.

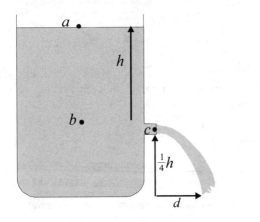

583. If the container is filled with water, and h is 20 m, the pressure at c is:

    A. 1 atm
    B. 2 atm
    C. 3 atm
    D. 4 atm

584. If the container is filled with water, and h is 20 m, the velocity of the water at c is:

    A. 5 m/s
    B. 10 m/s
    C. 20 m/s
    D. 40 m/s

585. If the container is filled with water, and h is 20 m, the pressure at b is:

    A. 1 atm
    B. 2 atm
    C. 3 atm
    D. 4 atm

586. If the container is filled with water, and h is 20 m, the distance d is:

    A. 5 m
    B. 10 m
    C. 20 m
    D. 40 m

587. If d is 10.0 m when the container is filled with water, what would be d if the container were filled with mercury? (Note: The specific gravity of mercury is 13.6)

    A. 1.36 m
    B. 10.0 m
    C. 13.6 m
    D. 136 m

588. If the pressure at b is 2 atm when the container is filled with water, what would be the pressure if the container were filled with mercury? (Note: The specific gravity of mercury is 13.6)

    A. 2 atm
    B. 14.6 atm
    C. 15.6 atm
    D. 27.2 atm

589. If the velocity at c is 2 m/s when the container is filled with water, what would be the velocity if the container were filled with mercury? (Note: The specific gravity of mercury is 13.6. Assume ideal conditions.)

    A. 2 m/s
    B. 14.6m/s
    C. 15.6 m/s
    D. 27.2 m/s

590. Which of the following graphs most accurately demonstrates how h changes with the fluid velocity v at point c?

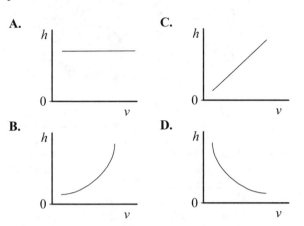

A.

B.

C.

D.

591. Which of the following graphs most accurately demonstrates how h changes with time t?

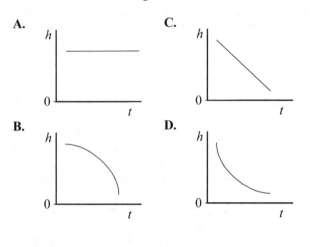

A.

B.

C.

D.

592. Which of the following is NOT true of an ideal fluid?

A. In an ideal fluid flowing through an irregular pipe, the same volume of fluid passes any given point at any given moment.
B. In an ideal fluid flowing through an irregular pipe, the same mass of fluid passes any given point at any given moment.
C. As the pressure increases in ideal fluid, the density remains the same.
D. In an ideal fluid, flow is always from high pressure to low pressure.

593. At what velocity does fluid flow from Tank B to Tank A in the diagram below?

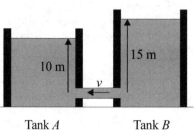

Tank A Tank B

A. 2.2 m/s
B. 10 m/s
C. 14 m/s
D. 17 m/s

594. The numbers below represent the volume flow rate (cm^3/s) of an ideal fluid into and out of the pipe shown. What is the flow rate at the end marked a?

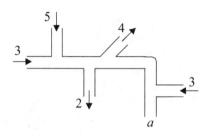

A. 3 cm^3/s out of the pipe
B. 5 cm^3/s out of the pipe
C. 2 cm^3/s into the pipe
D. 6 cm^3/s into the pipe

595. The container shown below is filled with an ideal fluid. Spigot a and b are at the same height. Spigot b has a larger cross-sectional area than spigot a. According to the Bernoulli Equation and the Equation of Continuity, how will the velocity and volume flow rate compare at the spigots a and b?

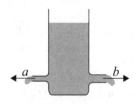

A. The velocity and flow rate will be greatest at a.
B. The velocity will be greatest at a, but the flow rate will be the same.
C. The velocity and the flow rate will be the same.
D. The velocity will be the same but the flow rate will be greatest at b.

Non-ideal Fluids (Real Fluids)

596. Which of the following characteristics of a fluid is most closely related to its viscosity?

   A. density
   B. intramolecular bond strength
   C. intermolecular bond strength
   D. pressure

597. Which of the following is the best explanation for the movement of water between the water tanks below?

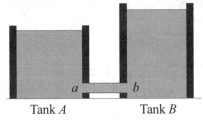

      Tank *A*   Tank *B*

   A. Water will move from Tank *B* to Tank *A* because Tank *B* has greater volume.
   B. Water will move from Tank *A* to Tank *B* because Tank *B* holds more mass of fluid.
   C. Water will move from Tank *B* to Tank *A* because the pressure is greater at *b* than at *a*.
   D. Water will move from Tank *B* to Tank *A* because the pressure is greater at *a* than at *b*.

598. Which of the following is the best explanation for the movement of water between the water tanks below?

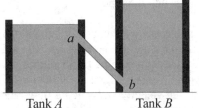

      Tank *A*   Tank *B*

   A. Water will move to the tank with the least volume of water.
   B. Water will move from Tank *A* to Tank *B* because the gravitational forces are greater than the pressure forces.
   C. Water will move from Tank *B* to Tank *A* because the pressure is greater at *b* than at *a*.
   D. Water will move from Tank *B* to Tank *A* because the pressure forces are greater than the gravitational forces.

599. Which of the following is the best explanation for the movement of water between the water tanks below?

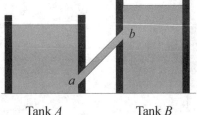

      Tank *A*   Tank *B*

   A. Water will move to the tank with the least volume of water.
   B. Water will move from Tank *B* to Tank *A* because the gravitational forces are greater than the pressure forces.
   C. Water will move from Tank *B* to Tank *A* because the pressure is greater at *b* than at *a*.
   D. Water will move from Tank *A* to Tank *B* because the pressure is greater at *a* than at *b*.

600. As a baseball spins, it drags air near its surface in the direction of its spin. The baseball shown below is traveling with a velocity *v* and spinning as shown. The trajectory of the ball will curve:

   A. to the right because air pressure will be lower on the right side of the ball.
   B. to the left because air pressure will be lower on the left side of the ball.
   C. out of the page because air pressure will be lower above the ball.
   D. into the page because air pressure will be lower below the ball.

601. In the pipe shown below a viscous fluid flows steadily from left to right. Fluid velocity is most likely the greatest at:

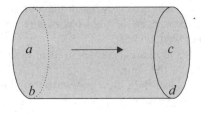

   A. *a*
   B. *b*
   C. *b* and *d*
   D. *a* and *c*

602. In the pipe shown in the previous question, which of the following decreases going from *a* to *b*?

- A. pressure
- B. velocity
- C. pressure and velocity
- D. neither pressure nor flow rate

603. 2 one liter containers are filled with the same viscous fluid via different size funnels. The cross-sectional area of the stem on the first funnel is twice as large as the cross-sectional area of the stem on the second funnel. If the first container is filled in 24 seconds, which of the following could be the time required to fill the second container?

- A. 24 s
- B. 42 s
- C. 48 s
- D. 54 s

Questions 604-607 refer to the chart below. The chart shows the summation of the cross-sectional areas of the different blood vessels of the body starting near the heart, working through the systemic circulatory system and back to the heart.

BLOOD VESSEL	CROSS-SECTIONAL AREA (CM^2)
Aorta	2.5
Small arteries	20
Arterioles	40
Capillaries	2500
Venules	250
Small veins	80
Venae cavae	8

604. According to the chart, where is blood velocity the lowest?

- A. Aorta
- B. Capillaries
- C. Small veins
- D. Venae cavae

605. Blood is a viscous fluid. Assuming the heart supplies all the force to push the blood through the circulatory system, and ignoring the effects of gravity, where is pressure likely to be the lowest?

- A. Aorta
- B. Capillaries
- C. Small veins
- D. Venae cavae

606. Which vessels have the greatest total volume of blood flowing past a single point in a given second?

- A. Aorta
- B. Capillaries
- C. Venae cavae
- D. The volume blood flow is the same for any point in the circulatory system at a given moment.

607. If the blood behaved ideally, where would the pressure be the greatest?

- A. Aorta
- B. Capillaries
- C. Small veins
- D. Venae cavae

Surface Tension

608. Which of the following is the best explanation for why the stream of water in a faucet attenuates as it falls?

- A. Atmospheric pressure squeezes the stream of water.
- B. The pressure in the stream decreases as its velocity increases allowing the cohesive forces between the molecules to attenuate the stream.
- C. The pressure in the stream increases as its velocity increases allowing the cohesive forces between the molecules to attenuate the stream.
- D. The density of the stream decreases as the velocity increases which results in a decrease in volume.

609. Below is a fluid in a glass tube. If the fluid molecules bond more strongly to the glass than to each other, which of the following represents the fluid in the tube?

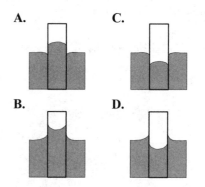

610. Below is a fluid in a glass tube. If the fluid molecules bond less strongly to the glass than to each other, which of the following represents the fluid in the tube?

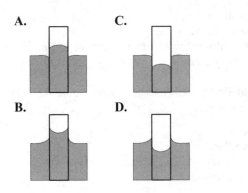

Solids

611. Which of the following best describes the difference between *stress* and *strain*?

A. *Stress* is what is done to a solid; *strain* is how the solid responds.
B. *Strain* is what is done to a solid; *stress* is how the solid responds.
C. *Stress* is a compressive force; *strain* is a tensile force.
D. *Strain* is net force applied to a solid; *stress* is the *strain* per unit area.

612. Strain is:

A. the force per unit area applied to an object.
B. the equivalent to the sum of Hooke's Law forces.
C. the result of the breaking of intramolecular bonds.
D. the fractional change of some dimension of an object due to applied stress.

613. The modulus of elasticity is:

A. equal to stress divided by strain.
B. equal to strain divided by stress.
C. equal to the force per unit area.
D. the fractional change in length of an object.

614. The modulus of elasticity is a constant for:

A. any particular shape.
B. any particular substance as long as the shape is the same.
C. any particular substance up to a certain maximum stress.
D. any particular substance under any stress.

615. Which of the following will change the modulus of elasticity used to calculate the stress applied on an object?

A. Changing the shape of an object.
B. Changing the force applied to an object.
C. Changing the temperature of an object.
D. Changing the size of an object.

616. A stress is applied to an object. When the stress is removed, the object returns to its original shape. The force with which the object pushes against the stress forces is:

A. conservative because it is equal and opposite to the stress forces.
B. conservative because mechanical energy is conserved.
C. nonconservative because it is *not* equal and opposite to the stress forces.
D. nonconservative because mechanical energy is *not* conserved.

Questions 617-625 refer to the Table below. The Ultimate strength represents the maximum stress applied to a specimen without fracture. (Note: Assume that the Young's Modulus is accurate up to the fracture point.)

Material	Density (kg/m^3)	Young's Modulus $(10^9 \ N/m^2)$	Ultimate Strength $(10^6 \ N/m^2)$
Steel	7860	200	400
Aluminum	2710	70	110
Glass	2190	65	50
Concrete	2320	30	40
Wood	525	13	50
Bone	1900	9	170

617. According to the table, which of the following can withstand the greatest amount of stress without breaking?

A. A cylinder of glass 1 meter long with a 10 cm radius
B. A human femur 0.5 meter long with a 10 cm radius
C. A cylinder of concrete 10 meters long with a 20 cm radius
D. A cylinder of aluminum 0.5 meter long with a 5 cm radius

618. According to the table, what is the maximum percent change in length withstood by a steel bar before it will break?

    A. 0.125 %
    B. 0.2 %
    C. 12.5 %
    D. 125 %

619. According to the table, a rod made from which of the following substances could stretch the farthest without breaking?

    A. steel
    B. aluminum
    C. glass
    D. wood

620. According to the table, what is the maximum height to which a concrete column could be made before it will collapse under its own weight?

    A. 10 m
    B. 1.0×10^2 m
    C. 1.7×10^3 m
    D. 1.3×10^6 m

621. According to the table, which of the following is the most flexible (expands the most without breaking)?

    A. steel
    B. glass
    C. wood
    D. bone

622. According to the table, which of the following is the most brittle (expands the least before breaking)?

    A. steel
    B. glass
    C. wood
    D. bone

623. A woman with a mass of 65 kg puts all her weight on one heel of her high-heel shoe. The cross-sectional area of the heel is 1 cm^2. According to the table, if she is standing on a pane of glass that is flat against the ground, does the glass break?

    A. No, because the stress is less than the ratio for the ultimate strength to Young's modulus for glass.
    B. No, because the stress is less than the ultimate strength of glass.
    C. Yes, because the stress is greater than the ratio for the ultimate strength to Young's modulus for glass.
    D. Yes, because the stress is greater than the ultimate strength of glass.

624. A wooden beam 3 m long has a cross-sectional area of 10 cm^2. If it is positioned vertically so that it supports 1.3×10^4 kg, what is its change in length? (Ignore the weight of the beam.)

    A. 3 mm
    B. 3 cm
    C. 33 cm
    D. 3 m

625. A wooden beam 3 m long has a cross-sectional area of 10 cm^2. It is positioned vertically so that it supports 1.3×10^4 kg. If a 6 m beam were used instead, the change in length of the beam would:

    A. decrease by a factor of 2.
    B. remain the same.
    C. increase by a factor of 2.
    D. increase by a factor of 4.

Questions 626-631 refer to the table below. The table gives the different moduli in GN/m^2 for various substances.

	Young's Modulus	Shear Modulus	Bulk Modulus
Aluminum	70	30	70
Steel	200	84	160
Copper	100	40	140
Lead	15	5.6	7.7
Mercury	-	-	27
Water	-	-	200

* Some values have been altered slightly to simplify calculations.

626. According to the table, which of the following is true concerning the apparent weight of lead in water at different depths?

    A. It is the same at all depths.
    B. It increases with depth.
    C. It decreases with depth.
    D. No effect of depth on the apparent weight lead in water can be derived from the table.

627. A force is applied to the top of a copper block as shown. If the bottom of the block is fixed to the ground, how far to the left will the top shift?

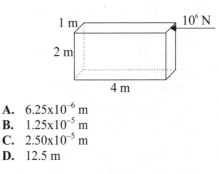

    A. 6.25×10^{-6} m
    B. 1.25×10^{-5} m
    C. 2.50×10^{-5} m
    D. 12.5 m

628. What is its approximate fractional change in volume of a 1 cm^3 cube of copper when it is submerged under water to a depth of 10 m?

A. 7×10^{-7}
B. 9×10^{-7}
C. 2.5×10^{-6}
D. 5×10^{-3}

629. The specific gravity of mercury is 13.6. According to the table, what will be the mass ratio of a very tall column of mercury compared to a column of water that is the same height?

A. 13.6
B. less than 13.6
C. greater than 13.6
D. 1

630. A large weight is hung from a cylindrical steel rod. The steel rod stretches 2 mm. If the steel rod were replaced with a copper rod, which of the following would result in a 2 mm stretching of the copper rod?

A. Using a copper rod that is twice as long as the steel rod
B. Using a copper rod that is half as long as the steel rod
C. Using copper rod that has twice the radius of the steel rod
D. Reducing the weight by a factor of 4

631. Which of the following experiences the greatest change in volume when removed from deep water?

A. aluminum
B. copper
C. steel
D. lead

632. A lead weight is placed on a movable piston above a closed container of mercury as shown. Which of the following does NOT change?

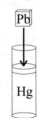

A. density of mercury
B. the height of the column
C. the Young's modulus for mercury
D. the specific gravity of mercury

Questions 633-635 refer to the diagram below. A uniform cylinder of an unknown solid is glued to the ceiling as shown with a very strong glue.

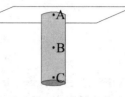

633. If the substance has a specific gravity of 1 and can withstand a maximum stress of 10^5 N/m^2, what is the maximum length of the cylinder before it breaks due to its own weight?

A. 1 cm
B. 10 cm
C. 1 m
D. 10 m

634. If the cylinder breaks due to the stress as applied in the diagram, at which point is it most likely to do so?

A. A
B. B
C. C
D. It is equally likely to break at all points.

635. Which shape of the unknown solid would be the most likely to break due to its own weight when hung in the orientation shown?

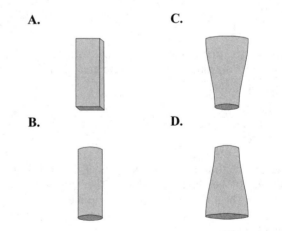

A.

B.

C.

D.

Wave Characteristics

636. A wave is a transfer of which of the following from one point to another?

    A. energy only
    B. momentum only
    C. mass and energy
    D. energy and momentum

637. If the frequency of a wave is 200 Hz, and the wavelength is 2 m, how much time is required for a single wave to pass by an observer?

    A. 0.005 s
    B. 0.050 s
    C. 200 s
    D. 400 s

638. If the frequency of a wave is 200 Hz, and the wavelength is 2 m, what is the velocity of the wave?

    A. 0.05 m/s
    B. 0.50 m/s
    C. 200 m/s
    D. 400 m/s

639. If the frequency of a wave is 200 Hz, and the velocity is 10 m/s, what is the wavelength?

    A. 0.05 m
    B. 0.50 m
    C. 20 m
    D. 2000 m

640. A longitudinal wave travels through the air. The net movement of the air molecules is:

    A. zero.
    B. in the direction of propagation of the wave.
    C. in the opposite direction of propagation of the wave.
    D. in the direction perpendicular to the propagation of the wave.

641. A transverse wave travels along a perfectly elastic string parallel to the ground. Any given point on the string:

    A. doesn't move.
    B. moves up and down.
    C. moves up only.
    D. moves left and right.

642. A 100 m rope is stretched tightly between two poles. When the rope is plucked near one pole, a wave with a wavelength of 25 cm reaches the other pole in 2 s. What is the frequency of the wave?

    A. zero, since a single wave cannot have a frequency.
    B. 12.5 Hz
    C. 200 Hz
    D. 400 Hz

643. A 20 cm wave is propagated through the following mediums. In which medium will the wave move the fastest?

    A. a tight, heavy rope
    B. a tight, light rope
    C. a loose, light rope
    D. The wave velocity depends upon the frequency of the wave.

644. Which of the following INCORRECTLY describes the relationship between a wave and the medium through which it propagates?

    A. Waves move faster through a medium that resists change.
    B. Waves move more slowly through a denser medium.
    C. Wavelength is inversely proportional to wave frequency.
    D. Wave velocity depends upon the wave frequency and wavelength, and is independent of the medium.

645. Which of the following determines the velocity of a wave?

    A. the frequency
    B. the wavelength
    C. the medium
    D. the amplitude

Questions 646-650 refer to the wave shown below.

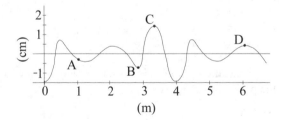

646. What is the approximate wavelength of the wave shown above?

    A. 1 m
    B. 3 m
    C. 4 m
    D. 6 m

647. If the wave above is moving at 2 m/s to the right, what is its frequency?

   A. 0.25 s^{-1}
   B. 0.5 s^{-1}
   C. 2.0 s^{-1}
   D. 8.0 s^{-1}

648. If the frequency of the wave shown is 2 Hz, and the wave is propagating to the right, how long will it take point A to pass the 5 m mark?

   A. 0.5 s
   B. 1.0 s
   C. 2.0 s
   D. 6.0 s

649. What is the amplitude of the wave?

   A. 0.5 cm
   B. 1.0 cm
   C. 1.5 cm
   D. 3.0 cm

650. If the amplitude of the wave were doubled, the frequency of the wave would:

   A. decrease by a factor of 4.
   B. decrease by a factor of 2.
   C. remain the same.
   D. increase by a factor of 2.

651. Which of the following would NOT increase the intensity of a harmonic wave?

   A. an increase in velocity
   B. an increase in frequency
   C. an increase in amplitude
   D. an increase in period

---

652. The equivalent S.I. units of intensity are:

   A. J/m^2
   B. kg/m
   C. W/m^2
   D. W/s

653. If ten ocean waves wash into shore each minute, what is the period of each wave?

   A. 1/6 s
   B. 6 s
   C. 10 s
   D. 60 s

Questions 654-658 refer to the diagram below. A sphere with mass m is placed at the surface of a very shallow pool (depth h) of a fluid with density ρ and oscillated a distance y every t seconds. Waves with a frequency f and amplitude A are generated on the fluid surface and propagate away from the sphere with a velocity v. The distance between the wave crests is given by x.

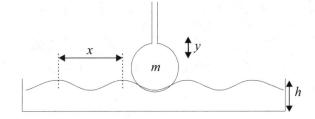

654. If y were increased, which of the following would have the greatest increase?

   A. x
   B. f
   C. v
   D. A

655. Which of the following changes, by themselves, would increase v?

   A. a decrease in t
   B. an increase in h
   C. an increase in ρ
   D. an increase in y

656. Which of the following gives the approximate velocity of the waves?

   A. $\sqrt{gh}$

   B. $\sqrt{gy}$

   C. $\sqrt{gx}$

   D. $\sqrt{\dfrac{g}{\rho}}$

657. Which of the following is the wavelength?

   A. x
   B. $2x$
   C. h
   D. y

658. If the wave generating apparatus were placed on the moon, and y remained the same, which of the following would occur?

   A. ρ would decrease.
   B. f would increase.
   C. x would increase.
   D. v would decrease.

659. A sound wave is:

   A. a longitudinal wave.
   B. a transverse wave.
   C. a gravity wave.
   D. an electromagnetic wave.

660. Sound emanating from a source is measured at 20 dB by an observer. In order to increase the intensity level to 40 dB, the rate of energy transfer must be:

   A. increased by a factor of 2.
   B. increased by a factor of 4.
   C. increased by a factor of 20.
   D. increased by a factor of 100.

661. Sound emanating from a particular source travels in all directions. This sound is measured at 20 dB by an observer standing 40 m away. In order to decrease the intensity level to 10 dB, approximately how far from the source must the observer be?

   A. 80 m
   B. 126 m
   C. 160 m
   D. 400 m

662. A wave is sent down a taught rope. Which of the following will change the velocity of the wave?

   A. changing the frequency of the wave
   B. changing the length of the rope
   C. changing the tension in the rope
   D. changing the amplitude of the wave

663. Sound waves move faster through water than through air. Which of the following is most likely the greatest contributing factor?

   A. Water has a greater density than air.
   B. Water is less compressible than air.
   C. Sound waves are longer in air.
   D. Sound waves have more energy in water.

664. As sound waves move through air, the pressure at any given point changes. The period of a sound wave is:

   A. the time between each pressure increase.
   B. the time between every two pressure increases.
   C. the time between a pressure increase and a pressure decrease.
   D. not related to the pressure changes.

665. Compared to a 440 Hz sound wave, a 880 Hz sound wave will travel:

   A. half as fast.
   B. the same speed.
   C. twice as fast.
   D. four times as fast.

666. A man stands between two sound sources that are each exactly 20 meters away. Each source generates a single sound pulse. If he hears both pulses at the same moment, one pulse at 20 dB and the other at 40 dB, which sound was generated first?

   A. The 20 dB pulse
   B. The 40 dB pulse
   C. Both were generated at the same time
   D. It is impossible to tell without knowing the frequencies of the sounds.

667. What are the equivalent SI units for dB?

   A. W/m^2
   B. W/s
   C. W
   D. Decibels represent a ratio and thus have no equivalent units in the SI sytem.

668. What purpose is served by measuring intensity level in terms of decibels and not W/m^2?

   A. Decibels measure absolute power as opposed to power per unit area.
   B. The decibel system is more accurate.
   C. Changes in decibels coincide more closely with the range of human sound perception.
   D. Decibels are used to honor Alexander Graham Bell.

669. The intensity of a wave will be most increased by an increase in which of the following?

   A. wavelength
   B. amplitude
   C. density of the medium
   D. velocity of the wave.

670. In deep water, the velocity of a surface wave is approximately proportional to the square root of the:

A. wavelength
B. amplitude
C. depth
D. density

671. In shallow water, the velocity of a surface wave is approximately proportional to the square root of the:

A. wavelength
B. amplitude
C. depth
D. density

672. If the average power of a sound wave is increased by a factor of 10, by how much does the intensity level increase?

A. 1 dB
B. 2 dB
C. 10 dB
D. 100 dB

673. A source creates a sound that is observed at 200 W/m². If the intensity level of the observed sound decreases by 20 decibels, what is the decrease in observed intensity?

A. 2 W/m²
B. 20 W/m²
C. 100 W/m²
D. 198 W/m²

674. A source creates a sound that is observed at 400 W/m². If the intensity level of the observed sound decreases by 10 decibels, what is the new observed intensity?

A. 40 W/m²
B. 80 W/m²
C. 100 W/m²
D. 390 W/m²

675. A sound source increases its average power output from 20 W/m² to 200 W/m². What is the corresponding increase in decibels to any observer?

A. 1 decibel
B. 10 decibels
C. 100 decibels
D. 180 decibels

676. A limiting factor to speed of audible sound in air is:

A. the root mean square velocity of the molecules.
B. the wavelength of the sound.
C. the frequency of the sound.
D. the pitch of the sound.

677. An increase in which of the following properties of the gas by itself, will decrease the speed of a sound wave through the gas?

A. pressure
B. density
C. temperature
D. volume

678. As the temperature of a gas increases, the speed of sound through the gas:

A. decreases
B. increases
C. The answer depends upon the density of the gas.
D. The answer depends upon the bulk modulus of the gas.

679. A sound wave moving through a tuning fork has a frequency f and wavelength λ. Which of the following is true of the sound wave when it passes into the air?

A. Both the wavelength and frequency remain the same.
B. Both the wavelength and frequency increase.
C. The wavelength decreases and the frequency remains the same.
D. The wavelength increases and the frequency remains the same.

Superposition, Phase, and Interference

Questions 680-682 refer to the diagram below. X, Y, and Z each represent a pair of waves produced by the same string.

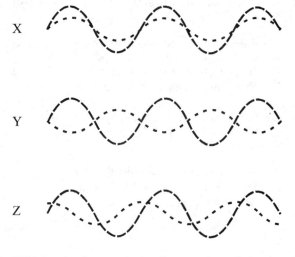

680. Which pair of waves in the diagram above is in phase?

A. X
B. Y
C. Z
D. both X and Y

681. Which pair of waves in the diagram above will experience only destructive interference?

   A. X
   B. Y
   C. Z
   D. both Y and Z

682. Which pair of waves in the diagram above will experience only constructive interference?

   A. X
   B. Y
   C. Z
   D. both X and Z

___

683. Two waves move toward each other along the same string. When they meet, they will:

   A. experience constructive interference but not destructive interference.
   B. experience destructive interference but not constructive interference.
   C. experience neither constructive nor destructive interference.
   D. experience both constructive and destructive interference.

684. Two waves move toward each other along the same string. When they meet, they will:

   A. reflect.
   B. refract.
   C. reflect and refract.
   D. neither reflect nor refract.

685. Two notes are played by two violinists. One note is played at 440 Hz, while the other is played at 436 Hz. An observer will hear a note at:

   A. 438 Hz with a beat frequency of 2 Hz.
   B. 438 Hz with a beat frequency of 4 Hz.
   C. 2 Hz with a beat frequency of 438 Hz.
   D. 4 Hz with a beat frequency of 438 Hz.

686. The beat frequency describes the change in:

   A. pitch
   B. intensity
   C. wavelength
   D. velocity

Questions 687-689 refer to the diagram below. Two low frequency sound waves are superimposed. The resulting pressure variation at a single point a distance x from the source is graphed below.

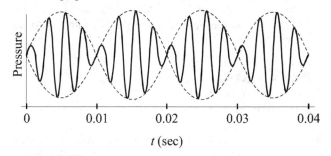

687. The beat frequency of the resulting sound wave is:

   A. 25 Hz
   B. 50 Hz
   C. 100 Hz
   D. 400 Hz

688. The frequency of the sound is:

   A. 25 Hz
   B. 50 Hz
   C. 400 Hz
   D. 800 Hz

689. Which of the following pairs of frequencies correspond to the original two sound waves?

   A. 42 Hz and 58 Hz
   B. 300 Hz and 500 Hz
   C. 350 Hz and 450 Hz
   D. 375 Hz and 425 Hz

___

690. A piano tuner plays an out of tune A note on his piano and then strikes his 440 Hz tuning fork. He notices a beat of 2 Hz. When he loosens the piano string and plays the note again, the beat goes to 4 Hz. What was the frequency of the note before he loosened the string? (Note: The A note is 440 Hz.)

   A. 438 Hz
   B. 440 Hz
   C. 442 Hz
   D. 444 Hz

691. A piano tuner plays an out of tune A note on his piano and then strikes his 440 Hz tuning fork. He notices a beat of 2 Hz. When he tightens the piano string and plays the note again, the beat remains at 2 Hz. What was the frequency of the note before he tightened the string? (Note: The A note is 440 Hz.)

   A. 438 Hz
   B. 440 Hz
   C. 442 Hz
   D. 444 Hz

692. A car travels at night at 10 m/s past a row of identical trees. Each tree is 1 m thick and 1 m from the nearest neighboring tree. A child watching the trees go by flickers a flash light on and off at a rate of 4 times per second. If the child can only see the trees when the flash light is on, how fast will the trees appear to the child to pass by?

   A. 1 tree each second
   B. 4 trees each second
   C. 9 trees each second
   D. 20 trees each second

693. A car travels at night at 10 m/s past a row of identical trees. Each tree is 1 m thick and 1 m from the nearest neighboring tree. A child watching the trees go by flickers a flash light on and off at a rate of 5 times per second. If the child can only see the trees when the flash light is on, how fast will the trees appear to the child to pass by?

   A. The trees will appear to be standing still.
   B. 1 tree each second
   C. 9 trees each second
   D. 20 trees each second

694. Two notes are played together. The resulting sound waves are summed and displayed by an oscilloscope. Which oscilloscope screen shows two notes with the closest frequencies?

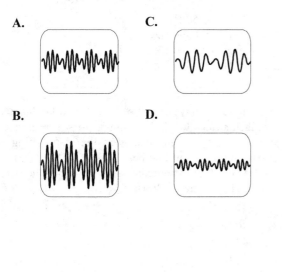

A.   C.

B.   D.

Questions 695-701 refer to the diagram shown below. When an instrument plays a note, the resulting sound is a combination of all the possible harmonics for that instrument in its momentary configuration. For instance, a musician changes notes on a violin by pressing the strings against the neck of the instrument, thus shortening the string length and changing the possible harmonics. A given shortened string will play at one time all the possible harmonics allowable by its string length. A given note is the same set of harmonics for all instruments. The diagram below shows the sound waves of the same note played by three different instruments.

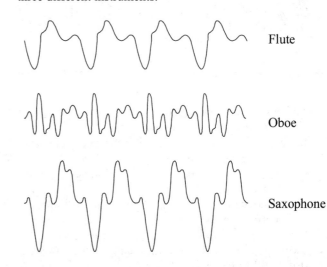

Flute

Oboe

Saxophone

695. Which of the following explains why a human can distinguish between the sound waves of the same note played by different instruments?

   A. The frequency is different for each instrument.
   B. The wavelength is different for each instrument.
   C. The relative intensities of each harmonic vary differently for the same instrument.
   D. The relative wavelengths of each harmonic vary differently for each instrument.

696. Which of the following properties is different for each sound wave shown in the diagram?

   A. velocity
   B. pitch
   C. beat frequency
   D. amplitude

697. How does the period of the first harmonic for the note played by the flute compare with the period of the wave form shown?

   A. The period for the first harmonic is half as great.
   B. The period for the first harmonic is the same.
   C. The period for the first harmonic is twice as great.
   D. The period for the first harmonic is four times as great.

698. How does the period of the second harmonic for the note played by the oboe compare with the period of the wave form shown?

A. The period for the second harmonic is half as great.
B. The period for the second harmonic is the same.
C. The period for the second harmonic is twice as great.
D. The period for the second harmonic is four times as great.

699. How does the period of the third harmonic for the note played by the oboe compare with the period of the wave form shown?

A. The period for the third harmonic is one fourth as great.
B. The period for the third harmonic is one third as great.
C. The period for the third harmonic is half as great.
D. The period for the third harmonic is the same.

700. If a higher note is played by the flute, which of the following properties of the sound wave must increase?

A. period
B. wavelength
C. amplitude
D. frequency

701. What phenomenon best explains why the same harmonics at different intensities can be superimposed to create the different waveforms as shown by the diagram?

A. interference
B. refraction
C. dispersion
D. reflection

---

702. One of the strings on a certain guitar is 36 cm long. What is the length of the first harmonic for this string?

A. 18 cm
B. 24 cm
C. 36 cm
D. 72 cm

703. One of the strings on a certain guitar is 36 cm long. What is the length of the third harmonic for this string?

A. 18 cm
B. 24 cm
C. 36 cm
D. 72 cm

704. One of the strings on a violin is 15 cm long. If the waves on the string move at 240 m/s, what is its fundamental frequency?

A. 240 Hz
B. 480 Hz
C. 800 Hz
D. 1600 Hz

705. A glass tube closed at one end is placed in front of a loud speaker fed by an audio oscillator of variable frequency. Air in the tube resonates when the speaker emits sound at a frequency of 425 Hz and 1275 Hz. What is the length of the tube? (Note: Assume the speed of sound is 340 m/s.)

A. 10 cm
B. 20 cm
C. 30 cm
D. 40 cm

706. A 30 cm violin string is placed in front of a loud speaker fed by an audio oscillator. What is the lowest frequency at which the audio oscillator can emit sound which will cause the string to vibrate? (Note: Waves propagate along the string at 264 m/s.)

A. 440 Hz
B. 880 Hz
C. 1320 Hz
D. 1760 Hz

707. A 30 cm violin string is placed near a loud speaker fed by an audio oscillator. When the oscillator emits sound over a frequency range of 500 Hz to 1500 Hz, the string vibrates only at 880 Hz and 1320 Hz. Which modes are these, respectively?

A. 1st and 2nd
B. 2nd and 1st
C. 2nd and 3rd
D. 3rd and 2nd

708. A 1 m glass tube is stood on end and partially filled with water. The air in the tube resonates when either a 440 Hz or a 1320 Hz tuning fork is vibrated at its opening. It does not resonate with a 147 Hz tuning fork. If the speed of sound in air is 340 m/s, approximately how deep is the water in the tube?

A. 19 cm
B. 42 cm
C. 50 cm
D. 81 cm

709. A 1 m glass tube is stood on end and partially filled with water. The air in the tube resonates when either a 440 Hz or a 1320 Hz tuning fork is vibrated at its opening. It does not resonate with a 147 Hz tuning fork. At which of the following frequencies will the air in the tube also resonate?

   A. 660 Hz
   B. 880 Hz
   C. 1760 Hz
   D. 2200 Hz

Questions 710-714 refer to the diagram below. A person dangles a rope and makes small circular motions with his hands. The rope takes on the shape as shown. *L* is the distance between the first two nodes.

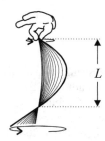

710. Which of the following describes the waveform shown in the diagram?

   A. The first harmonic of a system open at one end.
   B. The third harmonic of a system open at one end.
   C. The first harmonic of a system closed at both ends.
   D. The third harmonic of a system closed at both ends.

711. If *L* is 1 m, and the rope makes one revolution in 0.5 seconds, what is the velocity of the wave?

   A. 0.5 m/s
   B. 1.0 m/s
   C. 2.5 m/s
   D. 4.0 m/s

712. If increasing the frequency of the revolutions increases the tension in the rope, might the increased tension make it possible to generate the same harmonic at more than one frequency on the same rope?

   A. No, because a harmonic can have only one frequency for a given medium.
   B. No, because greater tension would produce the harmonic at a lower frequency.
   C. Yes, because greater tension would produce the harmonic at a higher frequency.
   D. Yes, because greater tension would produce the harmonic at a lower frequency.

713. Which of the following represents the fifth harmonic?

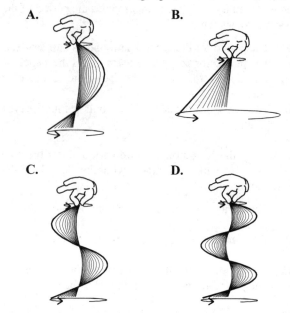

714. A longer rope with the same tension would result in:

   A. longer harmonics and lower resonance frequencies.
   B. longer harmonics and higher resonance frequencies.
   C. shorter harmonics and lower resonance frequencies.
   D. shorter harmonics and higher resonance frequencies.

Simple Harmonic Motion

715. Which of the following is NOT simple harmonic motion?

   A. An electron moving back and forth in ac current.
   B. The orbit of the earth around the sun as viewed from the side.
   C. A pendulum swinging at a small angle.
   D. A boy bouncing a yoyo in a steady rhythm.

716. Which of the following can NOT be described with a single sine wave function?

   A. A mass bouncing up and down hanging from a spring
   B. Any simple harmonic motion
   C. A guitar string vibrating at all its harmonics
   D. A fishing bobber bobbing up and down on a series of uniform water waves

717. Which of the following waves can NOT be represented by superimposing sine wave functions?

    A. The crying of an infant
    B. A square wave
    C. Any motion whatsoever.
    D. All of the above can be represented by an infinite number of superimposed wave functions.

718. Which of the following is true concerning a system in simple harmonic motion?

    A. Energy oscillates between potential and kinetic, but total energy remains constant.
    B. Energy oscillates between potential and kinetic, until total energy is exhausted.
    C. Energy oscillates between potential and heat, but total energy remains constant.
    D. Energy oscillates between heat and kinetic, but total energy remains constant.

719. Which of the following is true concerning a system in simple harmonic motion?

    A. The restoring force is inversely proportional to the displacement.
    B. The restoring force is directly proportional to the displacement.
    C. The restoring force is proportional to the square of the displacement.
    D. The restoring force is equal to the displacement.

720. Which of the following affects the period of motion of a mass bouncing on the end of a spring?

    A. the mass only
    B. the spring constant only
    C. the maximum displacement from the rest position only
    D. the mass and the spring constant only

721. A 2 kg mass bounces on the end of a spring completing one period every 2π seconds. What is the spring constant for the spring?

    A. 0.5 N/m
    B. 1 N/m
    C. 2 N/m
    D. 4 N/m

722. Which of the following is true concerning the period of oscillation for any system in simple harmonic motion?

    A. It is directly proportional to some resilient component of the system and inversely proportional to some inertial component of the system.
    B. It is directly proportional to some inertial component of the system and inversely proportional to some resilient component of the system.
    C. It is directly proportional to the square root of some resilient component of the system and inversely proportional to the square root of some inertial component of the system.
    D. It is directly proportional to the square root of some inertial component of the system and inversely proportional to the square root of some resilient component of the system.

723. A mass bouncing on the end of a spring has a period of motion T. If the spring is cut in half, and the mass is set in motion once again, what will be the approximate period of motion?

    A. $0.7T$
    B. $1.4T$
    C. $2T$
    D. $4T$

Questions 724-729 refer to the diagram below. A mass m is suspended by a spring with a spring constant k. The rest length of the spring is x_0, and it oscillates a distance Δx above and below its rest position. A very long string with a mass per unit length μ and constant tension T is attached to the mass as shown. The moving mass creates a wave on the string with a wavelength λ, a frequency f, an amplitude A, and a velocity v.

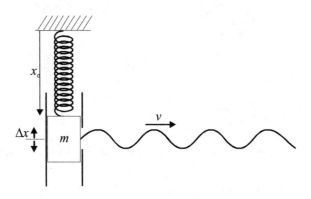

724. Which of the following is equal to the frequency of the wave on the string?

A. $\dfrac{v}{\Delta x}$

B. $\dfrac{1}{\Delta x}\sqrt{\dfrac{T}{\mu}}$

C. $\dfrac{1}{2\pi}\sqrt{\dfrac{k}{m}}$

D. $\dfrac{v}{A}$

725. Which of the following would increase the velocity of the wave on the string?

A. decreasing Δx
B. decreasing k
C. increasing m
D. decreasing μ

726. The wavelength of the wave on the string would be increased by which of the following:

A. increasing Δx
B. increasing k
C. decreasing m
D. decreasing μ

727. If the other end of the string were tied to a wall and the string were resonating at its third harmonic, which of the following would represent the length of the string? (Hint: Assume that a node exists at both ends of the string.)

A. $3\pi\sqrt{\dfrac{\mu k}{Tm}}$

B. $3\pi\sqrt{\dfrac{Tm}{\mu k}}$

C. $\dfrac{3\pi}{2}\sqrt{\dfrac{Tm}{\mu k}}$

D. $\dfrac{3\pi}{2}\sqrt{\dfrac{Tm}{\mu k}}$

728. When is the force on the mass due to the spring the greatest?

A. When the mass is at x_0
B. When the mass is at its maximum height
C. When the mass is at its minimum height
D. The force on the mass due to the spring is constant.

729. Which of the following is a graph of the kinetic energy of the mass versus x?

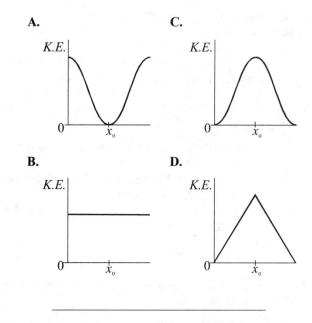

730-734 Questions 730-734 refer to the diagram below. A pendulum with a string length l and a bob mass m is pulled back to an angle θ and released. The period of motion is T. The tension in the string is τ.

730. In order for the motion of the pendulum to approximate simple harmonic motion, which of the following must be true?

A. T must be small.
B. l must be large.
C. θ must be small.
D. m must be small.

731. Which of the following will decrease the period of the pendulum?

A. placing the pendulum on the moon.
B. decreasing l
C. decreasing θ
D. increasing m

732. At what point in the swing of the pendulum is τ the greatest?

   A.   When θ is the greatest
   B.   When θ is zero
   C.   When θ is halfway between zero and θ_{max}
   D.   τ is constant throughout the swing

733. Which of the following is true if *m* is doubled?

   A.   The period decreases by a factor of 2.
   B.   The period increases by a factor of 2.
   C.   τ decreases by a factor of 2 at all positions during the swing.
   D.   τ increases by a factor of 2 at all positions during the swing.

734. If the θ is increased, τ will be:

   A.   greater at the top and the bottom of the swing.
   B.   less at the top and the bottom of the swing.
   C.   greater at the top of the swing and less at the bottom.
   D.   less at the top of the swing and greater at the bottom of the swing.

Questions 735-738 refer to the diagram below. A pendulum with string length *l* hangs inside a boxcar that is rolling down an incline at an angle β. The pendulum swings to a maximum angle θ. (Ignore friction. Assume β and θ are small.)

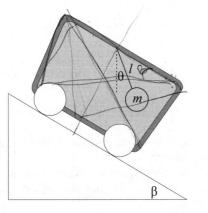

735. What is the resting position for the pendulum while the boxcar accelerates down the incline?

   A.   β to the right of vertical
   B.   β to the left of vertical
   C.   cosβ to the left of vertical
   D.   θ + β to the left of vertical

736. Which of the following represents the period of the pendulum while the boxcar accelerates down the incline?

   A. $2\pi\sqrt{\dfrac{g\sin\beta}{l}}$

   B. $2\pi\sqrt{\dfrac{g\cos\theta}{l}}$

   C. $2\pi\sqrt{\dfrac{l}{g\sin\theta}}$

   D. $2\pi\sqrt{\dfrac{l}{g\cos\beta}}$

737. How far from the vertical will the pendulum swing to the left while the boxcar accelerates down the incline?

   A.   θ
   B. $90^\circ + \theta$
   C.   θ + β
   D.   θ + 2β

738. If the cart is accelerated up the hill, the period will be:

   A.   the same as if it were stationary.
   B.   smaller than if it were stationary.
   C.   greater than if it were stationary.
   D.   zero.

Questions 739-741 refer to the diagram below. A *real* pendulum swings from a shifting peg. The peg moves back and forth horizontally in harmonic motion.

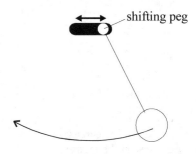

shifting peg

739. If the natural frequency of the pendulum is 0.2 Hz, at what frequency should the peg shift in order for the pendulum to attain the greatest height?

   A.   0.1 Hz
   B.   0.2 Hz
   C.   0.4 Hz
   D.   The greater the frequency of the shifting peg, the greater will be the height of the pendulum.

740. The pendulum is swinging while the peg is held still. If the peg begins to shift at exactly the resonance frequency of the pendulum, the amplitude of the oscillation of the pendulum will:

A. come to a complete stop.
B. increase to a certain maximum.
C. increase without bounds.
D. remain approximately the same.

741. If the peg is shifted at a frequency greater than the resonance frequency of the pendulum, the pendulum will:

A. swing higher.
B. swing lower at the same frequency of the shifting peg.
C. swing lower and irregularly.
D. stop swinging completely.

Questions 742-744 refer to the diagram below. A board with mass *m* and center of mass *C* sits on fixed, rotating rollers separated by a distance *L*. The coefficient of friction between the board and the rollers is μ. The board oscillates back and forth in simple harmonic motion at a frequency *f* with the center of gravity moving a distance *d* from the center of the rollers. The period of motion *T* is given below.

$$T = 2\pi\sqrt{\frac{L}{2\mu g}}$$

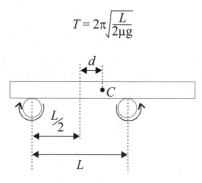

742. If a weight were placed on top of the board, which of the following would occur?

A. Both *f* and *d* would decrease.
B. Both *f* and *d* would increase.
C. Both *f* and *d* would remain the same.
D. *d* would decrease and *f* would remain the same.

743. If the distance between the rollers were increased by a factor of 4, *f* would:

A. decrease by a factor of 2.
B. remain the same.
C. increase by a factor of 2.
D. increase by a factor of 4.

744. Which of the following would occur if the direction of rotation of the rollers were reversed and their angular velocities doubled?

A. The board would be pushed off one end.
B. *T* would remain the same.
C. *f* would decrease by a factor of 2.
D. *d* would increase by a factor of 2.

The Doppler Effect

745. What property of waves creates the Doppler affect?

A. Waves diffract when moving through small opening.
B. Waves refract when changing mediums.
C. Wavelength is independent of wave amplitude.
D. Wave velocity is independent of the wave source.

746. If the source moves in the direction of a stationary observer, the observer observes the waves at a greater:

A. frequency.
B. wavelength.
C. amplitude.
D. velocity.

747. The speed of sound in air is 340 m/s. The sound from a jet moving through air at 100 m/s will move at:

A. 240 m/s
B. 340 m/s
C. 440 m/s
D. 34,000 m/s

748. Which of the following is true concerning the Doppler Effect and the wavelength of a wave?

A. Longer wavelengths are increased and shorter wavelengths are decreased.
B. Longer wavelengths are decreased and shorter wavelengths are increased.
C. Longer and shorter wavelengths are increased.
D. Different wavelengths are affected in the same manner.

749. If the source of a sound wave and the observer are stationary, and there is a steady wind blowing from the observer to the source, how will the Doppler Effect change the observed frequency?

A. The observed frequency will be greater.
B. The observed frequency will be smaller.
C. There will be no Doppler Effect.
D. The change in the frequency cannot be predicted.

750. The source of a sound wave is stationary. The observer is moving toward the source. There is a steady wind blowing *from the observer to the source*. How does the wind change the observed frequency?

A. The wind magnifies the Doppler Effect and increases the frequency.
B. The wind minimizes the Doppler Effect and increases the frequency.
C. The wind magnifies the Doppler Effect and decreases the frequency.
D. The wind minimizes the Doppler Effect and decreases the frequency.

751. The source of a sound wave is stationary. The observer is moving toward the source. There is a steady wind blowing *from the source to the observer*. How does the wind change the observed frequency?

A. The wind magnifies the Doppler Effect and increases the frequency.
B. The wind minimizes the Doppler Effect and increases the frequency.
C. The wind magnifies the Doppler Effect and decreases the frequency.
D. The wind minimizes the Doppler Effect and decreases the frequency.

752. Sound moves faster on a warm day than on a cold day. The Doppler Effect will be greater:

A. on a *warm* day because the velocities of the source and observer will be *less* significant compared to the velocity of sound.
B. on a *warm* day because the velocities of the source and observer will be *more* significant compared to the velocity of sound.
C. on a *cold* day because the velocities of the source and observer will be *less* significant compared to the velocity of sound.
D. on a *cold* day because the velocities of the source and observer will be *more* significant compared to the velocity of sound.

753. In 1845, Buys Ballot tested the Doppler Effect as follows. Trumpet players on a flatcar were moved toward stationary trumpet players via a locomotive. All trumpet players played an A note. Ballot stood between the stationary players and the moving train. What did Ballot expect to hear that would demonstrate the Doppler Effect?

A. A combined pitch lower than an A note.
B. A beat frequency.
C. A steady increase in the intensity of the A note.
D. A steadily increasing pitch as the train moved closer.

754. A sound source and an observer are both in motion. Which of the following will result in the greatest increase in observed frequency?

A. The source and the observer are both moving away from each other.
B. The source and the observer are both moving toward each other.
C. The source is moving toward the observer, but the observer is moving away from the source.
D. The source is moving away from the observer, but the observer is moving toward the source.

755. A certain star moves away from the earth. Light from the star will be shifted toward what color in the visible spectrum?

A. blue
B. green
C. red
D. yellow

756. The speed of sound is approximately 340 m/s. A police siren sounds at 1000 Hz. If a stationary observer hears the siren at 1100 Hz, what is the approximate speed of the police car?

A. 34 m/s toward the observer
B. 34 m/s away from the observer
C. 68 m/s toward the observer
D. 68 m/s away from the observer

757. An observer moves at 1/10 the speed of sound toward a stationary sound source. If the source emits sound waves with a wavelength λ, what is the approximate wavelength perceived by the observer?

A. $^1/_{10}\,\lambda$
B. $^9/_{10}\,\lambda$
C. $^{11}/_{10}\,\lambda$
D. $^{10}/_{9}\,\lambda$

758. Which of the following will result in the greatest increase in the observed frequency of sound?

A. The source moves toward the observer at 30 m/s.
B. The observer moves toward the source at 30 m/s.
C. The source moves away from the observer at 30 m/s.
D. A and B will result in exactly the same frequency change.

759. Humans can detect sound waves at a maximum frequency of 20 kHz. A certain dog whistle emits a frequency of 22 kHz. A person in a moving car blows the dog whistle. A second person standing by the road might hear the dog whistle if: (Note the speed of sound in air is 340 m/s.)

- **A.** the car is moving away from him at 34 m/s
- **B.** the car is moving toward him at 34 m/s
- **C.** the car is moving toward him at 374 m/s
- **D.** A human could never hear a dog whistle because the frequency is too high.

760. An interstellar gas circles the core of earth's galaxy. If the wavelength of the light reflecting off the gas coming toward the earth is 499 nm, and the wavelength of light reflecting off the gas moving away from earth is 501 nm, what is the speed of the gas?

- **A.** 4.2×10^4 m/s
- **B.** 1.2×10^5 m/s
- **C.** 6.0×10^5 m/s
- **D.** 1.5×10^{11} m/s

Electric Charge

761. Which of the following is true concerning the electrostatic force on a single Na^+ due to a single Cl^- in a crystal of NaCl?

  A. The force on the Na^+ is greater than the force on the Cl^- by a factor of 35/23.
  B. The force on the Na^+ is weaker than the force on the Cl^- by a factor of 35/23.
  C. The force on the Na^+ is the same magnitude as the force on the Cl^- and in the same direction.
  D. The force on the Na^+ is the same magnitude as the force on the Cl^- but in the opposite direction.

762. If the distance between two negatively charged ions is doubled, the force on one of them due to the other will:

  A. increase by a factor of 2.
  B. remain the same.
  C. decrease by a factor of 2.
  D. decrease by a factor of 4.

763. Which of the following is true concerning the electrostatic force on a single Na^+ due to a single SO_4^{2-} in a solution of Na_2SO_4?

  A. The force on the Na^+ is twice as great as the force on the SO_4^{2-}.
  B. The force on the Na^+ is half as great as the force on the SO_4^{2-}.
  C. The force on the Na^+ is the same magnitude as the force on the SO_4^{2-} and in the same direction.
  D. The force on the Na^+ is the same magnitude as the force on the SO_4^{2-} but in the opposite direction.

764. Which of the following is true concerning charge?

  A. A negative charge can be destroyed without destroying a positive charge.
  B. A positive charge can be created without creating a negative charge.
  C. A negative charge can be destroyed if a positive charge is destroyed at the same time.
  D. A positive charge can be destroyed without destroying a negative charge

765. Which of the following is true concerning a negatively charged metal wire?

  A. The charge is an intrinsic characteristic of the wire and cannot be separated from it.
  B. The wire contains more electrons than protons.
  C. The wire contains more protons than electrons.
  D. The wire contains an equal number of protons and electrons but the electrons have moved to one side to create the negative charge.

766. What are the units of the Coulomb's Law constant k?

  A. N
  B. $N\ m^2/C^2$
  C. $N\ C^2/m^2$
  D. $C^2\ m^2/N$

767. The strength of the electric field created by a point charge:

  A. increases directly with the distance from the charge.
  B. is inversely proportional to the distance from the charge.
  C. is inversely proportional to the square of the distance from the charge.
  D. depends upon the charge that is exposed to the field.

768. When placed a distance d from a positive point charge a positively charged particle has a potential energy U due to the electric field created by the point charge. If the charged particle is moved to a distance $2d$, which of the following represents its potential energy?

  A. $-U/2$
  B. $U/4$
  C. $U/2$
  D. $2U$

769. A negatively charged particle experiences a force F due to an electric field created by a positive point charge when it is placed a distance d from the positive charge. If the negatively charged particle is moved to a distance $2d$, which of the following represents the force on the negatively charged particle due to the electric field?

  A. $-F/2$
  B. $F/4$
  C. $F/2$
  D. $2F$

770. Which of the following does NOT represent equivalent units for electric field strength?

  A. $(J/m)/C$
  B. N/C
  C. V/m
  D. J/m^2

771. A particle with charge q experiences a force F when placed a distance d from a point charge. At distance d, the electric field has a strength E and a potential V. Which of the following represents the potential energy of the charge?

A. Fd
B. Eqd
C. Vq
D. Ed

772. A charged particle is moved from a great distance to a distance d from a point charge. At distance d, the electric field has a strength E and a potential V. Which of the following represents the work done per unit charge q?

A. V
B. Eqd
C. Vq
D. Ed/q

Questions 773-779 refer to the diagram below. A particle with charge q and mass m is moved through a constant electric field E a displacement d.

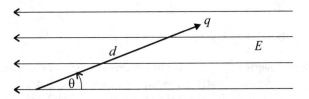

773. What is the change in voltage experienced by the charge q?

A. Ed
B. $Ed\cos\theta$
C. Eq
D. Edq

774. If the particle begins and ends at rest, how much work is done on the particle?

A. Edq
B. $Edq\cos\theta$
C. Ed
D. $Ed\cos\theta$

775. If q is positive and the charged particle is released after being moved the displacement d and stopped, the particle will move in the direction of:

A. d
B. $-d$
C. E
D. $-E$

776. As the particle is moved along d at a constant velocity, the force on the particle due to the electric field:

A. remains constant.
B. increases.
C. decreases.
D. The change in magnitude of the force depends upon whether the charge is positive or negative.

777. If q is positive, as q is moved along d the electric potential energy of q:

A. remains constant.
B. decreases.
C. increases.
D. The change in the electric potential energy of q depends upon whether it is accelerated or decelerated as it is moved along d.

778. E is least likely the result of:

A. a point charge nearby.
B. a point charge far away.
C. a parallel plate capacitor.
D. a very large, single charged plate.

779. Suppose q is positive, and a force F is applied in the direction d. If the force is equal in magnitude to Eq, the particle will:

A. move at a constant velocity along d.
B. accelerate in the direction of E.
C. accelerate in the direction exactly opposite to d.
D. accelerate at an angle up the page and to the left.

Questions 780-786 refer to the diagram below. E is the electric field created by q_1. V is the voltage at a given point in the field E. Assume that the electric field created by q_2 is negligible compared to E. k is Coulomb's Law constant. m_1 is the mass of q_1, and m_2 is the mass of q_2.

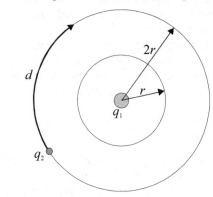

780. E can best be described as:

A. constant.
B. decreasing as r increases.
C. increasing as r increases.
D. increasing as q^2 increases.

781. What is the work done on q_2 when it is moved at constant velocity along the distance d?

   A. zero
   B. Vq_1
   C. Vq_2
   D. Edq_2

782. Which of the following represents the work done on q_2 when moved from its present position to a distance r from q_1?

   A. $\frac{1}{2}\, kq_1q_2/r$
   B. kq_1q_2/r
   C. $2\, kq_1q_2/r$
   D. kq_1q_2/r^2

783. If q_1 and q_2 have opposite charges, then when q_2 is moved from its present location to a distance r from q_1, the force on q_2 due to q_1:

   A. decreases by a factor of 4.
   B. remains the same.
   C. increases by a factor of 2.
   D. increases by a factor of 4.

784. If q_1 is positive, then when q_2 is moved from its present location to a distance r from q_1, the magnitude of the voltage experienced by q_2 due to E:

   A. decreases by a factor of 4.
   B. remains the same.
   C. increases by a factor of 2.
   D. increases by a factor of 4.

785. The strength of the electric field E at r is:

   A. half the field strength at $2r$.
   B. the same as the field strength at $2r$.
   C. twice the field strength at $2r$.
   D. four times the field strength at $2r$.

786. If q_1 and q_2 are both positively charged, and q_2 is released, what is the maximum velocity that can be achieved by q_2?

   A. $\sqrt{\dfrac{kq_1q_2}{m_2r}}$

   B. $\sqrt{\dfrac{kq_1q_2}{m_2r^2}}$

   C. $\sqrt{\dfrac{2kq_1q_2}{m_2r^2}}$

   D. $\sqrt{\dfrac{2kq_1q_2}{m_2r}}$

787. The Na^+/K^+ pump pumps three positively charged ions out of a neuron, while pumping 2 equally positively charged ions into the neuron. If this action establishes the an electric potential across the membrane, the direction of the electric field is:

   A. from the inside toward the outside.
   B. from the outside toward the inside.
   C. along the axon toward the axon terminals.
   D. along the axon away from the axon terminals.

788. Two positively charged masses are separated in deep space by a distance r. At this distance, the force of gravity happens to exactly counter the electrostatic force. At what other distance could this phenomenon be reproduced?

   A. This phenomenon would occur only at r and at no other distance.
   B. At $\frac{1}{2}\, r$.
   C. At $2r$.
   D. If the forces are equal at r, the forces must be equal at all distances.

789. Positively charged particle A starts at rest and is pulled from a great distance directly toward negatively charged particle B by the electric field created by particle B. If particle A has a velocity v when it is a distance $4r$ from particle B, what will be the velocity of particle A when it is a distance r from particle B?

   A. $\frac{1}{2}\, v$
   B. v
   C. $2v$
   D. $4v$

Questions 790-794 refer to the diagram below. The broken lines represent the paths followed by particles W, X, Y, and Z respectively through the constant electric field E. The numbers below the field represent meters.

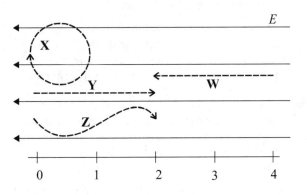

790. If the particles begin and end at rest, and all are positively charged, the same amount of work was done on which particles?

A. W and Y
B. W, Y, and Z
C. Y and Z
D. W, X, Y, and Z

791. If all particles started from rest, and all are positively charged, which particles must have been acted upon by a force other than that produced by the electric field?

A. W and Y
B. X and Z
C. X, Y, and Z
D. W, X, Y, and Z

792. If the particles are positively charged, which particles increased their electric potential energy?

A. X and Z
B. Y and Z
C. W, X, Y, and Z
D. Since the electric field is constant, none of the particles increased their electric potential energy.

793. Suppose particle Z has a charge of +2 C, and it begins and ends at rest. If E is 5 N/C, how much work is done on particle Z?

A. 10 J
B. 20 J
C. 40 J
D. 80 J

794. Suppose that the field strength E is 10 N/C and particle Y has a charge of –10 C. When particle Y is released from rest, it follows the path as shown and accelerates to a velocity of 10 m/s. What is the mass of particle Y?

A. 1 kg
B. 2 kg
C. 3 kg
D. 4 kg

Questions 795-800 refer to the diagram below. A very large, charged plate floats in deep space. Due to the charge on the plate, a constant electric field E exists everywhere above the plate. An object with mass m and charge q is shot upward from the plate with a velocity v and at an angle θ. It follows the path shown reaching a height h and a range R. Assume the effects of gravity to be negligible.

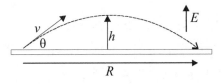

795. Which of the following must be true concerning the object?

A. q must be positive.
B. q must be negative.
C. m must be large.
D. m must be small.

796. Which of the following gives the vertical velocity of the object in terms of h just before colliding with the plate at the end of its flight?

A. $\sqrt{2gh}$

B. $\sqrt{2Eqh}$

C. $\sqrt{\dfrac{2mh}{Eq}}$

D. $\sqrt{\dfrac{2Eqh}{m}}$

797. Which of the following is true concerning all objects that follow the path shown when propelled with a velocity v at an angle θ?

A. They must have the same mass.
B. They must have the same charge.
C. They must have the same mass and the same charge.
D. Their mass to charge ratios must be the same.

Electricity and Magnetism

798. Suppose E is 10 N/C, m is 1 kg, q is –1 C, v is 100 m/s, and θ is 30°. What is h?

    A. 25 m
    B. 45 m
    C. 80 m
    D. 125 m

799. Which of the following will result in an increase in R?

    A. increasing both q and m by a factor of 2
    B. decreasing both q and m by a factor of 2
    C. increasing q by a factor of 2 while decreasing m by a factor of 2
    D. decreasing q by a factor of 2 while increasing m by a factor of 2

800. Which of the following is true concerning the flight of the projectile shown?

    A. Increasing the mass m decreases the maximum height h.
    B. Increasing the charge q increases the maximum height h.
    C. Increasing the mass m decreases the downward acceleration.
    D. Increasing the charge q decreases the downward acceleration.

Questions 801-802 refer to the diagram below. Three point charges are separated by the distances shown.

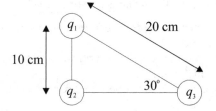

801. If all charges are equal, which of the following is true?

    A. The electrostatic force on q_2 due to q_1 is half as great as the electrostatic force on q_3 due to q_1.
    B. The electrostatic force on q_2 due to q_1 is equal to the electrostatic force on q_3 due to q_1.
    C. The electrostatic force on q_2 due to q_1 is twice as great as the electrostatic force on q_3 due to q_1.
    D. The electrostatic force on q_2 due to q_1 is four times as great as the electrostatic force on q_3 due to q_1.

802. If q_3 is 4 C and q_2 is 2 C, which of the following could represent the direction of the net force on q_1?

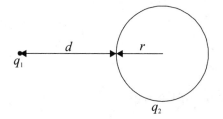

Questions 803-805 refer to the diagram below. Inside a vacuum chamber, a point charge q_1 is separated by a distance d from the surface of a hollow sphere with a radius r and made from a conducting material. The sphere has a charge q_2. (Note: k is the Coulomb's law constant.)

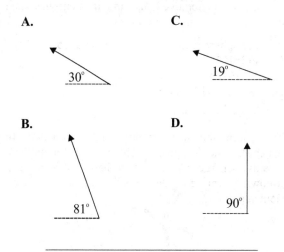

803. What is the electric field strength a distance $r/2$ from the center of the sphere?

    A. Zero, there is no electric field anywhere inside the sphere.
    B. kq_1/r^2
    C. $2kq_1/r$
    D. $kq_1/4r^2$

804. Which of the following most accurately represents the force on q_1 due to the charged sphere?

    A. $\dfrac{kq_1q_2}{r^2}$

    B. $\dfrac{kq_1q_2}{d^2}$

    C. $\dfrac{kq_1q_2}{(d+r)^2}$

    D. $\dfrac{kq_2}{r^2}$

805. When q_1 is removed, the force on the sphere changes. Which of the following represents the time between the moment q_1 is removed and the moment the sphere experiences any change in force?

   A. The sphere feels the change instantaneously.
   B. $d/(3 \times 10^8)$
   C. $(3 \times 10^8)/d$
   D. $(d + r)/(3 \times 10^8)$

---

806. The curve shown is made from a nonconducting material. It holds a positive charge on its top half and a negative charge on it bottom half. Which of the following represents the direction of the net electric field at point a?

   A. ↓

   B. →

   C. ↙

   D. ←

Movement of Charge

807. Electric charge moves through:

   A. conductors only.
   B. resistors only.
   C. conductors and resistors.
   D. neither conductors nor resistors.

808. Movement of charge is measured in:

   A. amps
   B. coulombs
   C. volts
   D. seconds

809. Which of the following is always true concerning an object with a net positive charge?

   A. The net charge on the object is the number of positive charges it holds.
   B. The net charge on the object is the number of negative charges it holds.
   C. The net charge on the object is the difference between the number of positive and negative charges it holds.
   D. The net charge on the object is the total number of positive and negative charges it holds.

810. A and B below are neutral conductors hanging from strings that do not conduct electricity. If a positively charged rod is placed near A as shown, and B is then separated from A:

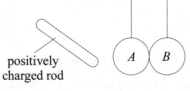

   A. both A and B will be positively charged.
   B. both A and B will be negatively charged.
   C. A will be positively charged and B will be negatively charged.
   D. B will be positively charged and A will be negatively charged.

811. Which of the following represents the equivalent units for amps?

   A. C/s
   B. V/m
   C. kg m/s
   D. C/m

812. An ohm (Ω) is a unit of:

   A. current
   B. resistance
   C. conductance
   D. electric field

813. Which of the following is true of current?

   A. Current can only be created by movement of electrons.
   B. Current moves through a resistor from low voltage to high voltage.
   C. Current is in the opposite direction to movement of electrons.
   D. Current is increased by resistance.

814. Which of the following is true for any circuit?

   A. The rate of flow of electrons is the same at any point in the circuit.
   B. The voltage drop in one complete trip around the circuit from any point is equal to the voltage of the battery.
   C. Any two resistors placed across the same voltage will have the same current.
   D. The voltage between two points in a circuit is independent of the path chosen to measure it.

815. What is the voltage across the resistor and the current through the resistor in the circuit shown below?

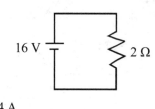

A. 8 V, 4 A
B. 16 V, 8 A
C. 16 V, 32 A
D. 32 V, 8 A

816. What is the voltage across the 3 ohm resistor and the current through the 3 ohm resistor in the circuit shown below?

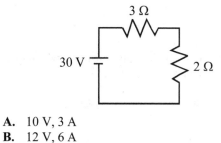

A. 10 V, 3 A
B. 12 V, 6 A
C. 18 V, 6 A
D. 18 V, 10 A

817. What is the voltage across the 2 ohm resistor and the current through the 2 ohm resistor?

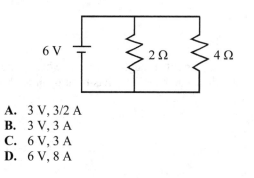

A. 3 V, 3/2 A
B. 3 V, 3 A
C. 6 V, 3 A
D. 6 V, 8 A

818. What is the voltage across the 2 ohm resistors and the current through either 2 ohm resistors?

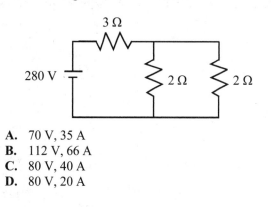

A. 70 V, 35 A
B. 112 V, 66 A
C. 80 V, 40 A
D. 80 V, 20 A

819. What is the voltage across the capacitor and the charge on the capacitor?

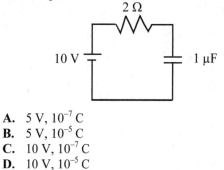

A. 5 V, 10^{-7} C
B. 5 V, 10^{-5} C
C. 10 V, 10^{-7} C
D. 10 V, 10^{-5} C

820. What is the voltage across the capacitor and the charge on the capacitor?

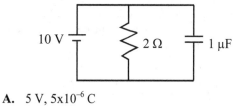

A. 5 V, 5×10^{-6} C
B. 5 V, 10^{-5} C
C. 10 V, 5×10^{-6} C
D. 10 V, 10^{-5} C

821. What is the potential difference across the capacitor and the charge on the capacitor?

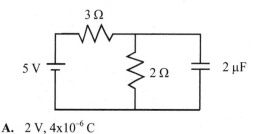

A. 2 V, 4×10^{-6} C
B. 2 V, 10^{-5} C
C. 5 V, 4×10^{-6} C
D. 5 V, 10^{-5} C

822. What is the potential difference across the capacitor and the charge on the capacitor after the switch is closed for a long time?

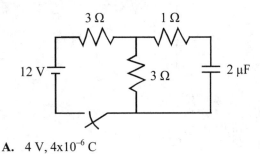

A. 4 V, 4×10^{-6} C
B. 4 V, 1.2×10^{-5} C
C. 6 V, 6×10^{-6} C
D. 6 V, 1.2×10^{-5} C

823. For the circuit in the previous question, what is the initial current across the 1 ohm resistor just after the switch is opened?

A. 1.0 A
B. 1.5 A
C. 2.0 A
D. 3.0 A

824. What is the voltage between points A and B?

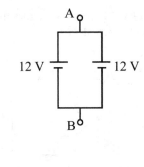

A. 0 V
B. 6 V
C. 12 V
D. 24 V

825. What is the current across the 3 ohm resistor?

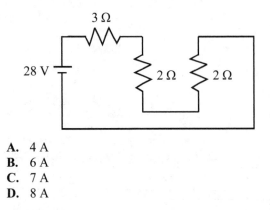

A. 4 A
B. 6 A
C. 7 A
D. 8 A

Questions 826-841 refer to the circuit shown below.

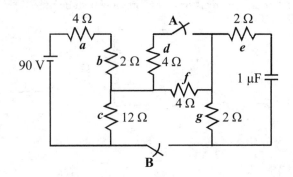

826. What is the current through resistor *a* when switch A and B have been open for a long time?

A. 0 A
B. 5 A
C. 9 A
D. 10 A

827. What is the current through resistor *g* when switch A and B have been open for a long time?

A. 0 A
B. 5 A
C. 9 A
D. 10 A

828. What is the power dissipated by resistor *a* when switch A and B have been open for a long time?

A. 20 W
B. 100 W
C. 200 W
D. 450 W

829. What is the current through resistor *a* when switch A has been closed and switch B has been open for a long time?

A. 0 A
B. 5 A
C. 9 A
D. 10 A

830. What is the current through resistor *a* when switch B has been closed and switch A has been open for a long time?

A. 0 A
B. 5 A
C. 9 A
D. 10 A

831. What is the current through resistor g when switch B has been closed and switch A has been open for a long time?

A. 3 A
B. 6 A
C. 9 A
D. 10 A

832. What is the current through resistor c when switch B has been closed and switch A has been open for a long time?

A. 3 A
B. 6 A
C. 9 A
D. 10 A

833. What is the power dissipated by resistor f when switch B has been closed and switch A has been open for a long time?

A. 36 W
B. 64 W
C. 90 W
D. 144 W

834. What is the potential difference across resistor f when switch B has been closed and switch A has been open for a long time?

A. 12 V
B. 24 V
C. 48 V
D. 90 V

835. What is the potential difference across the capacitor when switch B has been closed and switch A has been open for a long time?

A. 0 V
B. 12 V
C. 36 V
D. 90 V

836. What is the current through resistor a when both switch A and B have been closed for a long time?

A. 0 A
B. 5 A
C. 9 A
D. 10 A

837. What is the current through resistor d when both switch A and B have been closed for a long time?

A. 1.0 A
B. 2.0 A
C. 3.75 A
D. 5.25 A

838. What is the potential difference across the capacitor when both switch A and B have been closed for a long time?

A. 0 V
B. 9 V
C. 15 V
D. 90 V

839. How much energy is stored in the capacitor when both switch A and B have been closed for a long time?

A. 8.625×10^{-6} J
B. 1.125×10^{-4} J
C. 2.560×10^{-4} J
D. 6.400×10^{-4} J

840. Both switch A and B have been closed for a long time. If both switches are suddenly opened, what is the initial current through resistor e?

A. 1.0 A
B. 2.0 A
C. 3.75 A
D. 5.25 A

841. Both switch A and B have been closed for a long time. If only switch B is suddenly opened, what is the initial current through resistor g?

A. 0 A
B. 2.0 A
C. 3.75 A
D. 5.25 A

842. If one of the resistors is removed, what would happen to the current through the remaining resister?

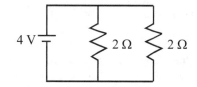

A. The current through the remaining resistor would increase by a factor of 2.
B. The current through the remaining resistor would remain the same.
C. The current through the remaining resistor would decrease by a factor of 2.
D. The current through the remaining resistor would decrease by a factor of 4.

Questions 843-846 refer to the diagram below.

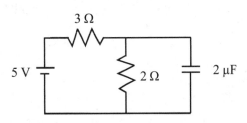

843. What is the energy stored in the capacitor?

    A. 1×10^{-6} J
    B. 2×10^{-6} J
    C. 4×10^{-6} J
    D. 8×10^{-6} J

844. If the area of the plates on the capacitor were doubled, the voltage across the capacitor would:

    A. decrease by a factor of 2.
    B. remain the same.
    C. increase by a factor of 2.
    D. increase by a factor of 4.

845. If the area of the plates on the capacitor were doubled, the energy stored in the capacitor would:

    A. decrease by a factor of 2.
    B. remain the same.
    C. increase by a factor of 2.
    D. increase by a factor of 4.

846. If the distance between the plates on the capacitor were doubled, the energy stored in the capacitor would:

    A. decrease by a factor of 2.
    B. remain the same.
    C. increase by a factor of 2.
    D. increase by a factor of 4.

---

847. What is the effective capacitance of the three capacitor unit below?

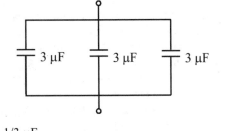

    A. 1/3 µF
    B. 1 µF
    C. 3 µF
    D. 9 µF

848. What is the effective capacitance of the three capacitor unit below?

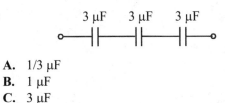

    A. 1/3 µF
    B. 1 µF
    C. 3 µF
    D. 9 µF

849. If a third resistor is added between A and B in the circuit below, what will happen to the effective resistance and the power used by the circuit?

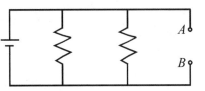

    A. The effective resistance will *decrease* and the power will *decrease*.
    B. The effective resistance will *decrease* and the power will *increase*.
    C. The effective resistance will *increase* and the power will *decrease*.
    D. The effective resistance will *increase* and the power will *increase*.

850. Approximately how long is required for an electron to move from one electrode to the other around the circuit connected to a typical car battery? (Assume about 4 m of wiring.)

    A. a fraction of a second
    B. several seconds
    C. several hours
    D. forever

Use the circuit below to answer questions 851-852.

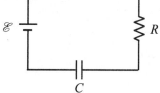

851. Which of the following represents the voltage versus time on the capacitor just after the switch is closed?

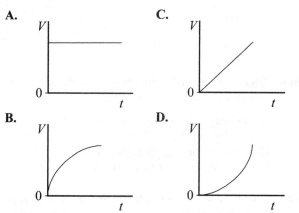

A.

C.

B.

D.

852. Which of the following represents the voltage versus charge on the capacitor as it is charging?

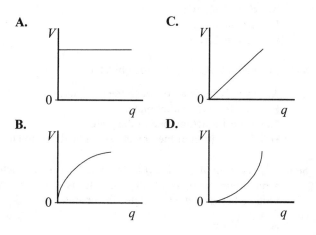

A.

C.

B.

D.

Questions 853-856 refer to the circuits below. All batteries have the same EMF.

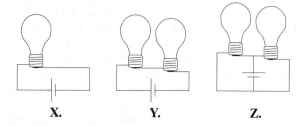

X.   **Y.**   **Z.**

853. Which circuit has the greatest current?

    A. X
    B. Y
    C. Z
    D. All have the same current.

854. Which circuit provides the most light?

    A. X
    B. Y
    C. Z
    D. All provide an equal amount of light.

855. Which circuit provides the least light?

    A. X
    B. Y
    C. Z
    D. All provide an equal amount of light.

856. In which circuit is the voltage across the effective resistance the greatest?

    A. X
    B. Y
    C. Z
    D. All have the same voltage.

AC Current

857. A power company supplies a home with alternating current (ac current). In ac current, electrons:

    A. move from the power company to the home.
    B. move from the home to the power company.
    C. move from the home to the power company and back.
    D. move back and forth in a very small space.

Questions 858-867 refer to the diagram below. Two experiments are set up as follows: An object with charge q and mass m is placed between two plates with equal and opposite charge. The plates are very large compared to the distance d between them. V is the voltage of the right plate relative to the left plate. The potential difference between the plates is adjusted each T seconds according to the V vs. t graph below each apparatus so that the object is accelerated back and forth exactly midway between the plates, coming very close to each plate but without making contact with either plate. (Diagrams are not drawn to scale.)

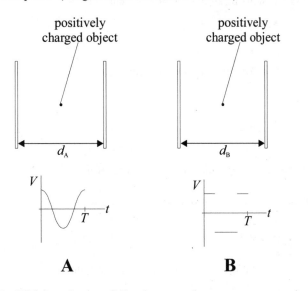

A   **B**

858. Which of the following graphs most accurately represents the velocity versus time for apparatus A?

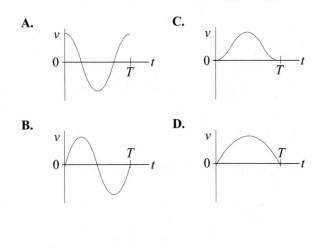

859. Which of the following graphs most accurately represents the velocity versus time for apparatus B?

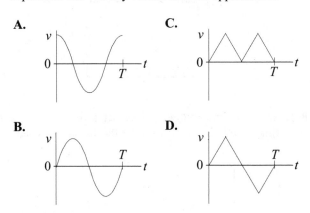

860. Which of the following is a possible initial starting point for the object in apparatus B?

   A. exactly midway between the two plates.
   B. ¼ d from the left plate.
   C. almost touching the right plate.
   D. The object may be started from any point.

861. How far does the object travel in T seconds in apparatus A and B respectively?

   A. d_A m, d_B m
   B. d_A m, $2d_B$ m
   C. $2d_A$ m, d_B m
   D. $2d_A$ m, $2d_B$ m

862. In apparatus A, where is the object at ½ T?

   A. exactly midway between the two plates.
   B. ¼ d from the either plate.
   C. almost touching one of the plates.
   D. The position of the object cannot be determined.

863. If d_B is 20 m, m is 1 kg, q is 2 C, and the object reaches a maximum velocity of 20 m/s, what is the maximum voltage between the two plates in apparatus B?

   A. 25 V
   B. 50 V
   C. 100 V
   D. 200 V

864. If the object in apparatus B reaches a maximum velocity of 20 m/s, what is the average speed of the object in the first T seconds?

   A. 0 m/s
   B. 10 m/s
   C. 14 m/s
   D. 20 m/s

865. If the object in apparatus A reaches a maximum velocity of 20 m/s, what is the rms velocity of the object in the first T seconds?

    A. 0 m/s
    B. 10 m/s
    C. 14 m/s
    D. 20 m/s

866. If the maximum voltages on both apparatus are equal, which of the following must be true?

    A. $d_A > d_B$ and the object reaches a greater speed in apparatus A than in apparatus B.
    B. $d_A > d_B$ and the object reaches a greater speed in apparatus B than in apparatus A.
    C. $d_A < d_B$ and the object reaches a greater speed in apparatus A than in apparatus B.
    D. $d_A < d_B$ and the object reaches a greater speed in apparatus B than in apparatus A.

867. If the maximum voltage in apparatus A is 100 V, what is the rms voltage?

    A. 14 V
    B. 50 V
    C. 71 V
    D. 100 V

Magnetism

868. All of the following are true of both magnetism and electricity EXCEPT:

    A. Like poles and charges repel; opposites attract.
    B. The strength of attraction and repulsion of electric charges or magnetic poles vary inversely as the square of the distance between the charges or poles.
    C. It is possible to isolate a single positive or negative electric charge or a single north or south magnetic pole.
    D. The forces of attraction or repulsion between two magnetic poles on either pole, or between two electric charges on either charge are of equal strength.

869. The S.I. unit for magnetic field strength is a:

    A. wortle
    B. newton
    C. tesla
    D. biot-savart

870. All of the following are true concerning magnetism EXCEPT:

    A. Breaking a magnet in half will create two magnets each with equal and opposite poles.
    B. The magnetic north pole is near the geographic south pole.
    C. The magnetic properties of a magnet are contained in every molecule of the magnet.
    D. A stationary charge can move a resting compass needle.

871. Which of the following is NOT true concerning a charge moving through a constant magnetic field?

    A. The force on the charge due to the field is proportional to the velocity of the charge.
    B. The force on the charge due to the field is proportional to the magnitude of the charge.
    C. The force on the charge due to the field is proportional to the strength of the magnetic field.
    D. The force is at a maximum when the velocity of the charge is in the same direction as the magnetic field.

872. Which of the following is true concerning a charge moving through a constant magnetic field?

    A. The direction of the force depends upon the angle between the velocity and the magnetic field.
    B. The force is always perpendicular to both the velocity and the magnetic field.
    C. The force is always perpendicular to the velocity and parallel to the magnetic field.
    D. The force is always parallel to both the velocity and the magnetic field.

873. Which of the following is true concerning an electric field created by a magnetic field?

    A. A nonconservative electric field is created by a changing magnetic field.
    B. A conservative electric field is created by a changing magnetic field.
    C. A nonconservative electric field is created by a constant magnetic field.
    D. A conservative electric field is created by a constant magnetic field.

874. What is the force on a 1 C charge moving at 1 m/s perpendicular to a magnetic field with a strength of 1 tesla?

    A. 0 N
    B. 1 N
    C. 2 N
    D. 3 N

875. A compass needle with a pole strength of 3 A•m is placed in a constant magnetic field with strength 3 tesla as shown. What is the net force on the compass needle?

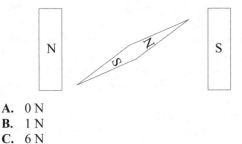

- **A.** 0 N
- **B.** 1 N
- **C.** 6 N
- **D.** 9 N

876. A piece of iron is wrapped by copper wire as shown. Which of the following is correct?

- **A.** A current in the wire will turn the iron into a magnet.
- **B.** If the iron is magnetized, a current will be produced in the wire.
- **C.** Both A and B are true.
- **D.** Neither A or B is true.

Questions 877-879 refer to the diagram below. A conducting coil is rotated at a constant speed in an external magnetic field as shown. A current is generated within the loop. *T* represents the time required for the loop to make one full rotation.

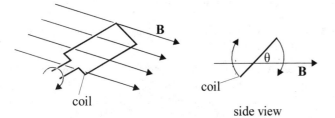

877. Which of the following most likely represents the current *i* generated within the coil as a function of time?

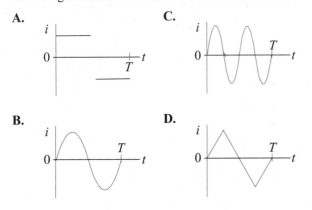

878. Which of the following most likely represents the force *F* on an electron within the coil as a function of θ?

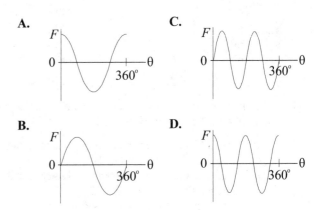

879. Which of the following would increase the current generated in the coil?

- **I.** increasing the speed of rotation of the wire
- **II.** increasing the size of the coil
- **III.** increasing the strength of the magnetic field

- **A.** I only
- **B.** II only
- **C.** I and II only
- **D.** I, II, and III

Questions 880-882 refer to the diagram below. A conducting bar is slid at a constant velocity *v* along two conducting rods. The rods are separated by a distance *l* and connected across a resistor *R*. The entire apparatus is placed in an external magnetic field *B* directed into the page.

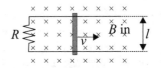

880. Which of the following represents the current *i* generated by the apparatus?

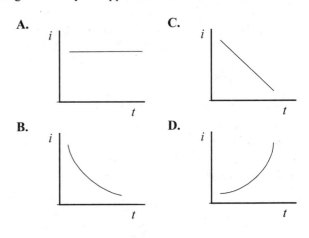

881. An increase in which of the following would NOT increase the current generated by the apparatus?

    A. v
    B. l
    C. R
    D. B

882. How will the current in the apparatus shown above be generated?

    A. sinusoidally
    B. clockwise
    C. counterclockwise
    D. There is not enough information to determine the direction of the current.

Questions 883-884 refer to the diagram shown below. A magnet is pulled through a stationary, conducting ring at a constant velocity v.

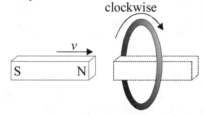

883. In which direction will the current in the ring be generated when the magnet moves completely through the ring?

    A. clockwise then counter clockwise
    B. counter clockwise then clockwise
    C. clockwise only
    D. counterclockwise only

884. The current induced by the magnet creates its own magnetic field. Which of the magnets below is oriented in such a position as to create a magnetic field similar to the magnetic field generated by the current in the ring?

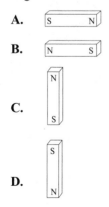

Questions 885-889 refer to the diagram below. Two long wires 1 and 2 separated by a distance d conduct current in opposite directions.

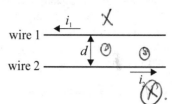

885. Which of the following statements is true?

    A. The magnetic field created by i_1 creates a net force on both wires.
    B. The magnetic field created by i_1 creates a net force on wire 1 only.
    C. The magnetic field created by i_1 creates a net force on wire 2 only.
    D. The magnetic field created by i_1 does not create a net force on either wire.

886. The magnetic field created by the moving charge is measured in tesla. Which of the following is equivalent to tesla?

    A. $N/(A \cdot m)$
    B. Nm/A
    C. NA/m
    D. $A \cdot m/N$

887. If d is doubled, the force on wire 1 due to the magnetic field created by i_2 will:

    A. decrease by a factor of 4.
    B. decrease by a factor of 2.
    C. remain the same.
    D. increase by a factor of 2.

888. Which of the following most accurately represents the direction of the net forces on wires 1 and 2 respectively due to all magnetic fields?

    A.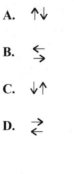
    B.
    C.
    D.

889. Which of the following describes the magnetic field created by i_1?

A. The field goes into the page above the wire and comes out of the page below the wire.
B. The field comes out of the page above the wire and goes into the page below the wire.
C. The field goes into the page above and below the wire.
D. The field comes out of the page above and below the wire.

---

890. A clockwise current of the same magnitude exists in each of the rings shown. At which center point shown is the magnetic field strength the greatest?

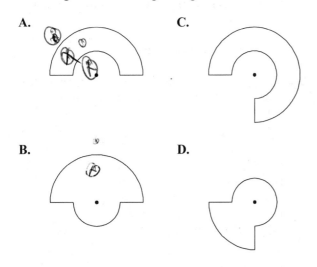

A.

C.

B.

D.

891. The circles represent currents, each of the same magnitude and in the direction shown. The radius of each circle is either r or $2r$. The dots are located midway between the loops and on the central axis. At which dot is the magnetic field the greatest?

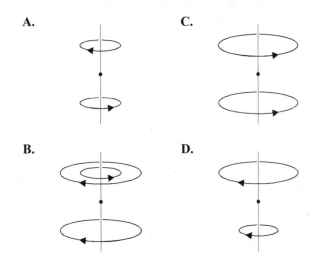

A.

C.

B.

D.

892. In which direction will a compass point if it is held directly over a wire carrying a strong current?

A. north
B. south
C. perpendicular to the wire
D. parallel to the wire

893. An electron moving in a circle at high speed generates a polarized electromagnetic wave called *synchrotron radiation*. Which of the following gives all possible orientations of the magnetic field, for any synchrotron radiation produced by the electron below?

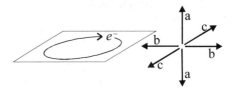

A. a only
B. b only
C. c and b only
D. a, b, and c

894. Which of the following gives possible directions of propagation for any synchrotron radiation produced by the electron in the previous question?

A. a only
B. b only
C. c and b only
D. a, b, and c

Light

895. What is the approximate speed of light in a vacuum?

A. 3×10^8 m/s
B. 3×10^8 km/s
C. 3×10^8 mph
D. 3×10^8 m/min

896. Which of the following most accurately describes light?

A. wave
B. particle
C. static electromagnetic field
D. wave and particle

897. Which of the following most accurately describes a photon?

A. A photon is an electric and magnetic wave *parallel* to each other and *perpendicular* to the direction of propagation.
B. A photon is an electric and magnetic wave *parallel* to each other and *parallel* to the direction of propagation.
C. A photon is an electric and magnetic wave *perpendicular* to each other and *perpendicular* to the direction of propagation.
D. A photon is an electric and magnetic wave *perpendicular* to each other and *parallel* to the direction of propagation.

898. Visible light is:

A. all possible wavelengths of electromagnetic radiation.
B. wavelengths of electromagnetic radiation between 390 nm and 700 nm.
C. wavelengths of electromagnetic radiation between 390 m and 700 m.
D. the only wavelengths of electromagnetic radiation that can penetrate Earth's atmosphere.

899. Which of the following lists light from highest to lowest energy?

A. orange, blue, ultraviolet, infrared
B. ultraviolet, blue, orange, infrared
C. infrared, orange, blue, ultraviolet
D. ultraviolet, infrared, blue, orange

900. White light:

A. has a wavelength of approximately 550 nm.
B. moves faster than colored light.
C. is a combination of all the wavelengths of visible light.
D. does not exist.

901. If red, yellow, and blue colors are mixed, the result is:

A. white
B. black
C. brown
D. purple

902. The sky is blue because it:

A. absorbs light at 390 nm.
B. reflects light at 390 nm.
C. absorbs light at 700 nm.
D. reflects light at 700 nm.

903. Which of the following is the approximate wavelength of an x-ray?

A. 5.2×10^{-11} m
B. 7.9×10^{-7} m
C. 3.0×10^{-7} m
D. 4.5×10^{-6} m

904. The index of refraction of a certain substance is 1.5. Light moves through that substance at a speed of:

A. 1.5×10^8 m/s
B. 2.0×10^8 m/s
C. 3.0×10^8 m/s
D. 4.5×10^8 m/s

905. The shapes below are made of glass and placed in a vacuum. Which line could be the path of a light ray as it travels through the shapes?

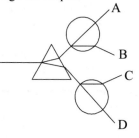

906. Which of the following pairs of angles must be equal?

A. the angle of incidence and the angle of refraction
B. the angle of incidence and the angle of reflection
C. the critical angle and the angle of refraction
D. the critical angle and the angle of incidence

907. If a light ray in air strikes the surface of an object at an angle of incidence of 60°, and refracts at 30°, what is the approximate index of refraction of the substance?

A. 0.58
B. 0.87
C. 1.7
D. 2.0

908. If a light ray in a substance strikes its surface from inside at an angle of incidence of 30°, and refracts into air at 60°, what is the approximate index of refraction of the substance?

A. 0.58
B. 0.87
C. 1.7
D. 2.0

909. When light moves from a medium with a low index of refraction to a medium with a higher index of refraction, the light:

A. slows down and bends toward the normal.
B. remains at the same constant velocity and bends toward the normal.
C. speeds up and bends toward the normal.
D. speeds up and bends away from the normal.

910. The object shown below is immersed in a fluid. The line represents the refracted path of a light ray. Which of the following can be deduced from the picture?

A. The light ray moves from left to right.
B. The light ray moves from right to left.
C. The index of refraction of the object is greater than the index of refraction of the surrounding fluid.
D. The index of refraction of the surrounding fluid is greater than the index of refraction of the object.

911. In order for total internal reflection to occur at the interface between two substances:

A. the index of refraction of the interfacing substances must be the same.
B. the index of refraction of the substance which the light is trying to leave must be *less* than the index of refraction of the substance which it is trying to enter.
C. the index of refraction of the substance which the light is trying to leave must be *greater* than the index of refraction of the substance which it is trying to enter.
D. one of the substances must be air.

912. Visible light of which color bends the most when entering glass from air?

A. yellow
B. green
C. violet
D. red

913. Visible light of which color bends the most when changing mediums?

A. yellow
B. green
C. violet
D. red

914. Which of the following is true of light striking a glass-air interface from the air side?

A. Total internal reflection may occur.
B. The intensity of the reflected light will always be greater than the intensity of the refracted light.
C. The intensity of the reflected light will always be less than the intensity of the refracted light.
D. The frequency of the refracted light will be the same as the frequency of the reflected light.

915. Which of the following is true when light strikes a glass-air interface from the glass side?

A. The frequency of the refracted light will increase.
B. The frequency of the refracted light will decrease.
C. The wavelength of the refracted light will increase.
D. The wavelength of the refracted light will decrease.

916. A prism bends different wavelengths of light to different degrees, in a phenomenon called chromatic:

A. dispersion
B. diffraction
C. interference
D. infraction

917. A certain animal swims at 4.0 m/s. If the animal takes the fastest path from its position on land to its home in the water, and that path is the one shown in the diagram below, how fast is the animal on land?

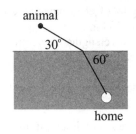

A. 2.0 m/s
B. 2.4 m/s
C. 6.8 m/s
D. 8.0 m/s

918. Water has an index of refraction of 1.3. Approximately how fast does light move through the water?

  A. 1.0×10^8 m/s
  B. 2.3×10^8 m/s
  C. 3.0×10^8 m/s
  D. 4.9×10^9 m/s

919. Light traveling through air strikes benzene ($n = 1.8$), which angle will be the smallest?

  A. the angle of reflection
  B. the angle of refraction
  C. the angle of incidence
  D. It can not be determined from the information given.

920. What is the approximate frequency of red light?

  A. 3.5×10^{-14} Hz
  B. 7.0×10^{-9} Hz
  C. 2.3×10^8 Hz
  D. 4.3×10^{14} Hz

921. If the frequency of light is doubled, the energy per photon:

  A. decreases by a factor of 2
  B. remains the same
  C. increases by a factor of 2
  D. increases by a factor of 4

922. A swimmer is submerged in a pool as shown. A lifeguard stands on the side. As drawn in the diagram:

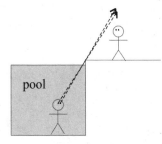

  A. the swimmer may be able to see the lifeguard but the lifeguard could not see the swimmer.
  B. the lifeguard may be able to see the swimmer but the swimmer could not see the lifeguard.
  C. both the lifeguard and the swimmer may be able to see each other.
  D. neither the swimmer nor the lifeguard could possibly see the other.

923. A one-eyed person standing in hip deep water sees a fish in the water one meter in front of him. The fish appears to be:

  A. closer and larger than it really is.
  B. closer and smaller than it really is.
  C. farther away and larger than it really is.
  D. farther away and smaller than it really is.

924. The person below views the coin in the water. The coin appears to be:

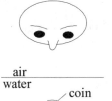

  A. closer and larger than it really is.
  B. closer and smaller than it really is.
  C. farther away and larger than it really is.
  D. farther away and smaller than it really is.

925. Which of the following would result in the greatest diffraction?

  A. small wavelengths moving through a small opening
  B. small wavelengths moving through a large opening
  C. large wavelengths moving through a small opening
  D. large wavelengths moving through a large opening

926. If the frequency of a simple harmonic, mechanical wave is doubled, its energy:

  A. decreases by a factor of 2.
  B. remains the same.
  C. increases by a factor of 2.
  D. increases by a factor of 4.

927. If the frequency of a photon is doubled, its energy:

  A. decreases by a factor of 2.
  B. remains the same.
  C. increases by a factor of 2.
  D. increases by a factor of 4.

928. If the amplitude of a simple harmonic, mechanical wave is doubled, its energy:

  A. decreases by a factor of 2.
  B. remains the same.
  C. increases by a factor of 2.
  D. increases by a factor of 4.

929. If the speed of a simple harmonic, mechanical wave is doubled, its energy:

A. decreases by a factor of 2.
B. remains the same.
C. increases by a factor of 2.
D. increases by a factor of 4.

930. Isaac Newton once wrote "To me the fundamental supposition itself seems impossible, namely, that the waves or vibrations of any fluid can, like rays of light, be propagated in straight lines, without a continual and very extravagant spreading and bending every way into the quiescent medium, where they are terminated by it." This statement indicates that Newton believed light did NOT exhibit:

A. interference.
B. diffraction.
C. refraction.
D. reflection.

931. Isaac Newton explained that light particles are strongly attracted to the surface of glass so that when they approach the surface from an angle, they receive an impulse that increases the perpendicular component of their velocity. This was most likely an attempt to use the particle theory of light to explain:

A. interference.
B. diffraction.
C. refraction.
D. reflection.

932. In the *photoelectric effect*, light falling on the surface of a metal ejects electrons from that metal. The kinetic energy of each electron is independent of intensity of the light. Einstein showed that the photoelectric effect demonstrates light is a:

A. wave because photons and electrons interfere.
B. wave because photons diffract.
C. particle because electrons reflect.
D. particle because photons make one-to-one collisions with electrons.

933. All electromagnetic waves are created by:

A. the acceleration of electric charge.
B. heat.
C. nuclear fission.
D. nuclear fusion.

934. White light strikes a glass surface from air at an angle of 30°. The light is split into colors in a phenomenon known as dispersion. What color light will have the greatest angle of refraction?

A. red
B. yellow
C. green
D. blue

935. White light strikes a glass surface from air at an angle of 30°. What color light will bend the most upon entering the glass?

A. red
B. yellow
C. green
D. blue

936. A triangular air pocket is cut from a rectangular piece of glass. Which of the following most closely resembles the chromatic dispersion that would occur if a ray of white light is shone through the glass and the air pocket?

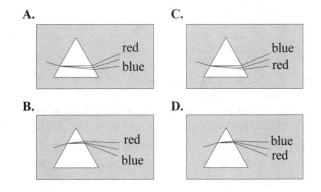

937. The index of refraction of the water in a certain murky pond is approximately 1.4. An alligator sits 1 m below the smooth surface of the pond. The alligators view of objects above the surface is restricted to a circular window at the surface with a radius of:

A. 0.5 m
B. 1 m
C. 2 m
D. 2.6 m

938. Two light sources produce light in phase with wavelength λ. The sources are placed 22.5λ and 45λ, respectively, from point *p*. The light sources are calibrated so that if either light is turned on without the other, the intensity of light at point *p* will be *I*. When both sources are turned on, the intensity of light at point *p* will be:

A. 0
B. 0.5 *I*
C. *I*
D. 2 *I*

939. If, in the previous question, point *p* were 23λ from both light sources, the intensity would be:

A. 0
B. *I*
C. 2 *I*
D. 4 *I*

940. The previous two questions exhibit the phenomenon known as:

A. refraction
B. interference
C. dispersion
D. diffraction

Mirrors and Lenses

941. Which of the following can make a real inverted image?

A. a convex lens
B. a convex mirror
C. a concave lens
D. a plane mirror

942. Which of the following cannot make a virtual image?

A. a convex lens
B. a convex mirror
C. a concave lens
D. All of the above can make a virtual image.

943. If a lens has a power of –1, the image it forms must be:

A. the same size as the object.
B. inverted.
C. virtual.
D. 1 m from the lens.

944. A plane mirror may form a virtual image:

A. behind the mirror only.
B. in front of the mirror only.
C. either in front of the mirror or behind the mirror.
D. A plane mirror cannot form a virtual image.

945. Real images are usually formed:

A. behind a concave mirror.
B. in front of a convex lens.
C. on the human retina.
D. behind a concave lens.

946. The focal distance of a plane mirror is:

A. zero
B. negative
C. positive
D. infinite

947. The radius of curvature of a convex mirror is:

A. zero
B. negative
C. positive
D. infinite

948. A woman of height *h* can see her entire body in a flat mirror. What is the minimum length of the mirror?

A. ¼ *h*
B. ½ *h*
C. *h*
D. Any mirror will work depending upon how far the woman stands from the mirror.

949. The magnification of a 3 cm object placed 5 cm from a certain lens is –1. Where is the image formed?

A. 5 cm in front of the lens.
B. 10 cm in front of the lens.
C. 5 cm behind the lens.
D. 10 cm behind the lens.

950. The magnification of a 3 cm object placed 5 cm from a certain lens is –1. What is the size of the image?

A. 1.5 cm
B. 3 cm
C. 6 cm
D. 5 cm

951. The magnification of a 3 cm object placed 5 cm from a certain lens is –1. What is the focal distance of the lens?

A. 0.4 cm
B. 0.5 cm
C. 2.5 cm
D. 5.0 cm

952. The magnification of a 3 cm object placed 5 cm from a certain lens is –1. What is the power of the lens?

    A. 1 diopter
    B. –1 diopter
    C. 40 diopters
    D. –40 diopters

953. A lens makes a 3 cm inverted image of a 6 cm object when the object is placed 10 cm from the lens. Where is the image formed?

    A. 5 cm in front of the lens.
    B. 5 cm behind the lens.
    C. 20 cm in front of the lens.
    D. 20 cm behind the lens.

954. A lens makes a 3 cm inverted image of a 6 cm object when the object is placed 10 cm from the lens. What is the focal distance of the lens?

    A. 3.3 cm
    B. –3.3 cm
    C. 10 cm
    D. –10 cm

955. A lens makes a 3 cm upright image of a 6 cm object when the object is placed 10 cm from the lens. What is the focal distance of the lens?

    A. 3.3 cm
    B. –3.3 cm
    C. 10 cm
    D. –10 cm

956. A concave mirror makes a 3 cm image of a 6 cm object when the object is placed 10 cm from the lens. What is the focal distance of the mirror?

    A. 3.3 cm
    B. –3.3 cm
    C. 10 cm
    D. –10 cm

957. In a flashlight, a concave mirror is used to create a beam of light with parallel rays. Where should the light source be placed?

    A. at the focal point of the mirror
    B. at twice the focal distance of the mirror
    C. at half the focal distance from the mirror
    D. at the radius of curvature of the mirror

958. A student compares a 1 diopter lens with a 10 diopter lens. He places an object in front of the 1 diopter lens, and adjusts the distance until an image appears 5 m from the lens. What should the student expect when he replaces the 1 diopter lens with the 10 diopter lens without changing the distance between the lens and the object?

    A. The image will be the same size.
    B. The image will be larger and closer to the lens.
    C. The image will be larger and farther from the lens.
    D. The image will be smaller and closer to the lens.

959. A student compares a 1 diopter lens with a 10 diopter lens. He places an object in front of the 1 diopter lens, and adjusts the distance until an image appears 5 m from the lens. What should the student expect when he replaces the 1 diopter lens with the 10 diopter lens and adjusts the distance between the lens and the object until an image appears 5 m from the lens?

    A. The image will be the same size.
    B. The image will be larger and the object will be closer to the lens.
    C. The image will be larger and the object will be farther from the lens.
    D. The image will be smaller and the object will be closer to the lens.

960. A student compares a 1 diopter lens with a –1 diopter lens. Which of the following findings is correct?

    A. The 1 diopter lens only magnifies images while the –1 diopter lens only minifies images.
    B. The 1 diopter lens only minifies images while the –1 diopter lens only magnifies images.
    C. Both lenses create the same size image for objects at the same distance.
    D. The –1 diopter lens produces only upright images, while the 1 diopter lens is capable of producing both upright and inverted images.

961. Photons A, B, and C leave the tip of a candle flame at the same moment and follow the respective paths shown in the diagram to form an image. Which photon arrives at the image first? (Note: $c = 3 \times 10^8$ m/s)

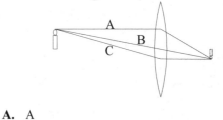

    A. A
    B. B
    C. C
    D. All arrive at exactly the same moment.

962. A 3 diopter lens is placed in contact with a 4 diopter lens. What is the power of the two lens system?

A. 0.75 diopter
B. 1 diopter
C. 7 diopters
D. 12 diopters

For questions 963-967, select the correct ray diagram for the object shown below.

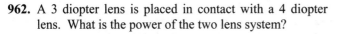

object

963.

A.

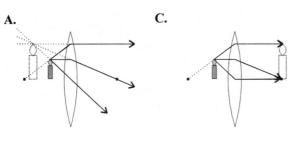

C.

B.

D.

964.

A.

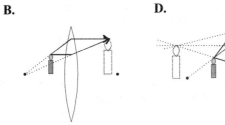

C.

B.

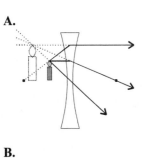

D.

965.

A. 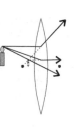   C.

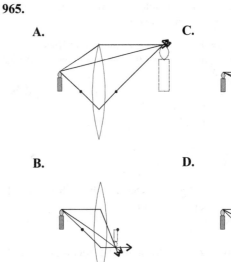

B.   D.

966.

A. 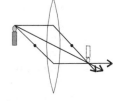   C.

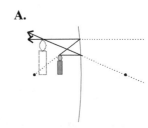 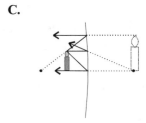

B.   D.

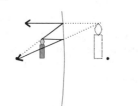 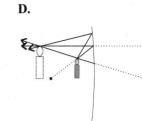

967.

A.   C.

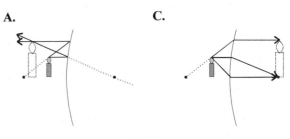

B.   D.

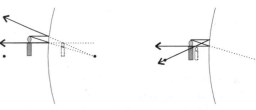 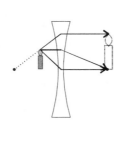 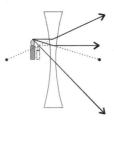

968. Which of the following could NOT be true concerning two lenses with different powers?

    A. Each lens could produce the same magnification.

    B. Each lens could produce the same size image of the same object.

    C. The object distance and image distance could be the same for both lenses.

    D. The image could be smaller than the object.

969. Which of the following is NOT true concerning ray diagrams?

    A. All horizontal light rays reflect through the focal point of any lens or mirror.

    B. Light rays striking the center of a thin lens move straight through the lens.

    C. Light rays coming through the focal point and striking a mirror are reflected horizontally.

    D. Light rays coming though the focal point and striking a convex lens are refracted through the second focal point.

Questions 970-975 refer to the *lens maker's equation*. The *lens maker's equation* is:

$$\frac{1}{f} = \left(\frac{n_L}{n_S} - 1\right)\left(\frac{1}{r_1} - \frac{1}{r_2}\right)$$

where n_S is the index of refraction of the surroundings, n_L is the index of refraction of the lens, f is the focal point of the lens, r_1 is the radius of curvature of the surface of the lens facing the object and r_2 is the radius of curvature of the surface of the lens opposite to the object. When the object faces a convex refracting surface the radius of curvature is positive; when the object faces a concave refracting surface the radius of curvature is negative.

970. Solid X has an index of refraction of 4. Liquid Y has an index of refraction of 2. What will be the power of a 30 diopter lens made from Solid A when submerged in Liquid Y?

    A. 10

    B. 15

    C. 30

    D. 60

971. What are the correct signs for the *lens maker's equation* for the convex lens shown below:

    A. r_1 is positive and r_2 is negative.

    B. r_1 is negative and r_2 is positive.

    C. r_1 and r_2 are both negative.

    D. r_1 and r_2 are both positive.

972. What are the correct signs for the *lens maker's equation* for the concave lens shown below:

    A. r_1 is positive and r_2 is negative.

    B. r_1 is negative and r_2 is positive.

    C. r_1 and r_2 are both negative.

    D. r_1 and r_2 are both positive.

973. If r_1 is greater than r_2, and both have positive values in the *lens maker's equation*, a glass lens in air will:

    A. have a positive power and converge light.

    B. have a positive power and diverge light.

    C. have a negative power and converge light.

    D. have a negative power and diverge light.

974. If the index of refraction of the surroundings is greater than the index of refraction of the lens, a convex lens will:

    A. have a positive power and converge light.

    B. have a positive power and diverge light.

    C. have a negative power and converge light.

    D. have a negative power and diverge light.

975. According to the *lens maker's equation*, which of the following lenses will have the greatest power?

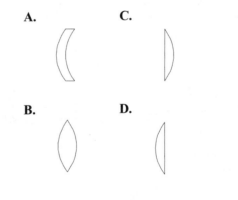

    A.   **C.**

    B.   **D.**

Questions 976-982 refer to the diagram below. Two converging lenses are separated by a distance l. An object is placed a distance x from Lens 1 as shown. The lenses have focal lengths f_1 and f_2 respectively.

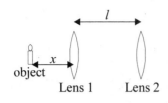

976. If x is less than f_1 and l is greater than f_2, then the final image must be:

   A. virtual and upright.
   B. virtual and inverted.
   C. real and upright.
   D. real and inverted.

977. If the image created by Lens 1 is formed to the right of Lens 2, the object distance for Lens 2 must be:

   A. negative
   B. positive
   C. less than f_2.
   D. greater than f_2.

978. If the image created by Lens 1 is formed to the right of Lens 2, the final image must be:

   A. virtual and upright.
   B. virtual and inverted.
   C. real and upright.
   D. real and inverted.

979. Suppose $l = 10$ cm, $f_1 = 24$ cm, $f_2 = 9$ cm, and $x = 6$ cm. Where is the final image formed?

   A. 18 cm to the right of lens 1
   B. 18 cm to the left of lens 1
   C. 18 cm to the right of lens 2
   D. 18 cm to the left of lens 2

980. Suppose $l = 10$ cm, $f_1 = 24$ cm, $f_2 = 9$ cm, and $x = 6$ cm. What is the approximate magnification of the final image?

   A. -0.15
   B. -0.75
   C. -1.3
   D. -2.0

981. Suppose $l = 28$ cm, $f_1 = 24$ cm, $f_2 = 9$ cm, and $x = 6$ cm. Where is the final image formed?

   A. 12 cm to the left of lens 2.
   B. 12 cm to the right of lens 2.
   C. 16 cm to the left of lens 2.
   D. 16 cm to the right of lens 2.

982. Suppose $l = 28$ cm, $f_1 = 24$ cm, $f_2 = 9$ cm, and $x = 6$ cm. What is the approximate magnification of the final image?

   A. 0.44
   B. 0.88
   C. 1.4
   D. 2.0

983. In which of the following situations must the *image* produced by a converging lens be *larger* than the *object*?

   A. The object is within one focal length of the pseudo focal point.
   B. The image is virtual.
   C. The image is inverted.
   D. The object is infinitely far from the lens.

984. Which of the following must produce an *image smaller than the object*?

   A. using a converging lens and placing the object anywhere within 2 focal lengths in front of the lens
   B. using a converging lens and creating an upright image
   C. using a diverging lens and placing the object anywhere in front of the lens
   D. using a flat lens and placing the object anywhere

985. Which of the following will NOT produce an image the same size as the object?

   A. placing an object two focal lengths in front of a converging lens
   B. placing an object two focal lengths in front of a concave mirror
   C. placing an object two focal lengths in front of a diverging lens
   D. placing an object anywhere in front of a plane mirror

986. For any spherical mirror or lens, there are two positions that the object can be placed to produce an image that is the same size as the object. If f is the focal length, the positions are:

   A. $0f$ and $2f$.
   B. $0f$ and $-2f$.
   C. $2f$ and $-2f$.
   D. f and $-f$.

987. An object is placed in front of a concave lens. Its image:

A. must be within one focal length in front of the lens.
B. must be within one focal length behind the lens.
C. must be in the same position as the object.
D. could be anywhere in front of the lens depending upon where the object is placed.

988. A converging lens produces an image twice the size of the object. The object is placed:

A. half a focal length in front of the lens.
B. one focal length in front of the lens.
C. two focal lengths in front of the lens.
D. half a focal length behind the lens.

Questions 989-992 refer to magnifying lenses. The human eye converges light forming an image on the retina, located about 2.5 cm behind the lens. The shape of the lens can be changed to focus on objects at distances from infinitely far off to about 25 cm. Magnifying lenses take objects closer than 25 cm and produce their enlarged images farther away than 25 cm. *Angular magnification*, which is NOT the same as lateral magnification (–i/o), is the angle subtended by the image divided by the angle subtended by the object if it were at 25 cm from the eye. For small angles when the object is just inside the focal point, the angular magnification of a simple magnifying lens can be approximated as:

$$m_\theta = 0.25P$$

where P is the power of the lens and 0.25 represents the minimum distance in meters that an object can still be brought into focus.

989. What is the angular magnification of a convex lens with a focal length of 5 cm?

A. 1.25
B. 5
C. 10
D. 20

990. A simple magnifier has an angular magnification of 5. How large will the image of a 3 cm object be, if viewed through this lens?

A. 3 cm
B. 6 cm
C. 9 cm
D. More information is required to determine the size of the image.

991.

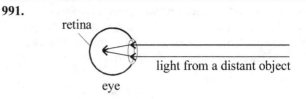

The lens of the eye above is unable to focus the image of a distant object onto the retina. Which lens could assist the eye to refocus the image onto the retina?

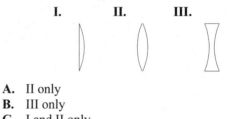

A. II only
B. III only
C. I and II only
D. I and III only

992.

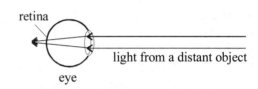

The lens of the eye above is unable to focus the image of a distant object onto the retina. Which lens could assist the eye to refocus the image onto the retina?

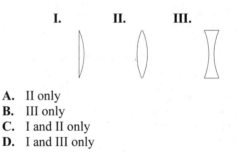

A. II only
B. III only
C. I and II only
D. I and III only

Questions 993-996 refer to the diagram below. A microscope uses a two-lens combination, the objective and the eyepiece, to enlarge an image. The distance between the focal points, or tube length (*s*), is adjusted so that an object placed just outside the focal distance of the objective will produce an image just inside the focal distance of the eyepiece. The magnification of a microscope is the product of the lateral magnification of the objective (–*i*/*o*) and the angular magnification of the eyepiece. (Angular magnification is described in questions 965). If we assume the distance between the focal points to be much greater than the focal lengths we arrive at the equation below. (Note diagram is not drawn to scale.)

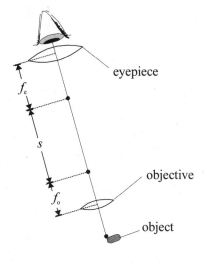

$$M = -\frac{s}{f_o}\frac{25\text{ cm}}{f_e}$$

993. The image created by the two-lens combination of the microscope is:

   A. virtual and inverted.
   B. virtual and upright.
   C. real and inverted.
   D. real and upright.

994. The lenses of a certain microscope are separated by a distance of 9.5 cm. The powers of the eyepiece and the objective are 100 and 200 diopters respectively. What is the magnification of the microscope?

   A. –400
   B. 400
   C. –400,000
   D. 400,000

995. A negative sign on the magnification indicates that the image is:

   A. virtual
   B. real
   C. inverted
   D. upright

996. A certain microscope has a magnification of 200. The powers of the eyepiece and the objective are 100 diopters each. What is the approximate *tube length*?

   A. 4 cm
   B. 8 cm
   C. 10 cm
   D. 12 cm

Questions 997-998 refer to the diagram below. A ship and an island are positioned as shown along the curved surface of the earth. A sailor on the ship sees a mirage of the island as shown.

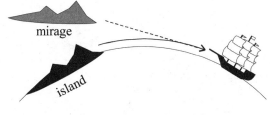

997. Which of the following is responsible for the mirage?

   A. diffraction
   B. refraction
   C. reflection
   D. dispersion

998. The graph below gives the air temperature versus height above the water. Which line most accurately represents the air temperature that produced the mirage?

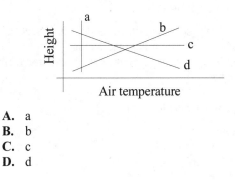

   A. a
   B. b
   C. c
   D. d

Questions 999-1001 refer to the diagram below.   A telescope can be made from two converging lenses. The distance s between the lenses is adjusted so that the focal points of the lenses coincide. The angular magnification m_θ can be approximated by the equation below.

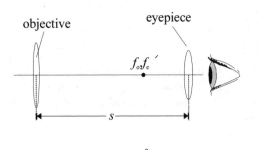

$$m_\theta = -\frac{f_o}{f_e}$$

999. The image seen by the observer is:

    A. virtual and upright
    B. virtual and inverted
    C. real and upright
    D. real and inverted

1000. Which of the following must be true in order for the telescope to work properly?

    A. f_e must be larger than f_o.
    B. f_o must be larger than f_e.
    C. f_o must be equal to f_e.
    D. f_o and f_e must both be negative.

1001. Which of the following commonly cause the image produced by the telescopes such as the one shown above to be out of focus?

    I. Perfectly spherical surfaces do not refract parallel light rays through the focal point.
    II. Different frequencies refract at slightly different angles.
    III. Light is diffracted as it comes through the front opening of the telescope.

    A. I only
    B. II only
    C. I and II only
    D. I, II, and III

Answers to 1001 Questions in MCAT Physics

Lecture 1

1. A is correct.

2. C is correct. The negative of a vector is a vector with the same magnitude (length) but pointing in the opposite direction.
3. C is correct.

Q R

$R - Q$

4. B is correct. In order to reduce the acceleration by a factor of 2, we must reduce the force by a factor of 2, while keeping it in the same direction.
5. D is correct. The vectors in answer choice D are not perpendicular to each other and so do not obey the Pythagorean theorem.
6. B is correct. The vectors in answer choice B sum to the opposite of vector Q.
7. D is correct. This is the definition of cross product. An MCAT example would be the force F on a charge moving through a magnetic field B with velocity v and charge q. $F = qv \times B$ or $F = qvB\sin\theta$.
8. A is correct. This is the definition of dot product. An MCAT example would be the work W on a particle due to a force F applied in a direction d. $W = F \cdot d$ or $W = Fd\cos\theta$.
9. D is correct. This is the Pythagorean theorem.
10. C is correct. Use the Pythagorean theorem. $20^2 = 16^2 + B^2$.
11. C is correct. In a 30-60-90 triangle, the side opposite to the $30°$ angle is half the hypotenuse. $B = C\sin30°$.
12. C is correct. You should recognize the lengths of the sides of this triangle for the MCAT. It is a 30-60-90 triangle.
13. B is correct. This is simple trigonometry. The cosine of any angle in a right triangle is equal to the length of the adjacent side divided by the length of the hypotenuse.
14. B is correct. This is the Pythagorean theorem.
15. D is correct. You should recognize the lengths of the sides of this triangle for the MCAT. It is a 30-60-90 triangle. The opposite side is ½ the hypotenuse.
16. A is correct. You should recognize the lengths of the sides of this triangle for the MCAT. It is a 30-60-90 triangle. The opposite side is ½ the hypotenuse.
17. D is correct. Displacement is the distance from the origin and is path independent.
18. B is correct. Horizontal velocity is horizontal displacement divided by the time. This is the same for all particles. Distance is different for all the particles, so speed, which is dependent upon distance, is different as well. The particles are moving in different directions at various times, so instantaneous acceleration is also different.
19. A is correct. Velocity is displacement divided by time. Displacement is zero.
20. D is correct. This is the definition of speed (speed = distance/time) where the distance is ½(2πr) since path C is a half circle.
21. A is correct. The vertical velocity is the vertical displacement divided by the time. The vertical displacement is zero.
22. D is correct. The vertical velocity is the vertical displacement divided by the time. Half way through the trip, the vertical displacement is 5. The time for half the trip is given by speed = distance/time, where distance is $2\pi r/4$. Thus vertical velocity equals $5/[(2\pi 5/4)/5\pi]$.
23. C is correct. Use the uniform linear motion equation: $x = \frac{1}{2}at^2$.
24. B is correct. Since we have constant acceleration, we can use $v_{avg} = (v_{final} + v_{initial})/2$
25. A is correct. Velocity equals displacement/time.
26. C is correct. Acceleration is change in velocity divided by time. Initial velocity is 1 m/s up; final velocity is 1 m/s down. The change in velocity is therefore 2 m/s. The time is found from speed equals distance divided by time. Distance is $2\pi r/2$. Thus $a = 2/[(2\pi 5/2)/1]$. $2/5\pi = 0.4/\pi$.
27. B is correct. The average velocity is the displacement divided by the time. The displacement is 10 m. The time is the distance divided by the speed. $t = 10/[(2\pi 5/2)/1]$
28. C is correct. Think of a particle moving in a circle at a constant speed. It has centripetal acceleration.
29. B is correct. A change in direction of motion is a change in velocity, which corresponds to a change in acceleration.
30. C is correct. Only choice C does not have constant acceleration, a requirement for the uniform linear motion equations.

31. B is correct. For a constantly accelerating particle, average velocity is $v_{avg} = (v_{final} + v_{initial})/2$.

32. B is correct. Acceleration is change in velocity divided by time. We can reason that the change in velocity is 10 m/s in 1 sec so the acceleration is 10 m/s^2.

33. C is correct. Since we have constant acceleration we can use $v = v_o + at$. We can reason that the particle will change its velocity by 10 m/s each second for a total of 20 m/s. Starting at 5 m/s, it finishes at 25 m/s.

34. B is correct. $v = v_o + at$. Or we can reason that the particle will change its velocity by 10 m/s each second for a total of 20 m/s. Ending at 5 m/s, it started at –15 m/s.

35. B is correct. $v = v_o + at$. The change in velocity was 10 m/s in 2 seconds or 5 m/s^2.

36. D is correct. $v = v_o + at$. The change in velocity is 10 m/s each second for 4 seconds. The final must be 40 m/s.

37. C is correct. $x = \frac{1}{2}at^2$. The initial velocity is zero, and the final is 40 m/s. The average must be exactly in the middle which is 20 m/s. 20 m/s for 4 seconds gives 80 m.

38. B is correct. $x = \frac{1}{2}at^2$. After one second the particle has gone 5 m. This is found by finding the initial velocity of zero, the final velocity of 10 m/s, the average in the middle is 5 m/s for 1 second gives 5 m. After two seconds, 20 meters. After 3 seconds 45 m.

39. C is correct. $v = v_o + at$. The acceleration is 10 m/s^2, so the velocity changes by 10 each second. That's 4.5 seconds to reach 45 m/s.

40. C is correct. $v_{avg} = (v_{final} + v_{initial})/2$. The average is between the initial and final, so 75 m/s is between 50 m/s and 100 m/s. 50 m/s is the initial velocity.

41. B is correct. $v_{avg} = (v_{final} + v_{initial})/2$. = distance/*time*. The average is between the initial (zero) and final (100 m/s), or 50 m/s. So the particle required 1 second to travel 50 m.

42. D is correct. $v_{avg} = (v_{final} + v_{initial})/2$. = distance/*time*. The average velocity is between the initial (zero) and final (100 m/s), or 50 m/s. Average velocity times time gives the displacement of 50 x4 = 200.

43. B is correct. $v_{avg} = (v_{final} + v_{initial})/2$. = distance/*time*. The average velocity is the displacement over time, so 240/4 gives 60 m/s average velocity. The final velocity is 100, and the average velocity is exactly between the initial and final. So the initial velocity must be 20 m/s.

44. D is correct. $v_{avg} = (v_{final} + v_{initial})/2$. = distance/*time*. The average velocity is displacement over time or 75/3 = 25 m/s. The average velocity is exactly between the initial velocity (10 m/s) and the final, so 25 m/s is exactly between 10 m/s and 40 m/s.

45. B is correct. $x = v_ot + \frac{1}{2}at^2$. From the previous problem we can figure out that the final velocity is 40 m/s, which represents a change of 10 m/s each second.

46. D is correct. $v^2 = v_o^2 + 2ax$. The average velocity is exactly between the initial (9 m/s) and final (16 m/s), so it is 12.5 m/s. At 12.5 m/s, the particle takes less than a second to travel 3.5 m, and less than a second to change its velocity by 7 m/s, so the acceleration must be greater than 7 m/s each second, so greater than 7 m/s^2.

47. C is correct. $v_{avg} = (v_{final} + v_{initial})/2$. = distance/*time*. The average velocity is exactly between the initial (30 m/s) and final (zero), or 15 m/s. Traveling at this average velocity for 3 seconds gives 45 m.

48. C is correct. $v_{avg} = (v_{final} + v_{initial})/2$. = distance/*time*. The average velocity is exactly between the initial (40 m/s) and final (10 m/s), or 25 m/s. Traveling at this average velocity for 3 seconds gives 75 m.

49. B is correct. $v_{avg} = (v_{final} + v_{initial})/2$. = distance/*time*. The average velocity is exactly between the initial (50 m/s) and final (20 m/s), or 35 m/s. Traveling at this average velocity over 105 m requires 3 seconds.

50. B is correct. Since $x = \frac{1}{2}at^2$, we know that x increases by a factor of four when t doubles and the particle starts at rest. x is the total distance; the question asks for distance with each consecutive second. This would be the total distance at $t = 2$ minus the distance at $t = 1$ s, or $4x – x$. Thus we know the distance increases by a factor of 3 from the first to the 2nd second.

51. C is correct. Since $x = \frac{1}{2}at^2$, we know that x increases by a factor of four when t doubles.

52. A is correct. $v_{avg} = (v_{final} + v_{initial})/2$. The distance is irrelevant. The average speed is exactly between the initial (40 m/s) and final (10 m/s) or 25 m/s.

53. B is correct. $v_{avg} = (v_{final} + v_{initial})/2$. = distance/*time*. The average velocity is exactly between the initial (50 m/s) and the final (20 m/s) or 35 m/s. At 35 m/s, 2 seconds is required to to 70 m.

54. C is correct. $a = (v_{final} – v_{initial})/t$. Acceleration is the rate of change in velocity. Velocity changes from –5 m/s to 5 m/s, or 10 m/s in one second. The acceleration is 10 m/s^2.

55. A is correct. $x = v_ot + \frac{1}{2}at^2$ where $a = (v_{final} – v_{initial})/t$. The displacement is the average velocity times time. The average is exactly between the initial velocity (–5 m/s) amd the final (5 m/s) so zero.

56. B is correct. $x = v_ot + \frac{1}{2}at^2$ where $a = (v_{final} – v_{initial})/t$ But there is a trick. x is displacement, not distance. To find distance, you must recognize that the particle travels half the distance in half the time. Thus, you plug in ½ the total time, only in the first equation and then solve for x and double your answer for the total distance.

57. A is correct. Use $v = v_o + at$, *where* $a = (v_{final} – v_{initial})/t$, but use ½ for t in the first equation because we want the speed halfway through the trip.

Answers and Explanations

58. B is correct. Use $x = v_0t + \frac{1}{2}at^2$, where $a = (v_{final} - v_{initial})/t$, but use $\frac{1}{2}$ for t in the first equation because we want the speed halfway through the trip.

59. C is correct. Use $x = v_0t + \frac{1}{2}at^2$, where $t = (v_{final} - v_{initial})/a$. Or, since the particle is reversing its direction to travel the same distance in the opposite direction, calculate the distance for one direction and double it for the total distance traveled. The distance in one direction is the average velocity times the time. The average velocity is exactly between the initial (10 m/s) and the final (zero), or 5 m/s. The 10 m/s² acceleration tells us that a change of 10 m/s in velocity requires one second. 5 m/s average velocity over one seconds gives a distance of 5 m in one direction. We double this for a total distance of 10 m.

60. B is correct. $t = (v_{final} - v_{initial})/a$. The change in the velocity is 20 m/s. 2 seconds is required to change the velocity by 20 at an acceleration of –10 m/s².

61. C is correct. Use $x = v_0t + \frac{1}{2}at^2$, where $t = (v_{final} - v_{initial})/a$ In order to find distance, you must divide the problem into 10 m/s to 0 m/s and 0 m/s to –20 m/s.

62. B is correct. Use $x = v_0t + \frac{1}{2}at^2$, where $t = (v_{final} - v_{initial})/a$.

63. C is correct. $t = (v_{final} - v_{initial})/a$

64. C is correct. Velocity is the slope. A change in velocity represents acceleration. W and Y have constant slope, so zero acceleration.

65. C is correct. Velocity is the slope. A change in velocity represents acceleration. W and Y have constant slope, but the slope for Y is zero.

66. C is correct. Slope is change in the y axis divided by change in the x axis, or m/s.

67. D is correct. The area under the curve is the product of the x and y axis, or meters times seconds.

68. B is correct. Velocity is the slope, A change in velocity represents acceleration. Only in X is the slope increasing.

69. C is correct. W, X, and Z have positive slopes, Y has a zero slope.

70. D is correct. All graphs have velocity greater than zero at all times.

71. D is correct. Slope is change in the y axis divided by change in the x axis, or (m/s)/s.

72. A is correct. The total area would assume that area beneath the x axis is positive. This indicates distance, not displacement.

73. B is correct. The horizontal distance from the x axis denotes velocity. In graph Y, this distance doesn't change.

74. C is correct. If acceleration is constant, velocity is constantly changing.

75. C is correct. The area under the curve is the x axis times the y axis; meters.

76. B is correct. Distance traveled is area under the curve. The area is a triangle; Area = ½ base times height.

77. C is correct. You can count the squares under both triangles in the first 6 seconds. Each square has the dimensions 5 m/s by 0.5 s, or 2.5 m. There are 18 squares in each triangle for a total of 90 m. You can also notice that both lines have a slope of 10, representing 10 m/s². Now use $x = \frac{1}{2}at^2$ for both triangles. Finally, you can also add the area of the triangles, which is Area = ½ base times height.

78. A is correct. The triangle under the x axis is negative for displacement because it represents the particle moving backwards.

79. B is correct. This is the slope; rise over run; 30/3.

80. B is correct. This is the value at the middle of the line, or $v_{avg} = (v_{final} + v_{initial})/2$.

81. C is correct. Since acceleration is constant (i.e. constant slope) use the velocity value at 2.5 seconds, which is midway between 2 and 3 s. Or use the formula: $v_{avg} = (v_{final} + v_{initial})/2$

82. B is correct. Between six and eight seconds, the slope is always positive, so acceleration is always positive. Since the line is always above the x axis between 6 s and 8 s, velocity is always positive.

83. C is correct. Since acceleration is constant in this interval, we can choose more convenient points to find the slope. Don't use 3.25 s and 5.5 s. Instead, use $(0 - {}^-30)/(6 - 3) = 10$.

84. D is correct. Acceleration is the slope, so acceleration is negative only where the slope is negative.

85. B is correct. The range is the horizontal velocity ($v\cos\theta$) times time in the air.

86. B is correct. Remember that t is the time for the entire flight of the projectile. If we examine only the second half of flight, the projectile drops from maximum height, and starts from an initial velocity of zero in ½t seconds. Using the equation: $x = \frac{1}{2}at^2$, but plugging in ½t for t, g for a, and h for x, we have: $h = \frac{1}{2}a(\frac{1}{2}t)^2$

87. A is correct. Use the trig function: the length of the opposite side (the vertical velocity) equals the length of the hypotenuse (v) times $\sin\theta$.

88. B is correct. Use the trig function: the length of the adjacent side (the horizontal velocity) equals the length of the hypotenuse (v) times $\cos\theta$.

89. C is correct. You should memorize this bit of trivia for the MCAT.

90. D is correct. For a projectile that is experiencing no air resistance, the mass is irrelevant to the flight.

91. D is correct. For a projectile that is experiencing no air resistance, the mass is irrelevant to the flight.

92. B is correct. You should memorize this for the MCAT.

93. D is correct. Maximum height is achieved by maximizing initial vertical velocity ($v\sin\theta$) The sine of an angle increases to 1 as the angle increases to 90°.

111
Copyright © 2003 EXAMKRACKERS, Inc.

94. B is correct. More trivia that you should memorize. Angles that are equidistant from 45° will result in the same range when there is no air resistance.

95. A is correct. The projectile must reach zero vertical velocity in order to change direction.

96. C is correct. The initial velocity v is a given, and is not affected by air resistance. Air resistance slows a projectile resulting in a smaller maximum height and shorter range. Time is trickier since air resistance decreases the trip upward, but increases the trip downward. Since air resistance has a greater affect on faster moving bodies, the trip upward is decreased by more that the trip downward is increased. (If you are using a parachute, balloon, or a feather to visualize air resistance, remember that the projectile in this problem goes up as well as down. The trip is still shortened. Try it yourself with a balloon.)

97. A is correct. As θ increases, the vertical velocity increases. The time of flight is directly proportional to the vertical velocity by $v = gt/2$

98. B is correct. There are no horizontal forces, thus no horizontal acceleration, thus no change in horizontal velocity.

99. A is correct. The barrel is the only thing applying a force upward to counteract gravity.

100. D is correct. The acceleration at all points in the path of a projectile is due to gravity.

101. D is correct. The initial vertical velocity of a projectile determines the time of flight. A and B have the same initial vertical velocity; 10 m/s. From $v = v_o + at$, we know that A and B are the same as C. The time in the air for the projectile in D can be found from $x = \frac{1}{2}at^2$.

102. B is correct. From $v = $ sqrt($2gh$), we see that doubling h increases the velocity by sqrt(2).

103. B is correct. From $x = \frac{1}{2}at^2$, we see that doubling x increases t by sqrt(2).

104. D is correct. From $x = \frac{1}{2}at^2$, we see that to double t, we must increase x by 4.

105. D is correct. From $v = $ sqrt($2gh$), we see that to double v we must increase h by 4.

106. C is correct. The acceleration of any projectile without air resistance is due only to gravity. Both projectiles have the same initial vertical velocity, so they will strike the ground at the same moment. Projectile B will have the same vertical velocity, but the horizontal velocity must also be added, making it greater than projectile A. Projectile B will travel the same vertical distance, plus some horizontal distance.

107. A is correct. $v = $ sqrt($2gh$), or average velocity is exactly between initial (10 m/s) and final (zero at the max height) or 5 m/s. Since acceleration is 10 m/s each second, a change of 10 m/s in velocity requires one second. Average velocity times time gives 5 m.

108. B is correct. The upward trip of a projectile with no air resistance mirrors the downward trip.

109. C is correct. $x = \frac{1}{2}at^2$. It will be in the air until it is moving 10 m/s downward. This is a change of 20 m/s. At an acceleration of 10 m/s each second, this will require 2 seconds.

110. A is correct. The maximum height is reached when final velocity is zero. $v = v_o + at$

111. C is correct. We assume from the question that the horizontal velocity is 20 m/s. The distance is the horizontal velocity times the time. The time for half the trip is found from $v = v_o + at$ where v is the vertical velocity, v_o is zero since when the animal reaches maximum height (halfway through the flight) its vertical velocity will be zero. We double t to find the time for the entire flight and multiply times 20 m/s.

112. A is correct. The horizontal velocity is irrelevant. We use $v = $ sqrt($2gh$)

113. B is correct. $v = $ sqrt($2gh$),

114. A is correct. $v = $ sqrt($2gh$)

115. D is correct. $v = $ sqrt($2gh$)

116. C is correct. Horizontal velocity remains constant; vertical is given. We use Pythagorean theorem to find the final vertical velocity. $15^2 + speed^2. = 25^2$. 20 m/s is the final vertical velocity. We use $v = $ sqrt($2gh$) to find the height.

117. B is correct. $x = \frac{1}{2}at^2$ gives half the time in the air.

118. C is correct. First find out how long the projectile is in the air, and then multiply air time by horizontal velocity. Air time is dependent entirely on vertical velocity. The vertical velocity is 20 m/s times sin30°, or 10 m/s. From $v = v_o + at$ we find that the time for the projectile to reach a maximum height is one second. Its maximum height is 20 meters (from $x = \frac{1}{2}at^2$ plus the 15 m of the platform.) The time required to fall from 20 m is 2 seconds from $x = \frac{1}{2}at^2$. The total flight is 3 second. 3 s times the horizontal velocity of approximately 17 m/s ($v$cosθ) gives approximately 51 m.

119. D is correct. Air time is dependent entirely on vertical velocity. The vertical velocity is 40 m/s times sin30°, or 20 m/s. From $v = v_o + at$ we find that the time for the projectile to reach a maximum height is two seconds. Its maximum height is 45 meters (from $x = \frac{1}{2}at^2$ plus the 25 m of the platform.) The time required to fall from 45 m is 3 seconds from $x = \frac{1}{2}at^2$. The total time is 5 seconds.

120. B is correct. First we must find the vertical velocity from the time of flight: $v = v_o + at$. 18 m/s is the initial vertical velocity. Now we add 25 m/s and 18 m/s using vector addition. They are perpendicular to each other and make a right triangle. Thus we use Pythagorean theorem: $18^2 + 24^2 = v^2$. Notice that this is a 3-4-5 triangle.

121. C is correct. The maximum height is reached in exactly half the flight time. If half the time in flight is 10 seconds, then the total flight took 20 seconds. Since the maximum height is reached in 10 s, we can use $v = at$ to find the initial vertical velocity, 100 m/s. This vertical velocity is equal to $v\sin\theta$, making q equal to $30°$. The horizontal velocity is $v\cos30°$. The horizontal velocity times the time gives 170 m/s x 20 s = 3400 m.

122. D is correct. Acceleration is 10 m/s². $a = F/m$ The heavier object has more inertia, so requires more force to change its motion at the same rate.

123. A is correct. Air resistance acts against motion. The air resistance is based on size and shape and will be the same for both balls, so the ball with the greater inertia will resist the change in its motion the most.

124. C is correct. If x is the vertical displacement, $x = x_0 + v_0t + \frac{1}{2}at^2$ for the dropped rock and $v^2 = v_0^2 + 2ax$ for the thrown rock. We find v_0 for the thrown rock from $v = \mathrm{sqrt}(2gh)$. If we solve for x in the second equation and set the first equation equal to the second equation, we can solve for the time they will meet. Then we can plug the time back into the first equation and solve for x. A much simpler way to solve this is to look at a v vs. t graph for both objects. The objects must meet at exactly halfway through their flight time. We can see by the area under the curve that this is ¾ of the way for the projectile moving up, and ¼ of the way for the projectile moving down. Notice that their velocities will be the same at this moment, which is predictable since their flights are mirror images of each other.

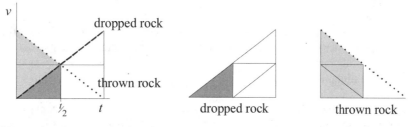

125. D is correct. Air resistance is a force against motion.

126. A is correct. You should know that air resistance increases with velocity, surface area, and air density.

127. A is correct. The greater mass won't change the force of air resistance, but it will add inertia, which increases the force required to change its motion.

128. B is correct. This question is designed to remind you that the effect of air resistance on heavy objects with a spherical shape is small. In other words, no air resistance is often a good approximation.

129. B is correct. The surface area, not the mass, changes the air resistance.

Lecture 2

130. C is correct. There are only four forces in nature: strong nuclear, weak nuclear, gravity, and electromagnetic.

131. B is correct. The force holding the barbell above the ground is the force applied to the barbell by the hands of the weightlifter. The fundamental force is the electrostatic repulsion between the molecules in the hands of the weightlifter and the molecules of the barbell.

132. D is correct. Mass is a quantitative measure of linear inertia.

133. C is correct. Of the choices, only weight is a vector and has a direction. Imagine the can and elephant in space. The elephant has the same inertia, mass, and size, but no weight. The can is not crushed in space.

134. B is correct. Weight is due to gravity. Gravity on the moon is less than on the earth. The mass is an intrinsic property to the ball and would not change. Since mass is a measure of linear inertia, the inertia would not change either. Momentum is mass times velocity. The question states that velocity remains the same, and we have established that mass does not change.

135. B is correct. This is a rotational inertia question. MCAT will probably <u>not</u> have any rotational inertia questions. Although mass is proportional to rotational inertia, the shape of the object also plays a role. These two balls have the same shape, so the difference in their rotational inertias is solely a function of their mass.

136. D is correct. Mass is a measure of the inertia of the block. The mass remains constant, so the inertia remains constant. Don't confuse inertia with momentum. The momentum of the block changes.

137. C is correct. This is a rotational inertia question. MCAT will probably <u>not</u> have any rotational inertia questions. This is really the same question as 136. These two balls have the same shape, so the difference in their rotational inertias is solely a function of their mass. Although the more massive ball has twice the inertia, the frictional force is also twice as great. ($F_{\mathrm{friction}} = \mu N$ where the normal force is proportional to the mass.)

138. B is correct. This is a rotational inertia question. MCAT will probably <u>not</u> have any rotational inertia questions. This is a really tough question. Although the balls have the same mass, they are not the same shape and therefore have different rotational inertias. What the MCAT would want you to know about this question is that the hollow ball has greater rotational inertia (and thus greater resistance to change in its motion) than the solid ball. Imagine a child's merry-go-round. If the children stand on the outside edge of the merry-go-round, it takes greater force to accelerate it at the same rate than if the children stand near the middle. Similarly, the ball with the mass concentrated toward its outside edge requires greater force to accelerate it at the same rate. At first this result may seem to contradict $F = ma$, because the force down the plane is

$mg\sin\theta$, while the force up the plane is static friction. Thus the net force on both balls appears to be the same ($mg\sin\theta -$ $\mu mg\cos\theta$). WRONG! This equation is not correct because static friction is <u>smaller than</u> or equal to $\mu mg\cos\theta$. Because the hollow ball has greater rotational inertia, it accelerates at a lesser rate, and the static friction on the hollow ball must be greater than the static friction on the solid ball. This question requires a qualitative understanding of rotational inertia, which is the maximum requirement for the MCAT. It is most likely more difficult than any MCAT question that you will encounter.

139. C is correct. Inertia is the tendency for an object to remain in its present state of motion, which really means its present linear and rotational velocity.

140. A is correct. There might not be any mass at the center of mass of an object. This is one example.

141. B is correct. This is really a torque problem. If the two balls were connected by a massless stick, where on that stick could you attach a string to hang the entire apparatus and keep it level? This spot is the center of gravity or mass. We will weight until the torque section to discuss how to solve this type of problem with torque. For now, the center of gravity will be twice as close to the object with twice the mass or three times as close to an object with three times the mass.

142. B is correct. The lead block is many times heavier than the foam, thus the center of gravity is many times closer to the center of the lead block; almost, but not quite, at its center.

143. C is correct. The problem above is an example where the geometric center is not the center of gravity. Whenever the object is not of uniform density, the geometric center might not coincide with the center of gravity.

144. C is correct. Of course, any situation that could actually occur will not violate Newton's laws (Classically speaking). Thus only C could be correct. A pendulum could not swing forever because it is acted upon by a net force of air resistance that changes its motion.

145. C is correct. C is a restatement of Newton's second law. A is wrong because the block experiences the pushing; it is the man that experiences the equal and opposite force. B violates Newton's second law. D is incorrect because the equal and opposite forces of Newton's third law always act on opposite bodies so they don't cancel each other out unless they occur within the same system.

146. A is correct. $F = ma$

147. A is correct. $F = ma$ Newton's 2nd law does <u>not</u> say "EXCEPT when the object is moving."

148. A is correct. $F = ma$ Newton's 2nd law does <u>not</u> say "depending upon the direction in which the body is moving."

149. A is correct. $F = ma$ Newton's 2nd law does <u>not</u> say "depending upon the direction in which the body is moving."

150. C is correct. $F = ma$

151. A is correct. $F = ma$

152. A is correct. Constant velocity means no acceleration and, by Newton's 2nd law, no net force.

153. C is correct. By Newton's 3rd law, the woman must experience a force equal and opposite to the force that she applies to the block. Since the block has less mass than the woman, the block will accelerate at a greater rate than the woman.

154. B is correct. The spaceship has 100 times more mass, and thus 100 times more inertia. Therefore, its acceleration will be 100 times less than the astronaut.

155. C is correct. Find the acceleration from $F = ma$. Next plug this into the linear motion equation $a = \Delta v/t$.

156. A is correct. Find the acceleration from $F = ma$. Next plug this into the linear motion equation $a = \Delta v/t$.

157. D is correct. The direction of the force is irrelevant. Use $F = ma$ and $a = \Delta v/t$.

158. D is correct. $F = ma$

159. A is correct. Constant velocity means no acceleration, which means no net force.

160. B is correct. The forces Q and R in the diagram are Newton's 3rd law forces, so they are always equal and opposite. The F in the equation is the magnitude of force on either body.

161. C is correct. The forces Q and R in the diagram are Newton's 3rd law forces, so they are always equal and opposite.

162. D is correct. The forces Q and R in the diagram are Newton's 3rd law forces, so they are always equal and opposite. If the masses are different, they will accelerate at different rates according to $F = ma$.

163. C is correct. From $F = GmM/r^2$ we see that the force on each mass grows greater as r decreases. From $F = ma$ we see that as F grows larger, a grows larger.

164. A is correct. To find the acceleration of the earth find the force from $F = GmM/r^2$, then divide by the mass of the earth M to get the acceleration.

165. D is correct. The gravitational force on the earth due to the object is equal and opposite to the force on the object due to the earth, which is mg.

166. D is correct.

167. C is correct. The mass of the person does not change regardless of the person's position. On the surface of the smaller planet, the distance between the centers of gravity of the person and the planet is smaller. From the formula $F = GmM/r^2$, we see that the force or weight is greater.

168. A is correct. $F = GmM/r^2$. Reducing the radius by a factor of 2, increases the gravitational force by four and the acceleration by four ($F = ma$).

169. A is correct. $F = GmM/r^2$. Reducing the radius by a factor of 2, increases the gravitational force by four and the acceleration by four ($F = ma$). You should know that the acceleration of a projectile is independent of its mass.

170. B is correct. $F = GmM/r^2$. Reducing the radius by a factor of 2, increases the gravitational force by four. Reducing the mass of an object by a factor of 2, reduces the force by 2. This is a net gain of a factor of 2.

171. C is correct. $F = GmM/r^2$ r is the distance between the center of gravities of the two objects.

172. B is correct. $F = GmM/r^2$. Reducing the radius by a factor of 2, increases the gravitational force by four and the acceleration by four ($F = ma$). You should know that the acceleration of a projectile is independent of its mass. From $x = \frac{1}{2}at^2$ we see that reducing the acceleration by a factor of four increases the time by a factor of 2.

173. A is correct. The acceleration of a projectile is independent of its mass, so ignore the mass difference. $F = GmM/r^2$. Decreasing the mass by a factor of 2, decreases the gravitational force by 2, but decreasing the radius of the planet by a factor of 2, increases the force by a factor of 4. There is a net increase in gravitational acceleration on planet B by a factor of 2. Force is proportional to acceleration. ($F = ma$). From $x = \frac{1}{2}at^2$ we see that increasing the acceleration by a factor of 2 decreases the time by a factor of sqrt(2).

174. B is correct. The mass of the rings is equal, so an object equal distances from the centers of gravity of both rings would experience a gravitational force of equal magnitudes from both rings.

175. B is correct. The mass of the rings is equal, so an object equal distances from the centers of gravity of both rings would experience a gravitational force of equal magnitudes from both rings. These forces would be equal and in opposite directions, thus they cancel each other out.

176. A is correct. This is a bit of trivia that you should know for the MCAT: The gravitational force everywhere inside a uniformly dense sphere or ring, due to that sphere or ring, is zero. However, the uniformly dense ring or sphere does not block the gravitational field due to other sources, so the force due to the smaller ring still affects a particle at position D.

177. C is correct. The bowling ball has 2,000 times more inertia, thus it requires a force 2,000 times greater to change its motion at the same rate.

178. C is correct. There is no air resistance in a vacuum.

179. B is correct. Don't do any math here. From $F = GmM/r^2$ and $F = ma$, we know that $F/m = g = GM/r^2$. Since r is the only change, and r increases, g decreases, but not to zero. Thus B must be correct.

180. C is correct. The force due to gravity near the surface of the earth is always mg.

181. B is correct. You should be able to figure this out with vectors, but you should also memorize this.

182. A is correct. You should be able to figure this out with vectors, but you should also memorize this.

183. A is correct. You should be able to figure this out with vectors, but you should also memorize this.

184. C is correct. The acceleration of the mass is $a = g\sin\theta$. The sine of an angle equals the length of the opposite side divided by the length of the hypotenuse, so $\sin 30° = 5/d$. The sine of 30° is ½, so $d = 10$. $d = \frac{1}{2}at^2$

185. C is correct. This is the same question as 184, since the mass of a projectile does not change the acceleration. (A mass on a frictionless plane is similar to a guided projectile since the force is constant and proportional to the mass.) The acceleration of the mass is $a = g\sin\theta$. The sine of an angle equals the length of the opposite side divided by the length of the hypotenuse, so $\sin 30° = 5/d$. The sine of 30° is ½, so $d = 10$. $d = \frac{1}{2}at^2$

186. A is correct. The acceleration is $g\sin\theta$, so it does not change. d is increased by a factor of 4. From $d = \frac{1}{2}at^2$ we see that t is doubled when d is increased by a factor of 4.

187. B is correct. The acceleration of the mass is $a = g\sin\theta$. The sine of an angle equals the length of the opposite side divided by the length of the hypotenuse, so $\sin\theta = 5/25$. $a = 2$ and $d = \frac{1}{2}at^2$

188. C is correct. The acceleration of the mass is $a = g\sin\theta$. The sine of an angle equals the length of the opposite side divided by the length of the hypotenuse, so $\sin\theta = h/d$. $a = gh/d$ and $d = \frac{1}{2}at^2 \Rightarrow d^2 = \frac{1}{2}ght^2$

189. A is correct. First find the velocity of the mass upon reaching the bottom of the incline. This can be done from conservation of energy: $\frac{1}{2}mv^2 = mgh$, or from the linear motion equation $v^2 = v_o^2 + 2ad$ where $a = g\sin\theta$. So $v = $ sqrt($2gd\sin\theta$). Next find the time from $v = x/t$. Thus $t^2 = x^2/2gd\sin\theta$. The sine of 30° is ½.

190. C is correct. The acceleration is given by $a = g\sin\theta$. Because there is no friction, the shape of the object is irrelevant. The net force is proportional to the mass, so acceleration is independent of the mass.

191. D is correct. All potential energy is converted to kinetic energy. Increasing the height increases the amount of potential energy.

192. C is correct. There is no acceleration along x; the net force is zero. Since the net force is zero, velocity must be constant.

193. A is correct. Acceleration is constant and has a component in the horizontal direction. Thus, the horizontal velocity increases.

194. C is correct. The easiest way to see this is to look at a velocity vs. time graph. The slope is acceleration and is constant. The area under the line is the distance traveled. Notice that there are three triangles under the 2nd second and only one triangle under the 1st second. The ratio is three to one for any constantly accelerating particle.

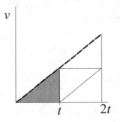

195. C is correct. Like the previous question, use the velocity vs. time graph to answer this question. There are five triangles beneath the 2nd to 3rd second segment of the line, compared to only one triangle beneath the zero to 1st segment.

196. A is correct. Because the object is moving at constant speed, the net force is the centripetal force. Centripetal force points toward the center of the circle circumscribed by the motion of the object.

197. C is correct. $a_c = v^2/r$

198. D is correct. Velocity is a vector, thus a change in direction but not magnitude still represents a change in velocity, which is acceleration.

199. B is correct. Since the speed of the object did not change, no work was done on the object, which means there was no net force in the direction of the displacement. Thus, all the net force was perpendicular to the motion at all times.

200. B is correct. $F_c = mv^2/r$

201. A is correct. This can be tricky. If we only use the formula $F_c = mv^2/r$, and reduce v by a factor of 2, we see that the radius needs to be reduced by 4 in order to keep the required centripetal force the same. However, from $F = GmM/r^2$ we see that when the radius is reduced by 4, the gravitational force is increased by 16. The moon would fall into the planet at this speed and distance. The equation that we must use is found by setting the centripetal force equal to the gravitational force, so that all the gravity is *used up* holding the moon in orbit. Thus $mv^2/r = GmM/r^2 => v^2 = GM/r$. From this equation we see that reducing the velocity by 2 results in an increase in the radius by a factor of 4.

202. B is correct. Since the speed of the object did not change, no work was done on the object, which means there was no net force in the direction of the displacement. However, any turn represents an acceleration, which requires a net force. Thus, all the net force must have been perpendicular to the motion at all times.

203. A is correct. $F_c = T = mv^2/r$

204. C is correct. If we ignore air resistance, then the gravitational force and the normal force cancel, leaving friction as the net force. The net force is in the direction of acceleration. The only acceleration is centripetal. Centripetal force always points toward the center of the circle.

205. D is correct. The force due to gravity is mg regardless of string length.

206. B is correct. $a_c = v^2/r$

207. A is correct. $g = a_c = v^2/r$ Gravity provides the centripetal force that maintains an orbit. If the centripetal force required is greater than the gravity, the orbiting object moves away from the planet; if the centripetal force required is less than gravity, the object falls toward the planet.

208. C is correct. Take the velocity from the previous problem and set it equal to the circumference of the earth ($2\pi r$) divided by the time: $v = d/t$

209. C is correct. This can be tricky. Start by setting the centripetal force equal to the gravitational force, so that all the gravity is *used up* holding the satellite in orbit. Thus $mv^2/r = GmM/r^2 => v^2 = GM/r$. From $v = d/t$ we see that the velocity is equal to the circumference ($2\pi r$) divided by the time necessary to make one orbit, or $v = 2\pi r/t$. Now, substitute for v in the previous equation to get: $(2\pi r/t)^2 = GM/r => 4\pi^2 r^3 = GMt^2$ Thus decreasing the mass of the planet (M) would result in an increase in the time necessary to make one orbit. Notice the mass of the satellite doesn't enter into the equation. Of course the radius of the planet does not affect its gravitational force nor the orbit of the satellite.

210. B is correct. Since the block is not moving, it is in equilibrium. Therefore, the net force is zero. Friction must be parallel to the contacting surfaces. Since friction is preventing the block from sliding down the plane, friction is in the direction up the plane. It is the only force pointing up the plane. Thus friction is equal to the sum of the forces acting down the plane, which is the normal force plus gravity, or $mg\sin\theta$. $\sin 30^\circ = \frac{1}{2}$.

211. B is correct. Since the block is not moving, it is in equilibrium. Therefore, the net force is zero. Friction must be parallel to the contacting surfaces. Since friction is preventing the block from sliding down the plane, friction is in the direction up the plane. It is the only force pointing up the plane. Thus friction is equal to the sum of the forces acting down the plane, which is the normal force, gravity, and the 5 N applied force ($5 + mg\sin\theta$). $\sin 30^\circ = \frac{1}{2}$.

212. C is correct. The maximum static frictional force is given by $f_{static\ max} = \mu mg\cos\theta$. The maximum static frictional force occurs just before the block begins to move. At that moment the block is in static equilibrium, so the net force is zero. That means that the force up the plane equals the force down the plane. The force down the plane is 7.3 N + mgsin30°. The force up the plane is static friction. Thus: μmgcos30° = 7.3 N + mgsin30°. sin30° = 0.5; cos30° = 0.87

213. B is correct. The maximum static frictional force is given by $f_{\text{static max}} = \mu mg$cosθ. The maximum static frictional force occurs just before the block begins to move. At that moment the block is in static equilibrium, so the net force is zero. That means that the force up the plane equals the force down the plane. The force down the plane is mgsin30°. The force up the plane is static friction. Thus: μmgcos30° = mgsin30°. sin30° = 0.5; cos30° = 0.87

214. B is correct. The maximum static frictional force is given by $f_{\text{static max}} = \mu mg$cosθ. The maximum static frictional force occurs just before the block begins to move. At that moment the block is in static equilibrium, so the net force is zero. That means that the force up the plane equals the force down the plane. The force down the plane is mgsinθ. The force up the plane is static friction. Thus: μmgcosθ = mgsinθ => μ = sinθ/cosθ

215. B is correct. Notice that in problem 214 the gravitational constant dropped out. Thus, this is the same as problem 213.

216. B is correct. Notice that in problem 214 the mass of the block dropped out. Thus, this is the same as problem 213.

217. D is correct. From problems 215 and 216 we see that answer choices A and B are wrong. For the MCAT, you should believe that the coefficient of kinetic friction is independent of the surface area and dependent only on the substances of the contacting surfaces.

218. D is correct. The block is in static equilibrium. There is no net force on an object in equilibrium.

219. A is correct. First we must discover if the block is moving. To do this, we see if the force down the plane (mgsinθ) will overcome the maximum static frictional force ($\mu_s mg$cosθ). $\mu_s$cos30° > sin30°, so the block does not slide, and the net force is zero.

220. B is correct. First we must discover if the block is moving. To do this, we see if the force down the plane (mgsinθ) will overcome the maximum static frictional force ($\mu_s mg$cosθ). $\mu_s$cos30° < sin30°, so the block does slide. The net force on the block while sliding is the force down the plane minus the kinetic frictional force up the plane $F_{\text{net}} = mg$sinθ – $\mu_k mg$cosθ (sin30° = 0.5; cos30° = 0.87) But don't do the math because only one choice is less than mgsinθ and greater than zero.

221. C is correct. First we must discover if the block is moving. (Notice that from problem 220, we already know that the block is moving. Whether or not it moves is independent of the mass.) To do this, we see if the force down the plane (mgsinθ) will overcome the maximum static frictional force ($\mu_s mg$cosθ). $\mu_s$cos30° < sin30°, so the block does slide. The net force on the block while sliding is the force down the plane minus the kinetic frictional force up the plane $F_{\text{net}} = mg$sinθ – $\mu_k mg$cosθ (sin30° = 0.5; cos30° = 0.87)

222. B is correct. Friction does not simply oppose motion. For instance, you can place your hand on the top of a book and move the book forward only by applying a frictional force on the book in the direction of its motion. A frictional force opposes the motion of an object with respect to the object that is applying that force. In the example of the hand moving the book, the hand is moving so the force of friction attempts to keep the book moving like the hand, or, in other words, keep the book stationary relative to the hand.

223. C is correct. The block is sliding so the friction must be kinetic. The velocity is constant so the net force must be zero. If the plane were frictionless, the block would have to accelerate.

224. B is correct. The friction is static because the contacting surfaces are not *sliding* relative to each other. The force opposes the motion of the car; if the friction is reduced (say the car is put on ice), the car moves forward more easily.

225. A is correct. The friction is static because the contacting surfaces are not *sliding* relative to each other. The force is in the direction of motion of the car; if the friction is reduced (say the car is put on ice), the car does not move forward.

226. C is correct. The net force on the car is the kinetic frictional force $\mu_k mg$cosθ. From $F = ma$ we can find the acceleration and plug this into $v^2 = v_o^2 + 2ax$. You could also solve this using the energy formula: $f_{\text{friction}}d = \frac{1}{2}mv^2$

227. C is correct. The net force on the car is the kinetic frictional force $\mu_k mg$cosθ. From $F = ma$ we can find the acceleration and plug this into $v = v_o + at$. You could also solve this using the impulse formula: $F\Delta t = m\Delta v$

228. A is correct. According to any undergraduate physics formulas, A is the only false statement. The distance and time needed to stop a vehicle is independent of mass and surface area of contact with the road. Refer to questions 226 and 227 to confirm this.

229. D is correct. The maximum static frictional force occurs just before the block begins to move. At that moment the block is in static equilibrium, so the net force is zero. That means that the force up the plane equals the force down the plane. The force down the plane is mgsinθ. The force up the plane is static friction. Thus: μmgcosθ = mgsinθ => μ = sinθ/cosθ. θ is the angle at which any block will slide; it is independent of mass.

230. D is correct. The net force on any block while sliding is the force down the plane minus the kinetic frictional force up the plane $F_{\text{net}} = mg$sinθ – $\mu_k mg$cosθ To find the acceleration, divide by the mass: $a_t = g$sinθ – $\mu_k g$cosθ. The acceleration is independent of the mass.

231. B is correct. If there were no friction, the ball would slide, not roll. Since the ball does not slide, the friction is static.

232. C is correct. At constant velocity, there is no net force, so the force of air resistance is equal to the force of gravity.

233. B is correct. $F = ma$, where F is the net force or $mg - f_{\text{air resistance}}$.

234. A is correct. The acceleration of the object in the absence of air resistance is g. At g, the object would be moving at 30 m/s after 3 seconds ($v = v_o + at$). We know that acceleration begins at approximately g and goes to zero by the end of the 3 seconds when the object is at constant velocity. Thus, we know that the average acceleration is something between g and zero, probably closer to $g/2$ than to g. The terminal speed must be much less than 30 m/s.

235. C is correct. The net force on both must be zero. Since, at terminal velocity, air resistance counteracts gravity, person A experiences twice as much air resistance.

236. B is correct. For the MCAT, tension in the string is equal to the force applied by the string to the ceiling <u>or</u> to the suspended object.

237. B is correct. For the MCAT, the tension is equal to the force applied by the rope on the strongman. Since in both cases the rope does not move, the net force on the rope is zero. Thus the building must apply as much force as any one strongman.

238. A is correct. As soon as the rope is released, it is no longer applying a force to anything. The tension is zero. If we examine the mass after the rope is released, it is accelerating at g. From $F = ma$ we know that the net force must be mg. Tension and gravity are the only forces acting on the mass, so tension must be zero.

239. A is correct. Before the man jumps, a tension is required to prevent the mass from falling. After the man jumps, the mass is falling because there is no tension to prevent it. Compare this question to 238. If we examine the mass after the man jumps, it is accelerating at g. From $F = ma$ we know that the net force must be mg. Tension and gravity are the only forces acting on the mass, so tension must be zero.

240. C is correct. If we examine the mass after the man steps on the elevator, it is accelerating at 3 m/s². From $F = ma$ we know that the net force must be 30 N. Tension and gravity are the only forces acting on the mass, and the tension is in the opposite direction. Since the mass is accelerating in the direction of mg, mg must be greater than T. mg must equal T plus ma. $mg = T + ma$.

241. B is correct. In effect, gravity is only allowed to work on the mass, but it is accelerating both the mass and the woman. Since the mass and the woman are the same weight, the acceleration is half of g. Thus tension is half mg. If we examine the mass first. We know that the mass accelerates downward because no horizontal force can be applied to the woman to prevent her movement. Since the mass accelerates downward, mg must be greater than T by an amount ma. $mg = T + ma$. Now we examine the woman. She accelerates toward the edge of the cliff, and the only force acting on her is T. Thus, $T = ma$. The masses and the accelerations are the same in both equations so we substitute to get: $mg = T + T$.

242. B is correct. In effect, gravity is only allowed to work on the mass, but it is accelerating both the mass and the man. Since the mass is ½ the weight of the man, the acceleration is 1/3 of g. Thus tension is 333 N. If we examine the mass first. We know that the mass accelerates downward because no horizontal force can be applied to the man to prevent his movement. Since the mass accelerates downward, mg must be greater than T by an amount ma. $mg = T + ma$. Now we examine the man. He accelerates toward the edge of the cliff, and the only force acting on him is T. Thus, $T = 2ma$. We substitute to get: $mg = T + T/2$.

243. B is correct. No matter how large the mass gets, its acceleration can never be greater than g, because it is gravity that is acting on it. Of course, the man will not be accelerated faster than the mass.

244. C is correct. The tension must be greater than mg and less than $2mg$ in order for the larger mass to accelerate downward and the smaller mass to accelerate upward, so the answer must be C. If you didn't see that they would accelerate this way, take the example to extremes; replace mg with a ping pong ball, and $2mg$ with a piano. It should be clear what will happen. To solve for tension examine the masses one at a time. First examine mass m. mass m experiences mg and T and accelerates upward, thus tension is greater than mg and $T = mg + ma$. Next examine mass $2m$. This mass experiences T upward, $2mg$ downward, and accelerates downward. Thus, $2mg$ is greater than T by $2ma$. $2mg = T + 2ma$. Of course the acceleration is the same for both masses or else the rope would shorten or lengthen. Substituting gives $2mg = mg + ma + 2ma \Rightarrow g/3 = a$.

245. C is correct. From 243 we know that the man will accelerate at g. To accelerate the man at g, the tension must be mg where m is the mass of the man.

246. B is correct. Hooke's law is $F = -kx$ The negative just indicates that the equation refers to the force applied <u>by</u> the object. Since the force applied <u>to</u> the object is equal and opposite, it is equal to kx, and ignoring the negative sign is usually harmless.

247. B is correct. $mg = kx$

248. C is correct. The net force will be the Hooke's law force ($F = k\Delta x$) in the direction of motion, so the acceleration will be in the direction of motion, resulting in an increasing in velocity. Since Δx will continue to decrease, the force will get smaller, resulting in a decreasing acceleration.

249. D is correct. $mg = kx$

250. D is correct. $mg + 30$ N $= kx$

251. D is correct. Imagine the spring stretches Δx when a mass is hung from one end creating a tension in the spring of mg. It is reasonable to assume that half of the spring accounts for half of the stretch. If we cut the spring in half and hang the same mass from half the spring, the tension is still mg. We already know that half the spring will stretch ½Δx when a tension of mg is applied. We can set the Hooke's law forces equal to each other since they are equal to the tension mg. Thus: $k_1\Delta x = k_2\Delta x/2 \Rightarrow 2k_1 = k_2$

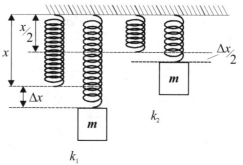

252. D is correct. Imagine hanging mass $m/2$ from one of the springs. Now hang a second mass $m/2$ from the second spring right next to the first. If you were to glue the two masses together, the change in spring length Δx would not be affected. Now you have a two spring system. Write Hooke's law for both equations, solve for Δx, and substitute. $mg/2 = k_1\Delta x$ and $mg = k_2\Delta x \Rightarrow k_2 = 2k_1$

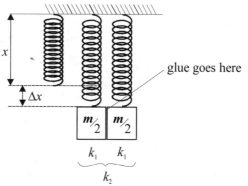

253. B is correct. $F = k\Delta x$ The length of the spring is irrelevant.

254. B is correct. $F = k\Delta x$ The length of the spring is irrelevant.

255. B is correct. Net force is more intuitive than acceleration and the two are directly proportional, so let's look at the problem in terms of net force. There are two forces acting on the spring: Hooke's law upward and gravity downward. Since the question says that the mass leaves the spring, the Hooke's law force must be greater initially. As Δx decreases, the Hooke's law force decreases, but the gravitational force remains constant. Somewhere before the Hooke's law force reaches zero, the two forces are equal making the net force zero. Up to this point, the net force, and thus the acceleration, have been decreasing. From this point, the Hooke's law force continues to decrease to zero, while the gravitational force remains constant creating a larger and larger net force downward. Since the question specifically asks about magnitude, we don't care about direction. The net force, and thus the acceleration, decreases, then increases.

256. B is correct. This question is a great example of how the MCAT can make very simple science, very tough. Everyone probably knows the formula: $F = k\Delta x$, but how do you apply it? Take the same spring and position it vertically. Now place a 50 N weight on top of it. The floor will apply a 50 N force upward, and it will compress 10 cm. 50 N = k(10 cm)

Lecture 3

257. D is correct. A system in equilibrium has no acceleration. It may be spinning at constant velocity.

258. A is correct. A system is in dynamic equilibrium if it is moving with a constant velocity. A system in static equilibrium is not moving. Both systems are treated the same with respect to calculations.

259. D is correct. A system that is not in equilibrium is accelerating.

260. B is correct. A system that is not in equilibrium is accelerating. By Newton's 2nd Law, the acceleration is proportional to the net force.

261. C is correct. Only answer C describes a system with no acceleration.

262. D is correct. A projectile is accelerating at g and is therefore NOT in equilibrium.

263. C is correct. The forces on the object are tension upward and *mg* downward. Since the mass is accelerating upward, tension must be greater than *mg*. Thus, $T = mg + ma$.

264. C is correct. The forces on the object are tension upward and *mg* downward. Since the velocity of the mass is downward, and it is decreasing, the velocity is changing toward the upward direction; the acceleration is upward. Since the mass is accelerating upward, tension must be greater than *mg*. Thus, $T = mg + ma$. Notice that the change in velocity and not the velocity is relevant.

265. A is correct. The forces on the object are tension upward and *mg* downward. Since the velocity of the mass is upward, and it is decreasing, the velocity is changing toward the downward direction; the acceleration is downward. Since the mass is accelerating downward, *mg* must be greater than tension. Thus, $T + ma = mg$.

266. B is correct. Velocity is constant, so the mass is in equilibrium; the net force is zero; the forces upward equal the forces downward; $T = mg$.

267. C is correct. The tension is greater than *mg*. The velocity of the mass must be changing in the upward direction. This leaves only answer C. If C is true, the mass is moving downward at any velocity and slowing down.

268. A is correct. The forces on the object are tension upward and *mg* downward. mg is greater than tension, so the acceleration is downward. Thus, $T + ma = mg$. $a = 2$ m/s^2. Since the motion is linear, and acceleration is constant, we use ($v = v_o + at$) to find the final velocity.

269. B is correct. Constant velocity indicates that the system is in equilibrium; the net force is zero. The force up the plane is the tension; the force down the plane is $mg\sin\theta$. $\sin30° = ½$

270. C is correct. Since the mass is accelerated up the plane, the forces up the plane must be greater than the forces down the plane by an amount *ma*. The force up the plane is tension; the force down the plane is $mg\sin\theta$. $T = mg\sin\theta + ma$. $\sin30° = ½$

271. C is correct. Since the mass is accelerated up the plane, the forces up the plane must be greater than the forces down the plane by an amount *ma*. The force up the plane is tension; the force down the plane is $mg\sin\theta$. $T = mg\sin\theta + ma$. Solve for *a* and plug into the equation: $v = v_o + at$

272. D is correct. The minimum force necessary to pull the mass up the plane is the force necessary to move it at constant velocity, thus the system is in equilibrium. The force up the plane equals the force down the plane. Since the mass is moving up the plane, the force of friction is down the plane. The force down the plane is $f_k + mg\sin\theta => \mu mg\cos\theta + mg\sin\theta$. $\sin30° = 0.5$; $\cos30° = 0.87$

273. B is correct. Since we want the mass to remain still, we want to put the system in equilibrium; make the net force zero. The force up the plane equals the force down the plane. Since the mass wants to slide down the plane, the frictional force is up the plane. First check to see what the maximum frictional force is: $f_{static\ max} = \mu mg\cos\theta$. Since this is less than the downward force of $mg\sin\theta$, we need to apply a force *F* on the mass in a direction up the plane in order to hold it still. Set the forces up the plane equal to the forces down the plane and solve for the applied force *F*. $mg\sin\theta = \mu mg\cos\theta + F$. $\sin30° = 0.5$; $\cos30° = 0.87$

274. A is correct. The mass is accelerating down the plane, so the downward forces equal the upward forces plus *ma*. $mg\sin\theta = \mu mg\cos\theta + T + ma$. $\sin30° = 0.5$; $\cos30° = 0.87$

275. B is correct. We want the velocity to change toward the downward direction, so we want the mass to accelerate in the downward direction, even while it is moving upward. This means that the forces downward will be greater than the forces upward by an amount *ma*: $mg\sin\theta + \mu mg\cos\theta = T + ma$. The moment that the mass reverses direction, it will have zero velocity. Use $v = v_o + at$ to find the acceleration. $\sin30° = 0.5$; $\cos30° = 0.87$

276. C is correct. Since we want the mass to remain still, we want to put the system in equilibrium; make the net force zero. The force up the plane equals the force down the plane. Since the mass wants to slide down the plane, the frictional force is up the plane. First check to see what the maximum frictional force is: $f_{static\ max} = \mu mg\cos\theta$. Since this is less than the downward force of $mg\sin\theta$, we need to apply a force *F* on the mass in a direction up the plane in order to hold it still. Set the forces up the plane equal to the forces down the plane and solve for the applied force *F*. $mg\sin\theta = \mu mg\cos\theta + F$. $\cos60° = 0.5$; $\sin60° = 0.87$

277. D is correct. This appears to be the same as the previous question. The difference is that the frictional force has changed directions. In this problem, the friction is trying to prevent the mass from sliding up the plane. Thus, $mg\sin\theta + \mu mg\cos\theta = F$

278. A is correct. Since the system is in equilibrium, the horizontal forces are equal: $T_1\cos\theta_1 = T_2\cos\theta_2$. As θ gets bigger, $\cos\theta$ gets smaller. $\theta_1 > \theta_2$, so $T_1 > T_2$

279. B is correct. The tension T_3 is independent of everything but the mass. $T_3 = mg$.

280. A is correct. Since the system is in equilibrium, the horizontal forces are equal: $T_1\cos\theta_1 = T_2\cos\theta_2$. and the vertical forces are equal: $mg = T_1\sin\theta_1 + T_2\sin\theta_2$

281. C is correct. Since the system is in equilibrium, the horizontal forces are equal: $T_1\cos\theta_1 = T_2\cos\theta_2$. and the vertical forces are equal: $mg = T_1\sin\theta_1 + T_2\sin\theta_2$

282. C is correct. The mass is accelerating to the right. The forces up equal the forces down; the vertical force up equals mg. The force to the right is greater than the force to the left by ma. Since there are no forces to the left, the horizontal component of the tension equals ma. Using the Pythagorean theorem: $ma^2 + mg^2 = T^2$

283. C is correct. Choose boat B as your system because both tensions are acting on boat B. Boat B moves at constant velocity to the left, so the forces to the left equal the forces to the right. The only force to the left is the tension in the rope between boats A and B. The forces to the right include both the tension in the rope between boats B and C, and the fluid resistance of the water. Thus the tension between boats A and B is greater than the tension between boats B and C.

284. B is correct. The system is in equilibrium, so the forces up equal the forces down. Choosing block B for the system to be analyzed, we have mg plus T_3 downward equals T_2 upward. m is the mass of block B.

285. C is correct. Now the block B is not in equilibrium; it is accelerating upward. Thus the force upward is greater than the force downward. $mg + T_3 + ma = T_2$. m is the mass of block B.

286. B is correct. You must realize that the greatest tension will be in T_1, thus T_1 will break first. Choose all three blocks for your system. The system is accelerating upwards, so the force upward is greater than the force downward: $T_1 = mg + ma$ where m is the sum of the masses of the blocks. Solve for a and plug into $x = \frac{1}{2}at^2$.

287. D is correct. The maximum reading occurs when the elevator is accelerating upward because, at this moment, the reading on the scale will reflect mg of the man and box, and ma. Choose the man and box as your system to analyze. When the elevator accelerates upward, the forces upward are greater than the forces downward by an amount ma. The force downward is mg (where m is the mass of the man and scale); the force upward is the normal force N. Thus, $N = mg + ma$. The normal force is applied by the scale; the scale reads the equal and opposite force to the normal force.

288. B is correct. The minimum reading occurs when the elevator is accelerating downward because, at this moment, the reading on the scale will reflect mg of the man and box minus ma. Choose the man and box as your system to analyze. When the elevator accelerates downward, the forces downward are greater than the forces upward by an amount ma. The force downward is mg (where m is the mass of the man and scale); the force upward is the normal force N. Thus, $N + ma = mg$. The normal force is applied by the scale; the scale reads the equal and opposite force to the normal force.

289. C is correct. The maximum tension is when the elevator accelerates upward. $T = mg + ma$.

290. D is correct. The apparent weight of the box is the force necessary to hold it up. The maximum will occur when the elevator accelerates upward. $W = mg + ma$.

291. C is correct. Once the box is released, it is in freefall, independent of any forces but gravity. The acceleration is g.

292. A is correct. To solve this problem, you must calculate the distance needed for the elevator to reach its maximum velocity (5 m/s as given in the paragraph above the diagram). This distance is the same as the distance necessary for the elevator to slow to a stop from maximum velocity. Use $v^2 = v_o^2 + 2ax$. This distance is 12.5 m to reach maximum velocity and 12.5 m to stop from maximum velocity. A trip from the first to the tenth floor is 45 m. Thus 12.5 m will be used to achieve maximum velocity and then to slow to stop. (Use this formula to figure both sections of the trip: $x = \frac{1}{2}at^2$ where $x = 12.5$ m and $a = 1$ m/s^2.) The remaining 20 m will be traveled at maximum velocity and will require $v = d/t$. Add the times together gives: $5 + 5 + 4 = 14$ s.

293. D is correct. This is a projectile problem. You want to throw a projectile straight up from the 1st floor to the 6th floor, and you want it to be in the air during the time that the elevator is moving. First find the time the elevator is moving. To solve this problem, you must calculate the distance needed for the elevator to reach its maximum velocity (5 m/s as given in the paragraph above the diagram). This distance is the same as the distance necessary for the elevator to slow to a stop from maximum velocity. Use $v^2 = v_o^2 + 2ax$. This distance is 12.5 m to reach maximum velocity and 12.5 m to stop from maximum velocity. A trip from the first to the sixth floor is 25 m; exactly enough distance for the elevator to reach maximum velocity and then slow to zero. (To find the time, use: $x = \frac{1}{2}at^2$ where $x = 12.5$ m, $a = 1$ m/s^2 and t will be the time for half the trip.) Now be sure to take the time for the whole trip and plug it into $x = v_o t + \frac{1}{2}at^2$ where $x = 25$ m and $t = 10$ s (Note: you must use $a = -10$ m/s^2 because acceleration is in the opposite direction of displacement and initial velocity.)

294. B is correct. The normal force is equal and opposite to the vertical component of the force F and the weight mg. The block will accelerate horizontally due to the horizontal component of the force F (horizontal component is $F\cos 60°$) $F = ma$

295. D is correct. The block does not accelerate vertically, so the normal force is equal and opposite to the vertical component of the force F and the weight mg ($N = mg + F\sin 60°$). The block will accelerate horizontally due to the horizontal component of the force F (The horizontal component is $F\cos 60°$) minus friction f ($f = N\mu$). Since the block accelerates to the left, the horizontal component of F is greater than friction by an amount ma. $F\cos 60° = (mg + F\sin 60°)\mu + ma$ ($\cos 60° = 0.5$; $\sin 60° = 0.87$)

296. B is correct. We want the plane to be in equilibrium. Find the net force on the plane as explained in the question, and apply a force equal and opposite in order to make the net force zero. You should recognize the ratio of the sides of a 30-60-90 triangle.

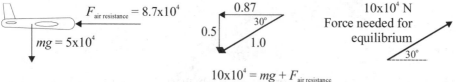

$$10\text{x}10^4 = mg + F_{air\ resistance}$$

297. C is correct. Torque equals the lever arm times the force when the lever arm is defined as the distance from the point of rotation to where the force acts at 90°. Since all the forces are equal, only the lever arm is different in each example. The lever arms are shown below. For the greatest torque, choose the longest lever arm.

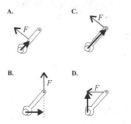

298. D is correct. To find the net torque on a system, you may choose any point as the rotational point. No net torque means that there is no angular acceleration, but there may or may not be angular velocity.

299. C is correct. Only the figure skater is changing her rate of rotation, and thus has angular acceleration.

300. C is correct. This is definitional.

301. C is correct. Torque equals the lever arm times the force when the lever arm is defined as the distance from the point of rotation to where the force acts at 90°. Since all the forces are equal, only the lever arm is different in each example. The lever arms are shown below. For the greatest torque, choose the longest lever arm.

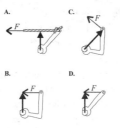

302. C is correct. The board is to be in equilibrium, thus the clockwise torques must equal the counter-clockwise torques. (Note: for the MCAT it is sufficient and expedient to view torque as a special *rotational force* pushing clockwise or counterclockwise. Torque is not a force, and cannot be added or subtracted to other forces.) If we choose as our point of rotation the point where the rope attaches to the board, we have counterclockwise torque 0.3*mg* due to the suspended mass and clockwise torque 0.2(12)*g* due to the mass of the board. (The weight of the board acts at its center of gravity 0.5 m from the left end.) Setting the torques equal gives the equation: $0.3mg = 0.2(12)g$

303. A is correct. The board is to be in equilibrium, thus the clockwise torques must equal the counterclockwise torques. If we choose as our point of rotation the point the fulcrum, we have counter-clockwise torque 0.3*mg* due to the mass at the left, and clockwise torques 0.6*mg* due to the mass suspended from the right end of the board and 0.2(3)*g* due to the weight of the board. (The weight of the board acts at its center of gravity 0.5 m from the left end.) Setting the torques equal gives the equation: $0.3(4)g = 0.2(3)g + 0.6mg$

304. B is correct. The board will not fall until the center of gravity of the mass, board and woman system is to the left of the large, stationary block, thus we want the center of gravity at the very edge. The center of gravity is the balancing point, so choose a point on the board directly above the edge of the block as your rotational point, and make the clockwise torque equal to the counter-clockwise torque. The counterclockwise torques are the weight of the woman 60*g* times her distance from the rotation point $(x - 3)$ and the weight of the board times the distance of its center of gravity from the rotational point 15*g*(2). The clockwise torque is the weight of the mass 75*g* times its distance from the rotational point $(3 - 1)$. Setting these equal gives: $60g(x - 3) + 15g(2) = 75g(3 - 1)$, where the *g* is 10 m/s². Of course you could choose any other point as your rotational point, but, if you do, don't forget to add the normal force upward at the edge of the block. The normal force is equal and opposite to the weight of the board, woman, and mass.

305. D is correct. The board is to be in equilibrium, thus the clockwise torques must equal the counter-clockwise torques. If we choose as our point of rotation the point where the rope attaches to the board, we have counterclockwise torque *x*4*g* due to the suspended mass and clockwise torque $(0.5 - x)(16)g$ due to the mass of the board. (The weight of the board acts at its center of gravity 0.5 m from the left end.) Setting the torques equal gives the equation: $x4g = (0.5 - x)(16)g$

306. A is correct. The board is to be in equilibrium, thus the clockwise torques must equal the counter-clockwise torques. If we choose as our point of rotation the fulcrum, we have counterclockwise torque Mg due to the mass of Mary times 7 m and the weight of the board $20g$ times 2 m, and clockwise torque Tg due to the mass of Tim times 3 m. Setting the torques equal gives the equation: $7Mg + 20g(2) = 3Tg$. We also know that $T + M = 180$

307. A is correct. The force on either end of the dipole is given by $F = Eq$ where E is the electric field inside the capacitor and q is the charge on either end of the dipole. Since the electric field inside a parallel plate capacitor is constant, and the charges on opposite ends of a dipole are equal and opposite, the force on each end is equal and opposite. There is, however, a net torque, which will cause the dipole to rotate.

308. D is correct. Choose the man and the pole as your system, but keep their centers of gravity separate. (You don't have to; it's just easier.) Since the man is balanced, the net torque about any point is zero. For the rotational point, you can choose where the man's feet touch the ground. The counterclockwise torque is the weight of the pole $25g$ times the distance shown as x in the diagram below. The clockwise torque is the weight of the man times 0.5. Thus: $25gx = 75g(0.5)$. $x = 1.5$ m. From trigonometry we know that the pole length times $\cos60° = x + 0.5 + x + 0.5 = 2x + 1$ => pole length $= 4x + 2 = 8$

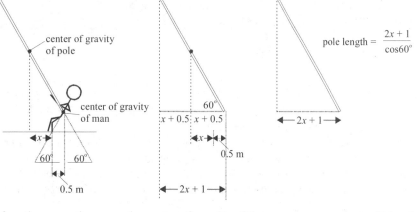

309. A is correct. Just before the crane tips over, the center of gravity of the crane-mass system will be above the right edge of the crane. If it goes beyond, the crane will tip over. Thus choose your rotational point to be the right edge of the crane. The counterclockwise torque is the weight of the crane $4,000g$ times the horizontal distance to the rotational point: 1.7 m. The clockwise torque is the weight of the mass mg times the horizontal distance to the rotational point: d. $4000g(1.7) = mgd$ The distance d is found through trigonometry to be $d + 1.7 = 22\cos30°$ $(\cos30° = \text{sqrt}(3)/2 \approx 1.7/2)$ Notice that the 1.7 cancels out when the equations are combined.

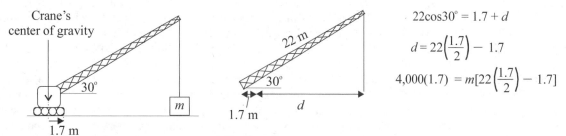

$$22\cos30° = 1.7 + d$$

$$d = 22\left(\frac{1.7}{2}\right) - 1.7$$

$$4,000(1.7) = m[22\left(\frac{1.7}{2}\right) - 1.7]$$

310. B is correct. This is an equilibrium problem, so the forces up $(T_1 + T_2)$ equal the forces down $(10g + 20g)$. Also, the counterclockwise torques equal the clockwise torques. Choosing the point of rotation to be where T_2 attaches to the board, gives the clockwise torque as $2.5T_1$, and the counterclockwise torque as $10g(5)$. Thus $T_1 = 200$ N. Plugging this value into the first equation gives $T_2 = 100$ N.

311. D is correct. This is an equilibrium problem, so the forces up $(T_1 + 10)$ equal the forces down $(10g + 8g)$. Also, the counterclockwise torques equal the clockwise torques. Choosing the point of rotation to be the right end of the board, gives the clockwise torque as $10(0.4)$ and T_1x and the counterclockwise torque as $10g(1)$ and $8g(0.5)$. Thus, $10(0.4) + T_1x = 10g(1) + 8g(0.5)$, and $(T_1 + 10) = (10g + 8g)$.

312. C is correct. This is an equilibrium problem. Remember, the frictional force f is <u>smaller than or equal to</u> μN. We are looking for the smallest possible value of μ. In order to avoid confusion, solve for the force f and then solve for μ. If we choose the spot where the rope attaches to the sign, we can quickly see that, for the sign to be in rotational equilibrium, mg must equal f; the torque equation is $0.2mg = 0.2f$. The forces upward equal the forces downward, so: $T\cos30° = mg + f$. Putting these two equations together, we have $T\cos30° = 2mg$ => $T = 2mg/\cos30°$. The forces left equal the forces to the right, so the normal force N equals $T\sin30°$. The force of static friction is $f \le \mu N = \mu T\sin30°$. Earlier we found that $T\cos30° = mg + f$. Solving for f and substituting, we have: $T\cos30° - mg \le \mu T\sin30°$ => $(\cos30°/\sin30°) - (mg/T\sin30°) \le \mu$. Earlier we found that $T = 2mg/\cos30°$. Substituting this value for T into the previous equation gives: $(\cos30°/\sin30°) - (mg\cos30°/2mg\sin30°) \le \mu$ => $(\cos30°/\sin30°) - (\cos30°/2\sin30°) \le \mu$ => $\frac{1}{2}(\cos30°/\sin30°) \le \mu$. (Note: $\sin30° = 0.5$; $\cos30° = 0.87$)

313. C is correct. This is a unit of force. If you are unsure of the units, think of a simple formula like K.E. $= \frac{1}{2}mv^2$ and plug in the units.

314. D is correct. Only D has units of energy.

315. D is correct. K.E. $= \frac{1}{2}mv^2$

316. C is correct. Gravity is a conservative force; mechanical energy is conserved. Initially, the energy is all mechanical mgh. All this energy is converted to kinetic energy.

317. C is correct. All the kinetic energy becomes potential energy: $\frac{1}{2}mv^2 = mgh$ => $v = \text{sqrt}(2gh)$

318. C is correct. 1280 J of kinetic energy turned to potential, thus $1280 = mgh$

319. B is correct. To solve this problem, we must calculate the maximum height of the projectile. The vertical velocity $v\sin60°$ gives the height from $v\sin60° = \text{sqrt}(2gh)$ => $h = 60$ m. From P.E. $= mgh$, we find that B is true.

320. B is correct. All the elastic potential energy is converted to kinetic energy: $\frac{1}{2}kx^2 = \frac{1}{2}mv^2$

321. C is correct. Gravitational potential energy is converted to elastic potential energy: $mgh = \frac{1}{2}kx^2$. Don't forget to add the 5 cm that the spring is compressed to the 45 cm, making $h = 50$ cm.

322. D is correct. The force due to gravity near the surface of the earth is given by both mg and Gmm/r^2, so we set them equal and solve for g.

323. D is correct. Ideal projectile motion is independent of mass, so both will have the same velocity at all times. Thus, only when their velocities are zero, will their kinetic energies be zero.

324. D is correct. Ideal projectile motion is independent of mass, so both will have the same velocity at all times. Thus, only when their velocities are zero, will their kinetic energies be zero.

325. B is correct. All its kinetic energy changes to potential energy; potential energy is proportional to height, thus at halfway the energies will be equal. Find the maximum height from $v = \text{sqrt}(2gh)$ and divide by 2.

326. A is correct. Both balls start with equal energy. All the elastic potential energy is converted to gravitational potential energy. Since gravitational potential energy is proportional to height and mass, the less massive ball will go proportionally higher.

327. B is correct. Both balls start with equal energy. All the elastic potential energy is converted to kinetic energy as the balls leave the spring. Since kinetic energy is proportional to mass but to the square of velocity, the less massive ball will have twice the velocity.

328. C is correct. This question is largely intuitive. The balls leave the spring at the same time, thus they have the same velocity. Velocity, not mass, dictates maximum height of a projectile. This means that 4 times as much work is done on the more massive ball.

329. C is correct. This question is largely intuitive. The balls leave the spring at the same time, thus they have the same velocity.

330. A is correct. When the springs at their rest length, just as the man touches the ground, the net force is mg. The spring force kx increases until it equals mg. At this moment the net force is zero, but the man has a maximum downward velocity. Now kx increases to greater than mg and the acceleration of the man increases from zero in the opposite direction until the springs are at maximum compression.

331. A is correct. Since the hands remain at equal temperatures, the energy transfer cannot be heat, so must be work. For B, there is no displacement, so no work. C is energy transfer as heat. For D, the force is gravity, a conservative force, and the force is 90° to the motion. There is no work. (Caution: MCAT may ask a question like "How much work is done by gravity?" Since work is the change in energy do to a force, a conservative force only does work, if we pretend that the potential energy associated with the conservative force does not exist. The question, as phrased, implies that we should make this assumption.)

332. A is correct. Work is equal to the force in the direction of displacement ($F\cos\theta$) times the displacement. $W = Fd\cos\theta$

333. B is correct. The work done on the block is manifested as kinetic energy. $W = Fd\cos\theta = \frac{1}{2}mv^2$

334. B is correct. Only B would not change the equation: $W = Fd\cos\theta$.

335. A is correct. $W = Fd\cos\theta$ The distance would be the greatest if the initial velocity were to the right.

336. B is correct. The work done on the block is manifested as kinetic energy. $W = Fd\cos\theta = \frac{1}{2}mv^2$

337. A is correct. The horizontal forces are equal, so the block doesn't move. There is no work done.

338. A is correct. The net horizontal force on the block is 90 N. $W = Fd\cos\theta$

339. D is correct. The normal force N is $mg + F\sin\theta = 100 + 50$. The frictional force f is $\mu N = 15$. The net force is $F\cos\theta - (f + 10) = 87 - (15 + 10) = 62$. Set the change in kinetic energy equal to the force times the distance: $\frac{1}{2}mv^2 = Fd$ => $\frac{1}{2}(10)v^2 = 62\times5$ => $v = \text{sqrt}(62) = 0.79$.

340. D is correct. Although D has the correct units, vt would represent the distance traveled if the velocity were constant at v, and mg is the force due to gravity, not the net force.

341. D is correct. Answer choices A, B, and C from the previous question each represent the work done on the block. These show that a change in q, d, or m would change the work done.

342. A is correct. See the previous question to understand A is correct. B, C, and D do not change because a block sliding down a frictionless plane is similar to a projectile; the forces are proportional to the mass, so changes in the mass don't change the motion.

343. A is correct. $W = Fd = mgd\sin\theta$.

344. B is correct. $W = mgh$

345. B is correct. $W = mgh$

346. C is correct. Hooke's law and gravity are conservative forces, so the mechanical energy is conserved.

347. B is correct. Since the molecules are attracted to each other, as they separate, their potential energy increases. Since energy is neither created nor destroyed, this energy must come from kinetic energy.

348. D is correct. The force applied by the astronaut is nonconservative.

349. C is correct. Conservative forces can't change the temperature of an object because mechanical energy is conserved leaving no energy for a temperature change. Conservative forces conserve mechanical energy, but they can redistribute energy among the forms of mechanical energy.

350. C is correct. This is definitional. Nonconservative forces transfer energy between mechanical and internal energy.

351. D is correct. Gravitational force is a conservative force. Since potential energy increased, kinetic energy decreased by the same amount. However, 144 J will decrease the velocity of a slow moving mass more than that of a fast moving mass. $\Delta\text{K.E.} = \frac{1}{2}m(v_{final}^2 - v_{initial}^2)$ Thus, the change in the velocity depends upon the initial velocity.

352. C is correct. Energy is always conserved; this is a universal law. Friction does not conserve mechanical energy. You may have been tempted by answer choice A. However, rub your hand on a stationary table. The table warms up without moving. This is not heat because the energy transfer is not due to a temperature difference but to a force. Work is done on the table.

353. D is correct. The block transfers some of its energy to the table via work done by friction. The energy transferred to the table does not necessarily equal the energy retained by the block. Even if these energies were equal, the change in temperature in each object would depend upon its heat capacity, which is a function of its size and what it is made of.

354. D is correct. When considering the energy transfer due to friction, we must take into account internal energy change. The frictional force times the distance is equal to the change in mechanical energy: $fd = \Delta\text{K.E.} + \Delta\text{P.E.}$, but this does not take into account the internal energy change of the block. Work by friction does not equal fd.

355. B is correct. A force perpendicular to motion (the tension in the string) does no work. Gravity is exactly countered by the vertical component of the tension in the string.

356. D is correct. $fd = \frac{1}{2}mv^2$

357. C is correct. $fd = \frac{1}{2}mv^2$

358. B is correct. Potential energy becomes kinetic energy, which is then dissipated by friction: $\mu mgd = fd = \frac{1}{2}mv^2 = mgh$

359. C is correct. Gravitational potential energy is changed to kinetic at the bottom of the ramp. Next, the frictional force times the distance equals the change in mechanical energy. Thus $\mu mgd = mgh + \frac{1}{2}mv^2$.

360. C is correct. $W = Fd$ where F is the net force in the direction of displacement. The negative sign indicates that the block lost energy.

361. D is correct. $W = Fd$, where F is the force of gravity. This is one of those strange questions that assumes that gravitational potential energy does not exist, thus the only change in energy of the block is kinetic. In reality, the block gains loses potential energy as well.

362. A is correct. $Fd = \Delta\text{K.E.}$ where F is the net force in the direction of displacement. The net force is 5 N. The distance is 10 m.

363. A is correct. $\Delta\text{K.E.} = \frac{1}{2}mv^2$ See the previous question to find $\Delta\text{K.E.}$

364. B is correct. The net force on the block is 5 newtons. This times the distance traveled gives the work done: $W = Fd$. The work done equals the change in the kinetic energy: $W = \Delta\text{K.E.} = \frac{1}{2}m(v_f^2 - v_o^2)$. Or use constant acceleration. The tension is less than the weight, so there is acceleration. $T + ma = mg$. The acceleration is 1.25 m/s². Now we use $v^2 = v_o^2 + 2ax$.

365. B is correct. Since the force is constant, this problem can be solved by substituting f/m for a in the equation $x = \frac{1}{2}at^2$. where $f = \mu mg$. You can also solve this problem using the equation impulse equals change in momentum: $ft = m\Delta v$

366. B is correct. Kinetic energy is dissipated by friction: $\mu mgd = fd = \frac{1}{2}mv^2$

367. B is correct. $W = Fd$

368. C is correct. $P = W/t$

369. B is correct. $P = W/t = 25mgh/t = 25\times60\times10\times2/50\times60 = 10$. The 25 represents the number of boxes. Don't forget to change 50 minutes to 3000 seconds.

370. C is correct. In order to keep the rocket moving at a constant velocity, the rocket's engines must supply enough force to counter gravity. $P = Fv = mgv$

371. C is correct. 100 W is the power. The power times the time equals the energy dissipated: $Pt = \Delta E$. The energy from climbing stairs is mgh times the number of stairs n. $Pt = nmgh$. Be sure to convert days to seconds and cm to m.

372. B is correct. $P = mgh/t$

373. A is correct. We know from $F = GmM/r^2$ that the force of gravity decreases. Thus, from power $P = mgv$ decreases as well.

374. D is correct. The rate at which work is done by gravity increases. The force is a constant mg, but the velocity, and thus the distance, increases with time.

375. A is correct. From $v = d/t$, we know that the train is 100 m from Lois. From $Fd = \frac{1}{2}mv^2$, we know that superman must apply a force of 5,000 N to stop the train. From $x = \frac{1}{2}at^2$ and $F = ma$, we know that when this force is applied to the train, it will stop in 20 seconds. $P = W/t = (\frac{1}{2}mv^2)/t$

376. D is correct.

377. A is correct. There is no energy transfer, so there is no power.

378. B is correct. $mgh/t = P$

379. A is correct. $mgh/t = P$ No change in h.

380. D is correct. $P = Fv$

Lecture 4

381. C is correct. Momentum is mass times velocity: $p = mv$

382. A is correct. Kinetic energy is: K.E. $= \frac{1}{2}mv^2$

383. D is correct. Mass is a quantitative measure of inertia.

384. C is correct. $Ft = mv$. The most difficult object to stop, is the one with the greatest momentum.

385. D is correct. The object with the greatest tendency to resist a change in its motion is the object with the greatest inertia.

386. C is correct. When the boy rolls off the sled, the boy and the sled will continue to move at the same speed unless some force is applied to either of them.

387. C is correct. $p = mv$

388. D is correct. The water from the rain has no horizontal momentum. It acquires horizontal momentum from the bucket. The total momentum of the bucket and all the water is conserved. Thus as the bucket fills with water, its mass increases and its velocity decreases.

389. D is correct. The bucket of water is losing water, so it is losing mass. Like the boy rolling off the sled, the leaking water takes its momentum with it. Thus the velocity of the bucket doesn't change, but its momentum decreases.

390. B is correct. $m_1v = (m_1 + m_2)v$ Total momentum is conserved.

391. B is correct. From the previous question, we see that when the mass is doubled in a completely inelastic collision, the velocity is cut in half. From K.E. $= \frac{1}{2}mv^2$, we see that the kinetic energy is also cut in half. Where did this energy go? It went to internal energy of the masses. If we knew the heat capacities of the masses, we could calculate the change in temperature.

392. C is correct. Calculate the horizontal and the vertical momentums separately. Both are conserved, independently of each other. $m_1v_{horizontal} + m_2v_{horizontal} = (m_1 + m_2)v_{horizontal}$

393. D is correct. Velocity of a single mass is never conserved in a collision.

394. D is correct. Each of the colliding objects by itself is NOT an isolated system, and each of their velocities will change when they experience the force of the collision and thus accelerate. (Acceleration means to change velocity.) Momentum is conserved for an isolated system, so the sum of the momentums of the colliding bodies will remain constant, but their individual momentums will change.

395. A is correct. Calculate the horizontal and the vertical momentums separately. Both are conserved, independently of each other. $m_1v_{horizontal} + m_2v_{horizontal} = (m_1 + m_2)v_{horizontal}$ and $m_1v_{vertical} + m_2v_{vertical} = (m_1 + m_2)v_{vertical}$ Draw the vectors and use the Pythagorean theorem to calculate the final velocity from the vertical and horizontal velocities. $v^2_{vertical} + v^2_{horizontal} = v^2$

396. B is correct. The horizontal momentum is remains constant, before, during, and after the collision.

397. C is correct. The objects do not necessarily remain at their same speed. For example, when one pool ball elastically collides with a second at rest, the first stops while the second continues at the original velocity of the first. A is true because elastic collisions can only involve conservative forces, because mechanical energy is conserved. B and D are definitional for elastic collisions.

398. C is correct. In an elastic collision, kinetic energy is conserved. $\frac{1}{2}m_1v^2_{initial} + \frac{1}{2}m_2v^2_{initial} = \frac{1}{2}m_1v^2_{final} + \frac{1}{2}m_2v^2_{final}$

399. C is correct. Mechanical energy is conserved.

400. C is correct. This question is designed to aid your intuition about collisions. Choice A and B violate conservation of momentum. The small object obviously cannot move to the right faster than the large object of it would move right through it. If the larger object were the same mass as the smaller object, conservation of momentum would allow for a maximum velocity of 5 m/s $[v = m_s + m_l)/m_s]$. Choice D violates conservation of energy, since the smaller object would have more energy than it had at the beginning of the problem. The graph below shows the final velocities of two colliding objects relative to their masses, when one of the objects are stationary. It was created from the formulas for conservation of momentum and conservation of kinetic energy (elastic only). v_o and v_1 are the initial and final velocities of the object that is initially moving. v_2 is the final velocity of the object that is initially at rest. m_1 and m_2 are their respective masses. Notice that the graph covers elastic collisions, inelastic collisions, and everything between them (partially elastic collisions). v_c represents the velocity of the combined masses in a fully inelastic collision. Since the second object is heavier, we look at the left half of the graph.

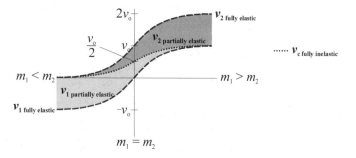

401. B is correct. This is also a question designed to test your intuition. Working the formulae would take a long time. From the graph in the answer to the previous question, we see that for this collision the final velocity of the lighter object must be less than $v_o/2$ if it moves to the right, regardless of the type of collision.

402. C is correct. This is also a question designed to test your intuition. Working the formulae would take a long time. From the graph in the answer to the two previous questions, we see that for this collision the final velocity of the lighter object must be greater than $v_o/2$ but less than $2v_o$, regardless of the type of collision.

403. B is correct. This is also a question designed to test your intuition. Working the formulae would take a long time. From the graph in the answer to question 400, we see that for this collision the final velocity of both objects must be to the right. Two pool balls colliding most closely represents a completely elastic collision of equal masses; one mass stops and the other continues at the original velocity. We would expect a larger mass to propel the smaller mass at greater than the original velocity. We would also expect that a larger mass would not be stopped in an elastic collision, but it would slow down.

404. D is correct. This is also a question designed to test your intuition. Working the formulae would take a long time. From the graph in the answer to question 400, we see that when $m_1 = m_2$, and the collision is fully elastic, v_1 is zero and $v_2 = v_o$. You can also imagine the pool balls from the explanation to question 403.

405. C is correct. This is also a question designed to test your intuition. Working the formulae would take a long time. From the graph in the answer to question 400, we see that when $m_1 < m_2$, and the collision is fully elastic, v_1 is negative and $v_2 < v_o$ but always positive. Imagine the locomotive and the ping pong ball from the explanation to question 403.

406. B is correct. Use the graph from the explanation to question 400, or imagine a locomotive colliding with a ping pong ball. Obviously, the ping pong ball will not slow the locomotive.

407. C is correct. You should be aware that the limit to the velocity of the lighter mass in the collision described is $2v_o$. See the graph in the explanation for question 400.

408. B is correct. To solve this, we must use conservation of momentum $[m_1v = (m_1 + m_2)v]$ and conservation of kinetic energy $(\frac{1}{2}m_1v^2_{\text{initial}} = \frac{1}{2}m_1v^2_{\text{final}} + \frac{1}{2}m_2v^2_{\text{final}})$ because it is an elastic collision. Notice that it can be solved without complicated calculations, but by considering conservation of momentum and kinetic energy. Answer A must be wrong, because from K.E. $= \frac{1}{2}mv^2$ we see that, if Choice A were true, energy would have to be created. Since we know that m_1 will bounce backward (see question 405), which represents negative momentum, the momentum of m_2 must be greater than the original momentum of m_1, (m_1v_o). Choices C and D do not give m_1 enough momentum.

409. A is correct. Use the graph from the explanation to question 400, or use conservation of momentum $[m_1v = (m_1 + m_2)v]$

410. C is correct. Mechanical energy and momentum must be conserved, so both bobs bounce to their original heights.

411. C is correct. Mechanical energy and momentum must be conserved.

412. A is correct. The initial momentum is zero, so the final momentums must add up to zero; they must be equal and opposite.

413. A is correct. Momentum of an isolated system is conserved.

414. C is correct. The center of mass of an isolated system will not move, so in order to move some mass to the right, some mass must be moved to the left. Or, momentum must be conserved, in order to move some mass to the right, some mass must be moved to the left.

415. B is correct. The center of mass of an isolated system will not move, so in order to move some mass to the right, some mass must be moved to the left. Or, momentum must be conserved, in order to move some mass to the right, some mass must be moved to the left. By climbing on top of the box, the man moves his mass to the right; the box must shift to the left to compensate.

416. B is correct. Whatever momentum the man gives to himself, he gives the box an equal and opposite momentum. The center of mass of the isolated system cannot be moved.

417. A is correct. In order to move to the rock in 3 s, the woman must give herself a velocity of 15 m/s. The woman has the same mass as the all the blocks together. If she gives them a leftward velocity of 15 m/s, momentum will be conserved with her rightward move of 15 m/s.

418. A is correct. Use conservation of momentum. The initial momentum is zero, so the final momentum must be zero. 5 blocks to the right at 6 m/s have a momentum of 150 kg m/s. The woman and the remaining blocks must have the same momentum to the left, so her velocity is found from 75 kg x 2 m/s = 150 kg m/s to the left. Now she gives the remaining blocks a velocity of 6 m/s so that their momentum is 25 kg x 6 m/s = 150 kg m/s. This is all of her remaining momentum. She must stop. The woman traveled 2 m/s for 2 s. Since she started at 45 m from the rock and traveled to the left, she ends at 49 m from the rock.

419. C is correct. She was accelerating while she applied a force to the block. After she releases the block, there is no force to provide an acceleration.

420. B is correct. This is a reverse collision; only momentum is conserved. Since there is nothing to push on, it is the only way that a rocket changes velocity in the vacuum of space.

421. A is correct. The change in motion would be the greatest for the object with the least tendency to resist that change, or the object with the least inertia.

422. D is correct. The change in momentum is proportional to the force: $Ft = \Delta mv$.

423. C is correct. Stopping force is proportional to the change in momentum: $Ft = \Delta mv$. Answer C has the greatest momentum.

424. D is correct. Starting force is proportional to the change in momentum: $Ft = \Delta mv$. Answer D has the least change in momentum per unit time.

425. B is correct. The direction of the change of motion is irrelevant. $Ft = m\Delta v$

426. C is correct. The area under the curve is the impulse, or change in momentum.

427. A is correct. To find the average force, find the area under the curve, and divide by the time.

428. D is correct. Use $F_{average}t = m\Delta v$.

429. C is correct. The average force on the mass in the first 20 seconds is equal and opposite to the average force on the mass in the second 20 seconds. In the first 20 seconds, the force on the mass, and thus the acceleration of the mass is always positive, and constantly changing, so A and B are incorrect. Since, in the first 20 seconds, the force on the mass is positive, the velocity is always increasing. The smallest velocity between 10 s and 20 s is greater than the greatest velocity between 0 s and 10 s, and the distance traveled must also be greater: $vt = d$

430. B is correct. The velocity of the first mass when it strikes the second is sqrt($2gh$). The collision is inelastic and the masses are equal so $mv_o = 2mv_f$. v_f is the initial velocity of the two mass system. The force of the mud is a type of friction so $Fd =$ the total change in mechanical energy. $Fd = \frac{1}{2}mv^2 + mgh$ where m is the mass of the two mass system and d and h are both the 1 cm penetration into the mud. Thus $Fd = \frac{1}{2} 2m \, 2gh/4 + 2mgd$

431. C is correct. The collision is inelastic, so momentum is conserved, but some kinetic energy is dissipated as internal energy. The force on the anvil is equal to the force on the hammer throughout the collision (Newton's third law), so the impulse that stops the hammer is equal to the impulse that goes into the anvil.

432. D is correct. During the collision between the sledgehammer and the anvil, the sledgehammer moves from very fast to very slow, while the anvil moves from zero to the same very slow speed. Thus, the hammer is always moving faster than the anvil from the moment of contact until they reach the same speed. Since the time of the collision is the same for both, the hammer must move a greater distance. A second way to view this is to realize that the mechanical energy acquired by a body is equal to the force over the distance that force is applied. In this collision, mechanical energy is kinetic. Since the change in kinetic energy is greatest for the hammer, and the force is the same for both the hammer and the anvil, the distance traveled is greater for the hammer. **Answer A and C** are the same concept. Change in momentum is impulse. Since both experience the same force over the same time, both experience the same change in momentum. **Answer B** is wrong because the hammer obviously slows down much more than the anvil speeds up.

433. D is correct. Change in velocity is not the same as the rate of change in velocity, which is acceleration. Without acceleration, we cannot find the force, and thus the distance over which the force acts or the time during which the force acts.

434. B is correct. An ideal machine changes force, never work.

435. D is correct. A real machine reduces force. However, in a real machine some energy is lost to internal energy through friction, and thus more work is required for the same job.

436. D is correct. Without a machine, 50 N of force would be required to lift a 5 kg object. Since a machine doesn't change work, the force is inversely related to the distance: $W = Fd$. When the force is decreased by a factor of 5, the distance must be increased by a factor of 5.

437. B is correct. Since the engineer can lift twice his own weight, the mechanical advantage is 2. An ideal machine does not change work. From $W = Fd$ we know that when the force is doubled, the distance is reduced by a factor of 2. This means that platform 2 will rise half as far as platform 1 will fall.

438. B is correct. Since the machine has a mechanical advantage, the platforms will only balance if twice the mass of the engineer is placed on platform 2. When less than twice the weight is placed on platform 2, the engineer and platform 1 will accelerate downward. The rate of their acceleration will be less than g since some upward force is applied by the 50 kg mass. See question #471.

439. C is correct. The net force on both masses is zero so velocity from the push remains constant. The work done on the mass is $m_2gh_2 + \frac{1}{2}m_2v_2^2$. $2m_1 = m_2$, $2v_2 = v_1$, and $2h_2 = h_1$ (See question #437. $v = h/t$ where t is equal for both platforms.). The work done on the mass in terms of the mass, height, and velocity of the engineer is $2m_1gh_1/2 + \frac{1}{2}2m_1(v_1/2)^2$ which is $m_1gh_1 + \frac{1}{2}\,\frac{1}{2}m_1v_1^2$.

440. D is correct. The total initial energy is m_1gh_1 where m_1 is the mass of the engineer. This must equal the total final energy, which is the kinetic energy of the engineer who has accelerated, and the potential and kinetic energy of the mass (or the work done on the mass).

441. B is correct. No matter how great the mass on platform 1, it is accelerated by gravity and could not change velocity faster than 10 m/s². Since platform 2 must move half the distance of platform 1 in the same amount of time, its max acceleration is half that or 5 m/s². Using the linear motion equation $v^2 = 2ax$ we have $v = $ sqrt(50) at the top height of platform 2. Using this velocity and the same equation to find how high the projectile goes once the platform stops, we have $50 = 2gh$. We get 2.5 m which we must add to the 5 m height of platform 2.

442. C is correct. From $W = Fd$ we know that to reduce the force by a factor of 10, we must increase the distance by a factor of 10. The ramp must be 10 times as long as the height.

443. D is correct. An ideal machine (a frictionless ramp in this case) will not change the work done by gravity on the ball. Thus, regardless of the incline, $mgh = \frac{1}{2}mv^2$

444. B is correct. The final velocity of the box is dependent upon the height of the ramp and not the mechanical advantage. The acceleration depends upon the mechanical advantage. The force is proportional to the acceleration. The acceleration is one half g, so the force is one half mg, so the mechanical advantage is 2 to 1.

445. C is correct. $W = \Delta PE + \Delta KE = mgh + \frac{1}{2}m(v_2^2 - v_1^2) = 5\times10\times1 + \frac{1}{2}\times5(4^2 - 2^2) = 50 + 30 = 80$ J.

446. C is correct. $W = mgh$. Because there is no friction, and the work is done against the conservative force of gravity, the work done is independent of the path taken. Warning: work is not a state function.

447. C is correct. $F = mg\sin\theta$; $\sin\theta = o/h = 7/21$

448. C is correct. This question has more calculations than would typically be found on the MCAT. However, it allows you to put several concepts together. Find the net force on the inclined plane, set this equal to ma. Remember that the sine is the opposite over the hypotenuse. Since force is constant for 4 seconds, we can use the uniform accelerated motion equations to find the distance.

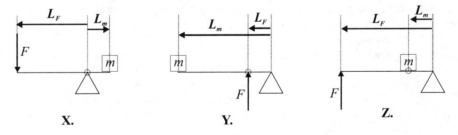

$F_{net} = F - mg\sin\theta = ma$

$d = \frac{1}{2}at^2$

$\sin\theta = \dfrac{h}{d}$

$d = \dfrac{1}{2}\dfrac{F - mg\dfrac{h}{d}}{m}t^2$

449. A is correct. $F = mg\sin\theta$; $\sin\theta = o/h = 4/36$

450. B is correct. If we define the lever arm as the distance from the rotational point to the point where the force is applied (in this case, all forces are perpendicular to all lever arms), then torque is force times lever arm: $\tau = Fl$. The lever arms for each lever are shown below. The lever arm for force F in X is 0.75 m, in Y it is 0.25 m, and in Z it is 1 m. The lever arm for the weight, mg, in X is 0.25 m, in Y it is 1 m, in Z it is 0.25 m. Since only in Y is the lever arm for the weight greater than the lever arm for the force, only Y requires a force greater than mg.

L_F L_m	L_m L_F	L_F L_m
X.	**Y.**	**Z.**

451. C is correct. Since the lever arm is inversely proportional to the force, the least force will be required by the lever with the greatest ratio for the lever arms of the force vs. the weight. See question #450.

452. A is correct. The minimum force is when the net force on the mass is zero so that the mass can move at a constant velocity. The net force will be zero when the net torque is zero. Setting the torques applied by the force and the weight equal to each other, we have: $Fl_{force} = mgl_{weight}$. See question #450 for the lever arms.

453. B is correct. The minimum force is when the net force on the mass is zero so that the mass can move at a constant velocity. The net force will be zero when the net torque is zero. Setting the torques applied by the force and the weight equal to each other, we have: $Fl_{force} = mgl_{weight}$. See question #450 for the lever arms.

454. D is correct. The minimum force is when the net force on the mass is zero so that the mass can move at a constant velocity. The net force will be zero when the net torque is zero. Setting the torques applied by the force and the weight equal to each other, we have: $Fl_{force} = mgl_{weight}$. See question #450 for the lever arms.

455. D is correct. An ideal machine can't change work. The force required by each lever would be different, but the work would be mgh for all the levers.

456. D is correct. The work done by each lever is the force times the distance over which the force was applied. Notice that the final height of each mass would be different, but the smallest mass would make up for lack of gravitational potential energy by having greater kinetic energy.

457. B is correct. The distance traveled by each mass is related to the ratio of its lever arms. To visualize this, simply turn any lever 90° and compare the distance traveled by the weight to the distance through which the force was applied. (Remember: the circumference of a circle is proportional to the radius: $C = 2\pi r$.) Since the lever arm for the force on Y is three times smaller than the lever arm for the weight, the mass travels three times farther than the distance through which the force is applied. In X the mass travels three times shorter; in Z, four times shorter.

458. C is correct. Now the final situation is different for each lever; the masses have different velocities. This is because the levers do not change work; the energy transferred into each mass is the same. Thus, the masses that change their height the most, have the smallest change in kinetic energy.

459. C is correct. As drawn, the table can only rotate about either point where the table legs meet the floor. It will only rotate if there is a net torque. The normal force on the table due to the ground is always equal and opposite to the weight of the man and table. This normal force is distributed evenly, or unevenly, between the table legs depending upon where the man positions his center of gravity. Lets choose the bottom of the left table leg as the point of rotation. As the man moves his center of gravity to the left the clockwise torque about this point is lessened; however, at the same time the normal force becomes greater on the left leg reducing the normal force on the right leg and reducing the counterclockwise torque made by the right table leg. Only if the man places his center of gravity to the left of the left table leg, can he defeat this compensation mechanism. This is because the normal force on the right table leg can only reduce to zero, and cannot be negative. Thus the right table leg can compensate for a decrease in clockwise torque, but it cannot compensate for the increase in counterclockwise torque that occurs when the man places his center of gravity to the left of the left table leg. No matter how hard the man pulls upward, his feet push downward with an equal and opposite increase in force. The net force applied by the man to the table is simply his weight, which must act in line with his center of gravity.

460. A is correct. We choose the point of rotation at the left end of the sheet. The center of gravity of the sheet is at its geometric center, so mg acts here creating a clockwise torque of 10,000 x 5. In order to lift the sheet at constant velocity, the tension T must create a counter clockwise torque of T x 10 equal to the clockwise torque.

461. A is correct. We choose the point of rotation at the left end of the sheet. The center of gravity of the sheet is at its geometric center, so mg acts here creating a clockwise torque of 10,000 x 5. The box creates a clockwise torque due to its weight times the lever arm: 1000 x 2. In order to lift the sheet at constant velocity, the tension T must create a counter clockwise torque of T x 10 equal to the clockwise torque.

462. C is correct. We choose the point of rotation at the left end of the sheet. The center of gravity of the sheet is at its geometric center, so mg acts here creating a clockwise torque of 10,000 x 5. The box creates a clockwise torque due to its weight times the lever arm: 1000 x 8. In order to lift the sheet at constant velocity, the tension T must create a counter clockwise torque of T x 10 equal to the clockwise torque.

463. D is correct. This problem is similar to question #459. The net force applied by the crane is its own weight, and must act in a vertical line with its center of gravity. No matter how hard the tension pulls up on the sheet, an equal an opposite increase in downward force occurs where the crane touches the sheet. Since the direction and position of the net force remains the same, the net torque remains the same, or zero.

464. D is correct. The tension in a single rope in an ideal pulley is the same throughout the rope. The force necessary to lift the mass is mg.

465. C is correct. The rope acting on the mass must have a tension mg in order to lift it. The lower pulley does not move relative to the mass, so the net force on this pulley must be zero. Since there are two tensions acting upward, their sum must be equal to mg. The two upward tensions must be equal to each other and equal to F because tension in a single rope in an ideal pulley is the same throughout the rope.

466. C is correct. The angle of the rope does not change this problem from the previous one. See the previous explanation for the answer.

467. D is correct. The tension in a single rope in an ideal pulley is the same throughout the rope. The force necessary to lift the mass is mg.

468. B is correct. The total tension in the ropes attached to mass must by equal to mg. Thus, the tension in each rope attached to the block is 30 N. Now examine only one of the pulleys attached to one of the ropes tied to the mass. This pulley does not move relative to the mass. Thus the net force on this pulley must be zero. Since there are two tensions acting upward, their sum must be equal to 30 N. The two upward tensions must be equal to each other and equal to *F* because tension in a single rope in an ideal pulley is the same throughout the rope.

469. B is correct. The rope acting on the mass must have a tension *mg* in order to lift it. The pulley does not move relative to the mass, so the net force on this pulley must be zero. Since there are two tensions acting upward, their sum must be equal to *mg*. The two upward tensions must be equal to each other and equal to *F* because tension in a single rope in an ideal pulley is the same throughout the rope.

470. C is correct. The rope acting on the mass must have a tension *mg* in order to lift it. The pulley does not move relative to the mass, so the net force on this pulley must be zero. Thus the tension upward must be equal to *mg*. The tension upward is $T\sin\theta$. The two upward tensions must be equal to each other and equal to *F* because tension in a single rope in an ideal pulley is the same throughout the rope. Thus $2T\sin\theta = mg$. $\sin 30^o = 0.5$

471. B is correct. Examine each mass as a separate system, starting with the mass on the left. Here $T + m2a = mg$ because the mass will accelerate downward at twice the acceleration of the other mass. The equation for the second mass is $2T = mg + ma$. Substituting for a in the first equation we have $T + m2[(2T - mg)/m] = mg$. This reduces to $5T - 2mg = mg$. $T = {}^3\!/_5\, mg$.

472. B is correct. This is the same question as the previous question with the normal force of the platform being analogous to the tension in the ropes of the pulley. The ideal machine inside the box might as well be the pulley of the last question. If the masses on both platforms are the same, the equation applies in the explanation to question 471 applies.

473. B is correct. From questions 472, we know that the normal force upward on the man is 600 N. Thus the net force is the weight of the man minus the normal force $1000 - 600$. $F = ma$. MCAT will probably not get this difficult, but this is a good problem for understanding.

474. C is correct. From questions 473 we know that platform 1 accelerates at 4 m/s^2 and platform 2 accelerates at 2 m/s^2. $x = \frac{1}{2}at^2$.

475. B is correct. As atomic weight goes up, the ratio of neutrons to protons for a stable atom increases up to as much as a 1.8:1 ratio.

476. B is correct. This is the best answer. Beta decay, alpha decay, and positron emission are all forms of radioactive decay. Energy is released because the atoms are converting to a more stable form.

477. D is correct. Definitional.

478. A is correct. A half-life is the time required for half the amount of a substance to decay.

479. C is correct. After on half-life ½ of a substance remains. In the next half-life, half of this or ¼ of the substance decays. This means that ¾ of the original amount decays in two half-lives.

480. D is correct. 2 hours is 4 half-lives of a substance with a 30 minute half-life. Going backwards, we double the final amount four times or 10x2x2x2x2 = 160.

481. A is correct. 2 days is 4 half-lives of a substance with a 12 hour half-life. Going forwards, we divide the initial amount by 2 four times or 400 x ½ x ½ x ½ x ½ = 25.

482. B is correct. Divide 240 grams by 2 until you get close to 30 g. 240/2 = 120; 120/2 = 60; 60/2 = 30. This represents 3 half-lives. 300 days/3 half-lives = 100 days/half-life.

483. B is correct. Divide 384 grams by 2 until you get close to 12 g. 384/2 = 192; 192/2 = 96; 96/2 = 48; 48/2 = 24; 24/2 = 12. This represents 5 half-lives. 5 half-lives x 10 hrs/half-life = 50 hrs.

484. D is correct. 15.15 minutes is 5 half-lives. 109/2 = 54.5; 54.5/2 = 27.25; 27.25/2 = 13.625; 13.625/2 ≈ 7; 7/2 = 3.5. So approximately 3.5 grams of polonium would remain. The rest would be lead and a very small amount of alpha particles. Thus, 109 − 3.5 = 105.5. 103.7 is the best answer.

485. A is correct. Subtract four from the mass number and 2 from the atomic number of U-238. This gives answer A.

486. A is correct. Since a negative charge (the beta particle) is created, a positive charge must also be created in order to maintain conservation of charge of the universe.

487. C is correct. Since a positive charge is created, a positive charge must be destroyed in order to conserve the charge of the universe.

488. D is correct. Since a negative charge is destroyed, a positive charge must also be destroyed in order to conserve the charge of the universe.

489. A is correct. The alpha decay removes 4 from the mass number and 2 from the atomic number. Each beta decay adds 1 to the atomic number. The net result is a decrease of 4 in the mass number and no change in the atomic number.

490. B is correct. Since the mass number changes by four, it must be alpha decay.

491. A is correct. The alpha decays remove 4 from the mass number and 2 from the atomic number with each decay. 7 times 4 is 28 and 7 times 2 is 14. Each beta decay adds 1 to the atomic number. The net result is a decrease of 28 in the mass number and a decrease of 8 in the atomic number. Count backwards 8 elements from U to find the identity of the new element.

492. A is correct. Beta decay does not change the mass number, but increases the atomic number by 1.

493. D is correct. Beta particle production is beta decay. Beta decay does not change the mass number, but increases the atomic number by 1.

494. A is correct. Since mass number changes by four, answer A is the easy answer.

495. B is correct. Positron emission results in a decrease of 1 in the atomic number and no change in the mass number.

496. B is correct. Electron capture results in a decrease of 1 in atomic number and no change in mass number.

497. B is correct. Alpha decay results in a decrease in mass number of four and a decrease in atomic number of 2.

498. A is correct. Gamma rays are photons.

499. A is correct. 335 hrs /67 hrs/half-life = 5 half-lives. $1000/2 = 500$; $500/2 = 250$; $250/2 = 125$; $125/2 = 56.5$; $56.5/2 = 28.25$. Close enough.

500. D is correct. The some of the contents will decay into something else, but the mass is conserved.

501. B is correct. Some of the mass of the complete atom is used as binding energy from the equation $E = mc^2$.

502. D is correct. Definitional.

503. D is correct. $E = mc^2$ gives you the number of joules. A volt is a joule per coulomb. Convert joules to electronvolts by dividing by 1.6×10^{-19} coulombs per charge on an electron.

504. C is correct. Iron has the greatest binding energy per nucleon. As mass number increases toward iron, binding energy generally increases, but as mass number increases away from iron, binding energy generally decreases.

505. C is correct. Iron-56 has the greatest binding energy per nucleon.

506. D is correct. U-235 is larger than iron-56, so it likely to undergo fission.

507. A is correct. Of the choices, only the hydrogen is smaller than iron-56, so it is the only one that is likely to undergo fusion.

508. B is correct. Hydrogen and helium are both light molecules so they will not release energy upon fission. Nuclear fusion releases energy from the sun.

509. B is correct. The energy of the sun comes from its rest mass energy: $E = mc^2$.

Lecture 5

510. C is correct. The MCAT answer is C. Molecules of an ideal gas do not experience forces. In a real gas, the forces are extremely small.

511. B is correct. The MCAT answer is B. Molecules of an ideal gas do not experience forces. In a real gas, the forces are extremely small. Molecules of a solid are bonded together permanently.

512. D is correct. All phases are capable of withstanding forces perpendicular to their surfaces. For instance, a gas can withstand the force of a stretched balloon. Only solids can permanently withstand forces that are not perpendicular to its surface.

513. A is correct. All phases are capable of withstanding forces perpendicular to their surfaces. For instance, a gas can withstand the force of a stretched balloon. Only solids can permanently withstand forces that are not perpendicular to its surface. This is because the only the bonds in a solid are not continually breaking and reforming.

514. C is correct. Water, a fluid, can permanently withstand only those forces that perpendicular to its surface.

515. A is correct. Although the water will have temporal resistance to the force due to its viscosity, it has no permanent resistance, and the boat will accelerate regardless of how small the force. However, the resistance will cause this acceleration to be less than F/m.

516. C is correct. All mass is affected by gravity. Gas particles move so fast and for such short distances, that the projectile path of the particle is nearly, but not quite, a straight line for its short trip.

517. A is correct. The extensive properties, which depend upon quantity, change; the intensive properties, which are intrinsic to the substance and not dependant upon quantity, do not change.

518. C is correct. Gases are easily compressible, creating a change in their densities. Liquids are thousands of times less compressible, and solids still thousands of times less so than liquids.

519. A is correct. Gasses are many times more compressible than liquids or solids.

520. A is correct. Gasses are many times more compressible than liquids or solids. When the gas is compressed, there is a change in volume resulting in a change in density.

521. C is correct. Again, gas is the most compressible.

522. C is correct. Projectile motion, even of a fluid, is independent of mass. Air resistance is negligible.

523. A is correct. No calculations are required. The alcohol jugs are lighter, so the machine could do the work more quickly. Power equals work per unit time. Work in this case is change in potential energy. Each jug of alcohol weighs 0.8 times as much as each water jug. Since power is constant, we must multiply time by 0.8 as well.

524. C is correct. Density and volume are inversely related. $\rho = m/V$

525. B is correct. The volume and mass remained the same, so the density remains the same. $\rho = m/V$

526. C is correct. In order to double the pressure, from $PV = nRT$, we know that the number of molecules was also doubled. This means that the mass was doubled without changing the volume. Density is directly proportional to mass. $\rho = m/V$

527. C is correct. You should know that ice is less dense than water. This means that the volume will decrease when ice melts. Thus the answer must be C or D. To find the exact volume ratio, use the specific gravity as follows.

$$m_{water} = m_{ice} \qquad 0.9 = \frac{\rho_{ice}}{\rho_{water}} = \frac{\dfrac{m_{ice}}{V_{ice}}}{\dfrac{m_{water}}{V_{water}}} = \frac{V_{water}}{V_{ice}}$$

528. B is correct. Water expands when it freezes. Only B can be correct.

529. A is correct. 1 L of water has a mass of approximately 1 kg at 25 $^{\circ}$C. This is a fact that you should know.

530. C is correct. The density of water is 1 g/cm^3. 12 grams of water divided by the density gives 12 cm^3.

531. A is correct. Since mercury has a specific gravity of 13.6, it has a density 13.6 times greater than water. 1 gram of water occupies 1 cm^3, so the same volume of mercury has 13.6 times as much mass.

532. B is correct. Water has a density of 1000 g/m^3. Lead is 11.6 times heavier, so the specific gravity of lead is 11.6.

533. B is correct. Density is mass divided by volume. The volume of the wood is 5x3x10=150 cm^3. 90 g/ 150 cm^3 = 0.6 g/cm^3 = 600 kg/m^3. (10^6 cm^3 = 1 m^3)

534. A is correct. Density is an intensive property, so it is independent of the amount of substance. The density of the second block is the same as the density of the first. Density is mass divided by volume. The volume of the first block is 4x3x10=120 cm^3. 60 g/ 120 cm^3 = 0.5 g/cm^3 = 500 kg/m^3. (10^6 cm^3 = 1 m^3)

535. A is correct. Density is mass divided by volume. The volume of the first block is 4x3x10=120 cm^3. 60 g/ 120 cm^3 = 0.5 g/cm^3 which is half the density of water.

536. D is correct. 760 mmHg approximates atmospheric pressure at sea level. (Note: 101,000 Pa is a closer approximation than 10^5 Pa, but less convenient for the MCAT.

537. B is correct. 1 Pa = 1/10^5 atm. 1 torr = 1/760 atm. 1 mmHg = 1/760 atm.

538. A is correct. Pressure is force per unit area.

539. C is correct. Pressure is defined such that the fluid pressure is independent of any submerged object. One such definition is the random kinetic energy of the molecules per unit volume.

540. A is correct. The gauge pressure is measured relative to atmospheric pressure. Thus we call atmospheric pressure zero. The pressure is independent of the depth of the pool, but dependent upon the depth at which the pressure is measured. It is a good idea to know that 10 m of water creates approximately 1 atm of pressure. $P = \rho gh$ = 1000 kg/m^3 x 10 m/s^2 x 10 m = 10^5 Pa = 1 atm.

541. B is correct. Now the diver is 20 m from the top. 10 m of water creates approximately 1 atm of pressure. $P = \rho gh$ = 1000 kg/m^3 x 10 m/s^2 x 20 m = 2x10^5 Pa

542. C is correct. Absolute pressure is gauge pressure plus the local atmospheric pressure. From question 540 we know that the gauge pressure is 10^5 Pa. Adding 10^5 Pa for the local atmosphere gives 2x10^5.

543. B is correct. Absolute pressure is never negative. The pressure inside the chest of a person inhaling is less than local atmospheric pressure, so 0.9 atm is the best answer.

544. C is correct. It is a good idea to know that 10 m of water creates approximately 1 atm of pressure. $P = \rho gh$ = 1000 kg/m^3 x 10 m/s^2 x 10 m = 10^5 Pa = 1 atm.

545. C is correct. The pressure at the bottom of the cylinder would be due to the weight of the air inside the cylinder. We know that this pressure is 1 atm, so $P = F/A = mg/A$ = 1 atm = 1.01x10^5 Pa. m = 1.01x10^4 kg.

546. C is correct. The heavier, or more dense, fluids will sink.

547. B is correct. Pressure is the total weight of the fluids directly over a given area divided by that area. p_2 has the most fluid above it, so it has the greatest pressure.

548. C is correct. The total pressure at a given point is due to the sum of the pressures created by all the fluids above that point regardless of the shape of the container. Fluids 1, 2, and atmospheric pressure are above p_3, so the pressure at p_3 is $\rho_1 gh$ + $\rho_2 gh$ + atm. = (500 kg/m^3 x 10 m/s^2 x 10 m) + (1000 kg/m^3 x 10 m/s^2 x 10 m) + 1 atm. Don't forget the 1 atm due to the local atmosphere.

549. B is correct. The total pressure at a given point is due to the sum of the pressures created by all the fluids above that point regardless of the shape of the container. Fluids 1, 2, 3, 5 m of fluid 4, and atmospheric pressure are above p_2, so the pressure at p_2 is $\rho_1 gh$ + $\rho_2 gh$ + $\rho_3 gh$ + $\rho_4 gh$ + atm. = (500 kg/m^3 x 10 m/s^2 x 10 m) + (1000 kg/m^3 x 10 m/s^2 x 10 m) + (2000 kg/m^3 x 10 m/s^2 x 10 m) + (4000 kg/m^3 x 10 m/s^2 x 5 m) + 1 atm. Don't forget the 1 atm due to the local atmosphere.

550. C is correct. The apparent weight loss is due to the buoyant force. The buoyant force is equal to the weight of the fluid displaced. The volume of fluid displaced is equal to the volume of the object. Since the actual weight of the object is 3 times the buoyant force, the object must have a density three times greater than the fluid, or a specific gravity three times greater than the fluid.

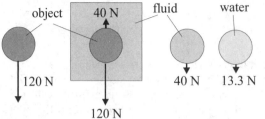

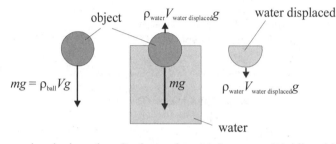

551. B is correct. The ball is ¾ as dense as water, so ¼ of the ball will float above the water. We can prove this by setting the buoyant force equal to the weight since the ball is in static equilibrium. $\rho_{ball}gV_{ball} = mg$. $\rho_{ball}gV_{ball} = \rho_{water}gV_{water\ displaced}$. The g's cancel, and after some algebra, we get $\rho_{ball}/\rho_{water} = V_{water\ displaced}/V_{ball}$. $= 750\ kg/m^3/1000\ kg/m^3$. $V_{water\ displaced}/V_{ball}$ is the fraction of the ball underwater. The rest of the ball is, of course, above water.

552. A is correct. M is grams per mol and n is moles. So the product Mn is grams. Dividing this by volume gives the density. From $PV = nRT$, we have $V = nRT/P$. Thus, density is PM/RT.

553. B is correct. Gases at the same pressure have the same number of particles, so air particles are, on average, 7 times more massive than helium. The volume of the balloon will be the same as the volume of displaced air at all altitudes, thus we need to have 7 times more helium in the same volume in order for helium to have the same density as air. From the equation for buoyant force we have: $\rho_{helium}Vg = \rho_{air}Vg$. If we have 7 times as many helium particles in the same volume, we must have 7 times the pressure.

554. C is correct. Of course the hot air balloon also follows the buoyant force equation: $\rho_{outside\ air}Vg = \rho_{air\ in\ balloon}Vg$. The volumes are equal at all altitudes, so the density will decide whether or not the balloon rises. Since the bottom of the balloon is open to the outside atmosphere, the pressures are equal at all altitudes. From $PV = nRT$, we know that increasing temperature at constant volume and pressure requires reducing the number of moles, and thus reducing the density, raising the balloon.

555. A is correct. The iceberg is 0.9 as dense as water, so 0.1 of the ball will float above the water. We can prove this by setting the buoyant force equal to the weight since the iceberg is in static equilibrium. $\rho_{ice}gV_{ice} = mg$. $\rho_{ice}gV_{ice} = \rho_{water}gV_{water\ displaced}$. The g's cancel, and after some algebra, we get $\rho_{ice}/\rho_{water} = V_{water\ displaced}/V_{ice}$. $= 900\ kg/m^3/1000\ kg/m^3$. $V_{water\ displaced}/V_{ice}$ is the fraction of the ice underwater. The rest of the ball is, of course, above water. Multiply by 100 to get percent.

556. B is correct. When the brick sinks, it displaces only its volume in water. When the brick is floated on Styrofoam, it displaces a volume of water equal to its weight. Since the brick is more dense than water, a greater volume of water is required to equal the weight of the brick.

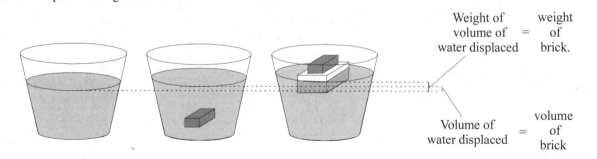

Weight of volume of water displaced = weight of brick.

Volume of water displaced = volume of brick

557. B is correct. All the battleship must do in order to float is to displace an amount of water equal to its mass. Since the buoyant force is actually created by pressure differences, and pressure is an intensive property (independent of amount), the water displaced does not have to remain in the pool with the battleship. The pressure is dependent upon depth, not volume.

558. C is correct. The apparent weight loss (250 N – 200 N = 50 N) is due to the buoyant force. The buoyant force is equal to the weight of the fluid displaced. The volume of fluid displaced is equal to the volume of the object. Since the actual weight of the object is 5 times the buoyant force, the object must have a density five times greater than the fluid, or a specific gravity five times greater than the fluid. (see question #550)

559. B is correct. Atmospheric pressure pushes the water up through the siphon, thus $P_{atmos.} = \rho gy$, where y is the height from the surface of the liquid to the top of the siphon. At a greater height than h, the absolute pressure would be lower than zero; an impossibility. (Remember: 10 meters of water creates 1 atm of pressure.)

560. B is correct. Same explanation as previous question.

561. C is correct. The absolute pressure in the siphon while the fluid is not moving is $1 \text{atm} - \rho gy$, where y is the difference between the liquid's surface and the point being measured in the siphon. A quick way to do this problem is to recognize that 10 m of water creates 1 atm.

562. D is correct. The pressure at the bottom is independent of the height of the siphon. The absolute pressure at the bottom of the container is given by $P = \rho gh + 1$ atm. (5 m of water creates approximately ½ atm.)

563. C is correct. Vacuums don't suck. Instead, this vacuum prevents atmospheric pressure from pushing down on one square centimeter of the top of the block. Thus the difference in the atmospheric pressure above and below the block is equal to the force applied by atmospheric pressure over one square centimeter. $F/A = P$. Thus $F = 10^5 \times 10^{-4}$. 10 N will lift 1 kg.

564. B is correct. The buoyant force pushes up at the center of the raft and is equal in magnitude to the total weight of the raft and man. If we choose the center of the raft as the point of rotation in a torque problem, the mass of the metal pushes down with a force of 1000 N and a lever arm of 2.5 m; the man pushes down with a force of 750 N and a lever arm of x. From $\tau_{counterclockwise} = \tau_{clockwise}$, we have $2500/750 = x$. x is the distance from the center; the question asks for the distance from the right side, which is $10 - (x + 5) = 1.67$.

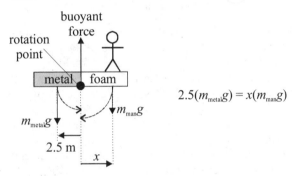

$$2.5(m_{metal}g) = x(m_{man}g)$$

565. D is correct. The pressure due to the fluid encompassed by h plus atmospheric pressure balances the pressure of the gas, thus $P_{gas} = \rho_{fluid}gh + P_{atmos.}$ $(0.8 \times 10^3 \times 10 \times 0.2) + 101,000 = 102,600$.

566. D is correct. Accelerating the container upward has the same affect as making the gravitational constant g greater. To see this, imagine standing on a scale inside an elevator as it accelerates upward. Your apparent weight mg is greater, but your mass remains the constant. To find the tension in the string when there is no acceleration, we set the buoyant force equal to tension plus weight: $\rho Vg = T + mg$. Since accelerating the container upward is equivalent to increasing g, we can increase g to see what happens. We see from the equation that doubling g will double the left side of the equation (the upward force), but it will not double the right side (the downward forces). In order to maintain equality, we must increase T. Thus T increases when we accelerate the container upward. Try plugging in some simple numbers to see for yourself. (Note: Notice that the buoyant force is not equal to ρVg when the fluid is accelerating.)

567. C is correct. If we assume constant density for both the solid and liquid, the buoyant force is equal to the weight of the fluid that the object displaces. The object displaces a volume of fluid equal to its own volume. Since densities don't change, the weight and amount of fluid displaced doesn't change, and the buoyant force remains constant.

568. A is correct. We can use an ideal fluid to approximate a real fluid. The energy of an ideal fluid is conserved as it flows. If the molecules have the same gravitational potential energy (which they would in a horizontal pipe), and greater kinetic energy due to greater uniform velocity, then they must have less kinetic energy due to random translational motion.

569. A is correct. From question #567, and from K.E. = 3/2 RT, where K.E. is the kinetic energy due to random translational motion of molecules and <u>not</u> their uniform velocity, we can conclude that the temperature is decreased when fluid velocity increases.

570. D is correct. When velocity decreases, the pressure goes up. When the temperature ($PV = nRT$), density, or cross-sectional area of pipe decreases the pressure goes down.

571. A is correct. $\Delta mv = F_{avg}\Delta t$. $P = F/A$. => $P = \Delta mv/A\Delta t$

572. C is correct. Volume flow rate remains constant in an ideal fluid.

573. B is correct. This is a characteristic of an ideal gas in the kinetic molecular theory, <u>not</u> an ideal fluid.

574. B is correct. The continuity equation $Q = Av$ shows that velocity is inversely proportional to cross-sectional area.

575. A is correct. The direction of flow for an ideal fluid cannot be determined by pressure changes. Even for a real fluid, other factors must be considered.

576. C is correct. The volume of fluid passing any point in a given second is the flow rate. For an ideal fluid the flow rate is independent of the length of the pipe. An ideal fluid obeys the continuity equation $Q = Av$. Since $A = \pi r^2$, doubling r will increase A by a factor of four, which will reduce v by a factor of four.

577. D is correct. The distance above the top of each fluid is related to $\frac{1}{2}\rho v^2 + 1$ atm. From $Q = Av$, we know that the velocities at a and c are equal and both larger than the velocity at b. Thus h_1 and h_3 rise to the same height, and h_2 rises higher than either.

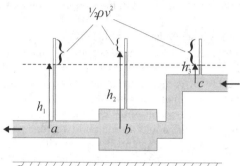

Diagram drawn to scale

578. D is correct. From $Q = Av$, we know that the velocities at a and c are equal and both larger than the velocity at b.

579. D is correct. The volume flow rate is constant throughout an ideal fluid.

580. C is correct. Pressure is proportional to either the kinetic energy in the random motions of the molecules or to the momentum represented in the random motion of the molecules. Both of these are proportional to the mass.

581. B is correct. The pressure at a given point in the small pipes would double, but twice as much pressure would be required to support the same volume of the heavier fluid.

582. A is correct. The fluid would not flow up and out of the pipes because the opening the tops would increase the pressure by 1 atm and thus increase the force downward. This would decrease each h.

583. A is correct. The pressure at the opening of the spigot is equal to atmospheric pressure.

584. C is correct. The energy of the water is equal everywhere. At the opening of the spigot, each water molecule has lost a potential energy of mgh, so it has gained an equal amount of kinetic energy $\frac{1}{2}mv^2$. Setting these equal and solving for velocity gives: $v = \sqrt{2gh}$.

585. C is correct. $P = \rho gh + 1$ atm. We assume that the velocity of the water at b is very nearly zero.

586. C is correct. The water behaves like a projectile. The time required to fall a distance $\frac{1}{4}h$ times the average horizontal velocity gives the distance d. From question #584 we know that the horizontal velocity is $\sqrt{2gh}$. From $x = v_0t + \frac{1}{2}at^2$, we have $\frac{1}{4}h = \frac{1}{2}gt^2$. Solving for t in the we get $t = \sqrt{\frac{1}{2}h/g}$. Thus $d = vt = \sqrt{2gh}\sqrt{\frac{1}{2}h/g} = \sqrt{(h^2)} = h$

587. B is correct. The weight of a projectile does not change its path. The path followed by the mercury would be the same as that followed by water. Notice that the equation for d in question #586 does not depend upon the mass or density of the fluid.

588. B is correct. $P = \rho gh + 1$ atm. If the pressure is 2 atm with water, then the guage pressure of water (ρgh) is 1 atm. The density of mercury is 13.6 times greater than water, so the gauge pressure would be 13.6 times greater. Adding the 1 atm gives 14.6 atm.

589. A is correct. The velocity would be the same because the velocity is independent of the mass or density of the fluid. (see question #584)

590. B is correct. $v = \sqrt{2gh}$, so $h = v^2/(2g)$

591. D is correct. Of course h decreases over time as the fluid drains. h is proportional to the volume above the spigot: $V = hA_c$. The volume flow rate Q is change in volume (or the volume lost from the container) over time so $Q = \Delta V/t = \Delta hA_c/t$. $\Delta h/t$ is the slope of the curve. Volume flow rate is also $Q = Av$, and we know from $v = \sqrt{2gh}$ that v decreases with time because h decreases with time. Thus, Q decreases with time and the slope decreases with time. Choice B has a slope that increases with time, and choice C has a constant slope.

592. D is correct. In an ideal fluid, pressure alone does not dictate the direction of flow. See questions #597-599.

593. B is correct. The difference in pressure between the two sides of the horizontal section of pipe is $P_1 - P_2 = \rho gy_1 - \rho gy_2$ where y_1 and y_2 are the depths in the respective tanks. This difference in pressure does work on the fluid per unit volume which is $\frac{1}{2}\rho v^2$. This gives $\rho gy_1 - \rho gy_2 = \frac{1}{2}\rho v^2$. The ρs cancel leaving; $g(y_1 - y_2) = \frac{1}{2}v^2$.

594. B is correct. What flows in, must flow out. 11 cm³/s flow into the pipe, and only 6 cm³/s are shown flowing out. 5 cm³/s more must be flowing out at end *a*.

595. D is correct. According to the Bernoulli's Equation, the velocities must be v = sqrt($2gh$). But if the velocities are the same, the flow rate must be greater at the larger spigot. Doesn't this violate the rule that volume flow rate is the same at all points in a conduit of ideal fluid? No. The volume flow rate rule says that volume of fluid flowing in must be equal to volume flowing out. For instance, imagine putting a vertical divider along the length of spigot *b*. You would not expect to change the velocity just because you divided the flow. This is a similar situation.

596. C is correct. Viscosity is created by intermolecular bonding.

597. C is correct. This is a horizontal pipe with constant cross-sectional area. In this simple case, fluid moves from high pressure to low pressure. Compare this to questions #598 and #599.

598. D is correct. The pressure is greater at the bottom of Tank *B* pushing water toward Tank *A*. See question #599.

599. B is correct. Questions 597, 598, and 599 are purposely placed in this order. Pressure is not the only thing driving fluid flow. Notice that the fluid moves in the direction of greater pressure in 599. A fluid flows in the direction that will dissipate its energy between gravity, velocity, and pressure. Often, it is easier to intuit the direction of flow than to find it mathematically.

600. B is correct. The air near the ball is dragged forward and collides with the air flowing past the ball creating a mass of slow moving air. Slow moving air has high pressure. On the other side of the ball, the air flows quickly past, creating a low pressure system. Greater pressure on one side of the ball pushes it to the left.

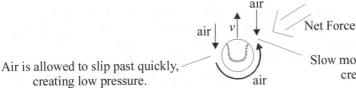

Air is allowed to slip past quickly, creating low pressure.

Slow moving air cushion builds here creating higher pressure.

601. D is correct. The viscous fluid drags along the sides of the pipe and is therefore slowed near the sides. However, even in a real fluid, the fluid must maintain its velocity or it will back up and the pipe will explode.

602. B is correct. Viscosity creates resistance toward the outer edge of flow. The resistance is countered exactly by an increase in pressure.

603. D is correct. Ignoring viscosity, the flow rate would be doubled for the first container: $Q = Av$. The viscosity has a greater effect on the narrower funnel. Thus the second container requires more than twice the time to fill.

604. B is correct. The velocity must be the lowest where the cross-sectional area is the greatest; $Q = Av$.

605. D is correct. In horizontal, viscous flow, pressure is analogous to voltage, both decrease in the direction of flow or current. $\Delta P = QR$ and $V = IR$. (Note: actually the cross-sectional area must also be constant in order to accurately apply the equation: $\Delta P = QR$.. However, the blood pressure drops fairly steadily as we move away form the heart.)

606. D is correct. The volume of blood flowing past a given section of the circulatory system must be the same, or there would be a buildup of blood at the lowest point, leading to an bursting of the vessel.

607. B is correct. The capillaries have the largest area, so, according to $Q = Av$ they would have the lowest velocity and according to Bernoulli's equation, they would have the greatest pressure.

608. B is correct. A is not a bad answer, but the major component is the cohesive forces between the molecules. The stream would form in the absence of atmospheric pressure.

609. B is correct. The attraction between the fluid molecules and the glass molecules pull the fluid up the tube. This is called *capillary action*.

610. C is correct. The attraction between the fluid molecules pull the fluid inward and down.

611. A is correct. Stress is the force applied to a solid divided its cross-sectional area; strain is the fractional change in some dimension of the solid.

612. D is correct. Strain the way in which an object responds to stress.

613. A is correct. This is the definition of a modulus.

614. C is correct. Although the shape of an object will change how it responds to stress, a modulus does not take shape into account. A modulus considers only the substance of the object and is a good approximation only up to a certain maximum stress called the yield point.

615. C is correct. Changing the temperature of a substance changes how it responds to stress, and thus changes its modulus elasticity.

616. B is correct. Since the force is proportional to the distance over which the object is deformed, the force is conservative. (Position dependent forces are always conservative.) Conservative means that the force conserves mechanical energy.

617. B is correct. The question asks for stress, not force. Stress is force per unit area, so the area of each object is irrelevant. The length is also irrelevant. Thus we just compare the ultimate strengths in the table. The ultimate strength is the greatest amount of stress an object can withstand without breaking.

618. B is correct. Typically the Young's modulus is inaccurate after the yield point is reached, which is before the fracture point is reached. However, the paragraph says to assume that the substances obey Young's modulus until they break. Use the ultimate strength (400×10^6 N/m^2) as the stress. Divide by the fractional change in length and set this equal to Young's modulus. Y = stress/fractional change in length.

619. D is correct. From question #618 we see that the maximum fractional change in length is the Ultimate strength divided by the Young's modulus.

620. C is correct. From the Table, the ultimate strength of concrete is 40×10^6 N/m^2. This is the maximum pressure that the concrete will withstand. $P = \rho g h$. $40 \times 10^6 = 2320 \times 10 \times h$.

621. D is correct. If each substance behaves according to its Young's Modulus until the breaking point (a somewhat unreal expectation), we can set the Young's modulus equal to the ultimate strength (stress) divided by the fractional change in length (strain). Solving for fractional change in length, bone has the greatest ratio of ultimate strength vs. Young's Modulus.

622. B is correct. This is the same as question #621 except that we look for the smallest fractional change in length. Glass is the smallest.

623. B is correct. To discover if the glass breaks, we see if her weight creates a pressure greater than the ultimate strength of glass. Her weight of 650 N distributed over 1 cm^2 = 0.0001 m^2 creates a pressure of 6.5×10^6 N, a pressure less than the ultimate strength of glass.

624. B is correct. This is a straight Young's modulus problem. The weight divided by the cross-sectional area of the beam is the stress applied to the beam. The change in length divided by the original length is the strain. Young's modulus = stress over strain: $Y = (F/A)/(\Delta l /l)$. 13×10^9 N/m^2 = $(1.3 \times 10^5$ N / 0.001 m$^2)/(\Delta l / 3$ m) : $\Delta l = 0.03$ m

625. C is correct. From the formula, the original length is directly proportional to the change in length.

626. B is correct. The apparent weight is the actual weight minus the buoyant force. In other words, if we put a lead ball on a scale underwater, the scale would display the apparent weight? The buoyant force is equal to the product of the density of the fluid displaced, the volume of the fluid displaced, and the gravitational constant g. The actual weight is equal to the product of the density of the object, the volume of the object, and the gravitational constant g. Since lead has a lower bulk modulus than water, it has a greater decrease in volume under pressure. This decrease in volume creates an increase in density. As the lead ball sinks and the pressure increases, the density of the lead ball increases faster than the density of water. The volume of the lead ball is always equal to the volume of water displaced, so the difference between the actual weight and the buoyant force increases. Thus, the apparent weight increases. (**Warning:** On the MCAT, fluids are considered incompressible unless otherwise defined, so the buoyant force will be the same at all depths on the MCAT.)

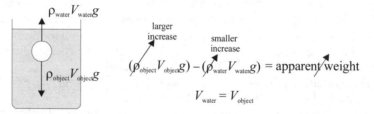

627. B is correct. This is a shear stress, so we use the shear modulus. 40×10^9 N/m^2 = $(F/A)/(\Delta x/h)$. $F = 10^6$ N The area to be used is the top of the block. $A = 4$ m^2. $h = 2$ m. Solve for Δx.

628. A is correct. We use the bulk modulus: $B = P/(\Delta V/V)$. $P = \rho g h = 10^5$ Pa. Thus 140×10^9 N/m^2 = 10^5 Pa / $(\Delta V/V)$ where $\Delta V/V$ is the fractional change in length.

629. C is correct. If we ignored any change in volume, we would have a 13.6 to 1 mass ratio. However, the pressure on the mercury would be 13.6 times greater than the pressure on the water, and mercury has a lower bulk modulus. A lower bulk modulus indicates a greater change in volume for the same amount of pressure and thus a greater change in density. In this case, the density increases with pressure. Thus the density of mercury toward the bottom of the column would be greater than 13.6 times the density of water. Since the volumes are the same, the mass ratio is greater than 13.6 to 1.

630. B is correct. We can manipulate the equation for Young's modulus to be $\Delta l = F l_o/AY$. This problem replaces steel with copper. The Young's modulus for copper is half that of steel, so we are increasing the change in length by a factor of 2. In order to compensate and keep Δl constant, we can reduce the length of the copper rod by a factor of 2. Answer choice A would do the opposite. Answer choice C would increase the cross-sectional area by a factor of 4. Answer choice D would decrease the force by a factor of 4.

631. D is correct. The substance with the lowest bulk modulus will experience the greatest change in volume when exposed to a change in pressure.

632. C is correct. The Young's modulus is a constant. The mercury experiences a change in volume according to the bulk modulus equation. A change in volume creates a change in density, height of the column, and specific gravity.

633. D is correct. 10^5 N/m^2 is equivalent to approximately 1 atm or the pressure created by 10 m of water. Since the object has a specific gravity of 1, the object has the same weight as water. 10 m of the object will create the stress required to break the object.

634. A is correct. Point A holds up the weight of the entire object. The other points hold up only the weight beneath them.

635. D is correct. Object D has the smallest cross-sectional area at the top where the stress is the greatest. Stress = $F/A = mg/A$. A specific substance can withstand a specific amount of stress. Thus mg must be smaller for object D or it will break.

Lecture 6

636. D is correct. The medium of a wave remains undisturbed after the wave has passed; mass is not permanently displaced.

637. A is correct. The time required for one wave to pass a given point is the period. $T = 1/f$.

638. D is correct. $v = f\lambda$ This wave moves 400 m/s.

639. A is correct. $v = f\lambda$

640. A is correct. By definition, the medium of a longitudinal wave moves back and forth parallel to the propagation of the wave, but the final displacement of the medium is zero.

641. B is correct. By definition, the medium of a transverse wave moves back and forth perpendicular to the propagation of the wave.

642. C is correct. $v = f\lambda = d/t : f = d/\lambda t = 100/(0.25 \times 2) = 200$

643. B is correct. $v^2 = T/\mu$ where T is the tension of the rope, and μ is the mass per unit length.

644. D is correct. The velocity of a wave is independent of the wavelength and frequency, and dependent upon the medium through which the wave travels. In other words, changing the frequency of a wave will not change its velocity, but will change its wavelength. In order to change the velocity, the medium must be changed.

645. C is correct. The velocity of a wave is independent of the wavelength, frequency, or amplitude, and dependent upon the medium through which the wave travels. In other words, changing the frequency of a wave will not change its velocity, but will change its wavelength. In order to change the velocity, the medium must be changed.

646. C is correct. The wave function repeats itself every four meters.

647. B is correct. Since the wavelength is 4 m, ½ wavelength would pass a given point each second. This is the frequency. $v = f\lambda$

648. A is correct. Point A is 1 m away from the five meter mark. If the frequency is 2 Hz, 2 waves pass a given point each second. This means that the period is ½ s, or that it would require 0.5 seconds for one wave to pass a given point, or that the wave moves one wavelength every ½ second.

649. C is correct. The amplitude is the maximum displacement, which is 1.5 cm.

650. C is correct. Frequency is independent of amplitude. (Gravity waves are an exception that is unlikely to appear on the MCAT).

651. D is correct. Intensity is directly proportional to the square of the frequency. Since frequency is inversely related to period, increasing the period would decrease the intensity.

652. C is correct. Intensity is the rate of energy transfer over a surface area.

653. B is correct. Ten waves per 60 seconds equals one wave every six seconds.

654. D is correct. Surface waves (or gravity waves) are difficult, and knowledge of surface waves will be limited on the MCAT. Questions 654-658 probably require a little more knowledge than what will be required by the MCAT. In shallow water, the velocity of the surface wave is dictated by the medium and independent of wave length. Thus, $v = f\lambda$. Since the medium is not changed in this question, v is constant for this question: C is incorrect. The restoring force on a pendulum and on a surface wave is gravity. Like the height of a pendulum, the amplitude of the surface wave does not change the period of motion. Period is inversely related to frequency, so frequency is unaffected: B is incorrect. If frequency and velocity are constant, then wavelength is unaffected: A is incorrect. The bobbing of the mass m dictates the height of the wave, which is the amplitude A.

655. B is correct. In order to change v, we must change the medium. For surface waves in shallow water, $v = \text{sqrt}(gh)$ where h is the depth of the water.

656. A is correct. For surface waves in shallow water, $v = \text{sqrt}(gh)$ where h is the depth of the water.

657. A is correct. The wavelength is the distance from peak to peak, or trough to trough.

658. D is correct. $v = \text{sqrt}(gh)$ and $v = f\lambda$. g is smaller on the moon, so velocity would decrease. The frequency is dictated by t, the period. Since t does not change, frequency remains constant and λ must decrease.

659. A is correct. By definition, a sound wave is longitudinal; the medium moves in parallel and antiparallel with the direction of propagation.

660. D is correct. A 10 dB increase is an increase in intensity by a factor of 10, so a 20 dB increase is an increase by a factor of $10 \times 10 = 100$.

661. B is correct. A decrease of intensity level by 10 dB is a decrease in intensity by a factor of 10. Since the sound travels in all directions, it is dissipated over a spherical surface with area $4\pi r^2$. The formula for the relationship between the intensity and the distance r from the source is:

$$I = \frac{P}{4\pi r^2}$$

In order to decrease intensity by a factor of 10, radius must be increased by a factor of the sqrt(10) or 3.16. 3.16 x 40 = 126. Don't do all the math; round the numbers off and choose the closest answer.

662. C is correct. In order to change the velocity of a wave, the medium through which the wave travels must be changed. $v =$ sqrt(T/μ) where T is the tension and μ is the mass per unit length.

663. B is correct. The velocity of sound is given by $v =$ sqrt(β/ρ) where β is the bulk modulus (resistance to change) and ρ is the density. Water's greater density would tend to slow it down. However, it's greater bulk modulus more than compensates for the density. Liquids are thousands of times less compressible than gases, thus their bulk moduli are thousands of times greater.

664. A is correct. In a sound wave, the molecules start at a resting point, move together, move apart, and then move back to their resting point. When they move together, this is high pressure. They move together once each period.

665. B is correct. The medium, not the frequency, dictates the speed of a wave.

666. C is correct. The velocity of the wave is independent of the intensity.

667. D is correct. The formula for dB is dB = 10 log(I/I_o). The units for I cancel.

668. C is correct. Humans do not hear twice the intensity as being twice as loud. Decibels more closely coincide with human perception.

669. B is correct. The intensity of a sound wave is given by $I = \frac{1}{2} \rho \omega^2 A^2 v$ where ρ is the density, ω is the angular frequency ($\omega = 2\pi f$), A is amplitude, and v is velocity. Wavelength is inversely related to frequency, so choice A is wrong.

670. A is correct. This is one of the few wave types where velocity is dictated by a property of the wave. In deep water, surface wave velocity follows the formula: $v =$ sqrt($g\lambda/2\pi$).

671. C is correct. $v =$ sqrt(gy) where y is the depth of the water. Compare this formula for shallow water waves with the formula for deep water waves in question #670.

672. C is correct. Average power and intensity refer to the same thing for waves and may be interchangeable on the MCAT. A tenfold increase in intensity corresponds to an increase of 10 decibels.

673. D is correct. A 20 dB decrease is a decrease in intensity by a factor of 100. Dividing the original intensity by 100 gives 200/100 = 2 W/m^2. This is the new intensity, but the question asks for the change in intensity, which is 198 W/m^2.

674. A is correct. A decrease in intensity of 10 dB is equivalent to a decrease in intensity by a factor of 10. 400/10 = 40 W/m^2.

675. B is correct. An increase in intensity by a factor of 10 is equivalent to an increase of 10 dB.

676. A is correct. Since the molecules must move back and forth in order to carry a sound wave, their speed is a limiting factor to sound velocity through air. Sound velocity through air is slower than, but on the same order as, the root mean square velocity of the molecules.

677. B is correct. $v =$ sqrt(β/ρ); since pressure is related to bulk modulus $v =$ sqrt(P/ρ), and since pressure is related to temperature through the ideal gas law $v =$ sqrt($\gamma RT/M$) where R is the gas constant, T is temperature, M is molecular weight, and γ is a constant to adjust for the temperature changes due to the adiabatic nature of the gas expansion. From these equations, an increase in density will decrease the speed of sound, and an increase in temperature or pressure will increase the speed of sound.

678. B is correct. $v =$ sqrt($\gamma RT/M$) where R is the gas constant, T is temperature, M is molecular weight, and γ is a constant to adjust for the temperature changes due to the adiabatic nature of the gas expansion.

679. C is correct. Frequency always remains constant when a wave passes from one medium to the next. Since the wave travels more slowly through the air than through the tuning fork, the wavelength must decrease. $v = f\lambda$.

680. A is correct. Since waves in phase have the same wavelength, the same points of zero displacement, and coincidental positive and negative slopes.

681. B is correct. This pair of waves is 180° out of phase. Their displacements are in the opposite direction at every point, so they will only experience destructive interference.

682. A is correct. This pair of waves is in phase. Their displacements are in the same direction at every point, so they will only experience constructive interference.

683. D is correct. Since the waves pass through each other, every point of one wave will interfere with every point of the other at some time during the collision. This means that there will be moments when the summing displacements of both waves are in the same direction (constructive interference), and other moments when they are in the opposite direction (destructive interference).

684. D is correct. The two waves will momentarily experience interference as they pass through each other, and then continue on unaffected by the collision. Refraction is a change in speed due to a transfer to a new medium. Reflection is a change in direction after rebounding with a new medium.

685. B is correct. The observed frequency will be the average of the two frequencies: $(440 + 436)/2 = 438$. The intensity of this average frequency will pulsate at the beat frequency which is the difference of the two frequencies: $440 - 436 = 4$.

686. B is correct. The beat is the cyclical change in intensity which occurs at a frequency equal to the difference in frequency of the two sound sources.

687. C is correct. The period of a beat is the time between maximum intensities. The square of the pressure is proportional to the intensity. Thus, the horizontal distance between the antinodes in the diagram represents the period of the beat, which is 0.01 sec. The reciprocal of the period is the frequency: $1/0.01 = 100$ Hz.

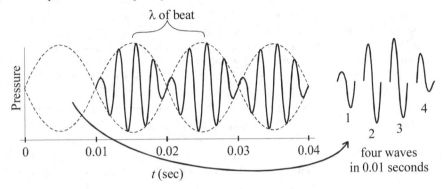

688. C is correct. Count the number of waves in a given section and divide by the time. From $t = 0$ to $t = 0.01$ there are four waves. $4/0.01 = 400$ cycles per second. (See the diagram in question #687.)

689. C is correct. The beat frequency is 100 Hz (See question #687). The average frequency is 400 Hz (See question #688). The original two sound waves differ by the beat frequency, so they must be 100 Hz apart. They also must be an equal distance from the average frequency, so they must be 350 and 450 Hz.

690. A is correct. The original out of tune A note must have been 438 or 442 since it created a beat frequency of 2 Hz with the 440 Hz tuning fork: Beat frequency $= f_1 - f_2$. When the piano string was loosened, the velocity of the wave, and thus the frequency, must have decreased: $v = \sqrt{T/\mu}$ where T is tension; $v = f\lambda$ where λ remains constant because the string length is not changed. When the frequency decreased, the beat frequency increased, so the frequency moved away from 440 Hz. Therefore, the original out of tune note was 438 Hz.

691. A is correct. The original out of tune A note must have been 438 or 442 since it created a beat frequency of 2 Hz with the 440 Hz tuning fork: Beat frequency $= f_1 - f_2$. When the piano string was tightened, the velocity of the wave, and thus the frequency, must have increased: $v = \sqrt{T/\mu}$ where T is tension; $v = f\lambda$ where λ remains constant because the string length is not changed. When the frequency increased, the beat frequency remained constant, so the frequency must have increased to 442 Hz, the only other frequency that would produce a beat of 2 Hz.

692. A is correct. Five trees pass each second. (Five trees and five spaces equal 10 m.) This is a frequency of 5 trees per second. The frequency of the flashing light and the frequency of the passing trees create a beat frequency of : $5 - 4 = 1$.

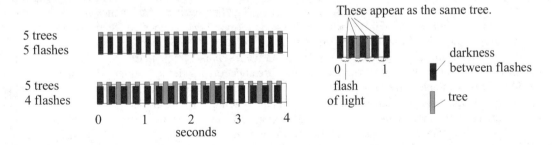

693. A is correct. See question #692.

694. C is correct. The period of a beat is the time between maximum intensities. A, B, and D show four maximum intensities in the given time. Choice C shows two maximum intensities in the given time. A higher beat frequency indicates two notes further apart.

695. C is correct. The passage says that each wave form represents the same note, and that a note is the same set of harmonics. This means that A, B, and D are not true.

696. D is correct. Choice A is wrong because the medium dictates the velocity of sound. Choice B is wrong because pitch correlates with frequency, and frequency is the same for each note. Choice C is wrong because each wave represent a single note, so there is no beat frequency. Choice D is correct. The amplitude is different for each note.

697. B is correct. The wave form shown is a combination of all the harmonics for that note. The first harmonic would have the same wavelength, and thus the same frequency and period.

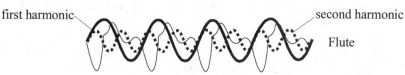

first harmonic / second harmonic / Flute

698. A is correct. From the equation $L = n\lambda/2$ where $n = 1, 2, 3\ldots$ for each harmonic, we see that the second harmonic has half the wavelength of the first, so the period is half as long. From question #967 we know that the period of the note is the same as the period of the first harmonic. Notice in the diagram above that the amplitudes are different for the first and second harmonic. It is the sum of these harmonics that gives the wave its irregular shape. For the oboe, the ratio of the amplitudes is different, so the oboe sound wave has a different shape. This is the difference that the ear perceives when we hear the same note on different instruments.

699. B is correct. From the equation $L = n\lambda/2$ where $n = 1, 2, 3\ldots$ for each harmonic, we see that the third harmonic has one third the wavelength of the first, so the period is one third as long. From question #967 we know that the period of the note is the same as the period of the first harmonic.

700. D is correct. Velocity is dictated by the medium through which the wave travels, air. Higher pitch correlates with higher frequency. Amplitude may remain unchanged. Period and wavelength must decrease with higher frequency: $f = 1/T$ and $v = f\lambda$.

701. A is correct. The addition of waves is called interference. The waveforms are created by the summing of harmonic waves of various amplitudes. The ratios of the amplitudes of the harmonic waves in a harmonic series vary with each instrument.

702. D is correct. L is 36 cm. $L = n\lambda/2$ where $n = 1, 2, 3\ldots$ for each harmonic.

703. B is correct. L is 36 cm. $L = n\lambda/2$ where $n = 1, 2, 3\ldots$ for each harmonic.

704. C is correct. $v = f\lambda$ where λ is found from the equation $L = n\lambda/2$ where $n = 1, 2, 3\ldots$ for each harmonic. $L = 15$ cm. Don't forget to convert cm to m.

705. B is correct. The oscillator sets up sound waves that become trapped in the tube. The tube resonates with one end open and one end closed. Thus tube length $L = n\lambda/4$ ($n = 1, 3, 5\ldots$). The air in the tube has a wavelength $\lambda = v/f$. Putting the equations together: $L = nv/4f$. The frequencies are in the proportion to represent the first and the third harmonic, thus when $f = 425$, $n = 1$. When $f = 1275$, $n = 3$.

706. A is correct. The oscillator sets up sound waves that strike the violin string at a certain frequency. If the frequency is a resonance frequency of the string, the energy and thus the vibration of the string increases to a maximum. The lowest resonance frequency is the longest harmonic, or the first harmonic. The first harmonic is twice the length of the string length L. From $v = f\lambda$ we get 440 Hz.

707. C is correct. The oscillator sets up sound waves that strike the violin string at a certain frequency. If the frequency is a resonance frequency of the string, the energy and thus the vibration of the string increases to a maximum. The string has several resonance frequencies which correlate to its harmonics. The resonance frequencies are given by the equation $L = nv/2f$ where $n = 1, 2, 3\ldots$ Thus n and f are directly proportional. The first resonance frequency in this example must be 440 Hz, the second 880 Hz, and the third 1320 Hz, because (from the formula) the distance between any two consecutive frequencies must be equal to the first resonance frequency. Since there was no resonance between 880 Hz and 1320 Hz, they must be consecutive resonance frequencies.

708. D is correct. It is the air in the tube that is resonating, so we are concerned with the length of the open space in the tube. This is an open ended resonance so we use the formula $L = nv/4f$ (see question #704). This means that the longest distance between frequencies is equal to $f = nv/4L$ where $n = 1, 3, 5\ldots$ If 440 Hz were the resonance frequency of the third harmonic, the tube would resonate at 147 Hz and each 247 Hz after that. The question says that it does not resonate at 147 Hz. Thus 440 Hz must be the first resonance frequency. Using the equation, $L = 19$ cm. 1 m − 19 cm = 81 cm.

19 cm

1 m

709. D is correct. From question #708 we know that these frequencies are the first and third harmonics. The distance between successive harmonics is equal to the first harmonic or 440 Hz. The fourth harmonic does not exist, so the next resonance frequency is the firth harmonic or 1320 + 880 = 2200 Hz.

710. B is correct. Don't be fooled! L here is not the length of the string L in the equation: $L = n\lambda/4$. You can see by the picture that length of the string = $3\lambda/4$ making this the third harmonic in an open ended system.

711. D is correct. If L is 1 m, then the wavelength is 2 m. One revolution represents one period, so the frequency is 2 Hz. The velocity is: $v = f\lambda$, so the velocity is 4 m/s.

712. C is correct. Usually a medium has only one frequency for a given harmonic. The difference in this case is that by increasing the frequency, we are increasing the tension in the string and, in effect, actually altering the medium. From $v =$ sqrt(T/μ) we know that increasing the tension in the string increases the velocity of the wave. From $v = f\lambda$ we know that frequency and velocity are proportional to each other. From question #705 ($L = nv/4f$) we see that velocity is proportional to string length, while frequency is inversely proportional. Thus, as velocity increases, frequency increases by the same proportion resulting in the same string length at any velocity and frequency. (Since the string is not perfectly elastic, there is a shortening of the wavelength that complicates calculations.) In this particularly odd situation, we can achieve resonance for any harmonic at any frequency on the same string. Note: It is a very good idea to try this experiment at home. A long string of beads or a telephone cord work particularly well. Try to establish different harmonics and then change the frequency.

713. C is correct. $L = n\lambda/4$. You can see by the picture that length of the string $= 5\lambda/4$ making this the fifth harmonic in an open ended system.

714. A is correct. The tension dictates the velocity of the wave. Assuming the tension remains the same, then, from question #705 ($L = nv/4f$), f must decrease when L increases and v remains constant.

715. D is correct. Simple harmonic motion is any motion that can be described with a sign wave. The yoyo is the only motion that is not simple harmonic. It is, however, harmonic motion, which is any cyclical motion.

716. C is correct. The guitar string is actually the sum of many sine waves, since each harmonic is a sine wave with a different frequency. (See questions #695-701)

717. D is correct. Any wave can be recreated by summing sine waves.

718. A is correct. Total energy is conserved in simple harmonic motion. Energy oscillates from one form to another.

719. B is correct. This is true of all simple harmonic motion. For instance, a mass bouncing on a string is in simple harmonic motion. The restoring force is proportional to the displacement and given by Hooke's law: $F = -k\Delta x$.

720. D is correct. The period $T = 2\pi$ sqrt(m/k). MCAT is unlikely to require you to memorize this equation. However, all periods of simple harmonic motion will be proportional to the square-root of some inertial component (like m), and inversely proportional to the square-root of some elastic component (like k).

721. C is correct. The period $T = 2\pi$ sqrt(m/k). MCAT is unlikely to require you to memorize this equation.

722. D is correct. This is true in all cases. However, be careful with a pendulum, where the restoring force is the weight and the inertial component the mass times the length of the string. The mass cancels leaving gravity g the resilient component, and length l the inertial component.

723. A is correct. $T = 2\pi$ sqrt(m/k). Cutting a spring in half, doubles its spring constant (Question 251).

724. C is correct. This is the frequency of motion of a mass on a spring. The frequency passes unchanged to the medium of the string.

725. D is correct. The velocity of a wave is dictated by the medium. Only a change in the medium will change the velocity. The medium of the wave on the string is the string itself.

726. D is correct. There are two important points to notice here: 1) The frequency of the wave is created by the oscillating mass. 2) The frequency of oscillations remains constant when a wave is transferred from one medium to the next (in this case, the bouncing mass to the string). Choice A is wrong because increasing Δx would not change the frequency of the mass ($f = 1/2\pi$ sqrt(k/m). The velocity is dictated by the medium (the string), so if frequency remains the same, λ remains constant ($v = f\lambda$). B is incorrect because a increase in k would raise the frequency and lower the wavelength ($f = 1/2\pi$ sqrt(k/m), but would not change the characteristics of the string which dictates the velocity of the wave on the string. C is incorrect for the same reasons. D would increase the velocity via the equation: $v =$ sqrt(T/μ) where T is tension and μ is mass per unit length. The frequency would still be dictated by the bouncing mass, so the wavelength would have to compensate for the greater velocity by getting longer.

727. B is correct. A node at both ends means this is a harmonic closed at both ends. Therefore:

$$L = \frac{n\lambda}{2} \quad \text{where } n = 3 \text{ for the third harmonic.} \qquad \lambda = \frac{v}{f} \qquad v = \sqrt{\frac{T}{\mu}} \qquad f = \frac{1}{2\pi}\sqrt{\frac{k}{m}}$$

$$L = \frac{n}{2}\frac{v}{f} = \frac{3}{2}\sqrt{\frac{T}{\mu}}\,2\pi\sqrt{\frac{m}{k}} = 3\pi\sqrt{\frac{Tm}{\mu k}}$$

728. C is correct. The force on the mass due to the spring is given by Hooke's law: $F = -k\Delta y$, so it is directly proportional to Δy. Here we distinguish Δy from Δx. As defined in the passage, x equals zero at the rest point of the spring when the mass is attached. At this point, the net force is zero, so Hooke's law equals gravity and $\Delta y = mg/k$. Because this is simple harmonic motion, energy of the mass is constant throughout the bounce. At the top of the bounce, the energy is elastic potential and gravitational potential ($\frac{1}{2}k\Delta y_t^2 + mgh$), at the bottom of the bounce the energy is $\frac{1}{2}k\Delta y_b^2$. Setting these two energies equal, we see that Δy_b is greater than Δy_t. Thus the force on the mass due to the spring is greater at the bottom than at the top.

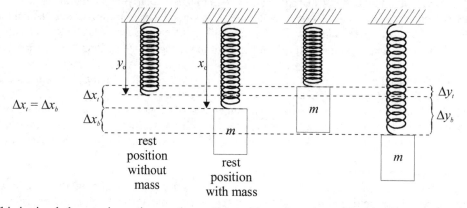

729. C is correct. This is simple harmonic motion, so the graph must be a sine wave. The kinetic energy will be the greatest as the mass moves through the resting point of the spring.

730. C is correct. This limit on the approximation of simple harmonic motion by a pendulum is typically ignored by the MCAT.

731. B is correct. $T = 2\pi\sqrt{L/g}$. Placing the pendulum on the moon would decrease g. The period of a pendulum is independent of θ and m.

732. B is correct. The net force in the direction of tension is equal to the centripetal force. The magnitude of the tension in the string is given by $\tau = mg\cos\theta + mv^2/L$. Both v and $\cos\theta$ are maximized when θ is $0°$. (Note: Don't let the directions of the arrows confuse you. The diagram below shows the vector equation; the formula, $\tau = mg\cos\theta + mv^2/L$, gives magnitude.)

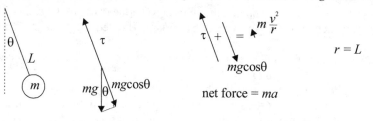

733. D is correct. From the answers to questions #731 and #732, we see that the period is unaffected by mass, and the tension is directly proportional to the mass.

734. D is correct. The tension in the string is given by $\tau = mg\cos\theta + mv^2/L$. At the top of the swing velocity is zero and the equation becomes: $\tau = mg\cos\theta$. At the bottom of the swing, θ becomes zero and the tension is given by: $mg + mv^2/L$. As θ increases, the height from which the pendulum is swung increases, which increases the velocity at the bottom of the swing. As θ increases, $mg\cos\theta$ decreases. Thus the tension increases at the bottom of the swing and decreases at the top.

735. B is correct. The mass and the cart are accelerating down the incline plane at $g\sin\beta$ (See question #182). The net force on the mass must be $mg\sin\beta$.

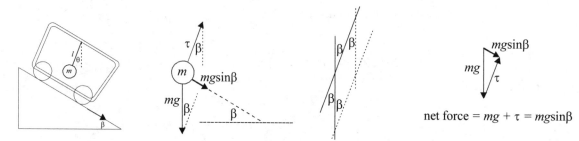

This pendulum is most easily viewed from this reference frame. In other words, rotate the page so that β is horizontal, and substitute $g\cos\beta$ for g in any equation. We can do this because in this reference frame, $mg\cos\beta$, not mg, is now the restoring force for the pendulum. If you were standing inside the box, and the box accelerated smoothly down the incline forever, you would think that up was along the string of the resting pendulum. It would seem to you that you were stationary and that your weight was $mg\cos\beta$. If you dropped a ball, it would fall at $mg\cos\beta$ and at an angle β to the left of vertical.

736. D is correct. The frame of reference has been changed. Replace g with $g\cos\beta$ in the formula for the period of a pendulum. (See question #735).

737. D is correct. The frame of reference has been changed. (See question #735). In the new reference frame, the maximum angle from the new rest position is given by $\beta + \theta$. This is how far is will swing to either side from the rest position. This means that it will swing to the left of vertical by an amount $\theta + 2\beta$.

738. B is correct. From question #736, we know that, since $g > g\cos\beta$, the period would decrease if we applied a force $mg\sin\beta$ on the cart to hold it stationary on the incline. This is because we would be increasing our restoring force back to mg. If we now push even harder up the incline, our frame of reference (see question #735) begins to rotate in the other direction and our restoring force increases still further. Imagine accelerating rapidly up the incline. You would feel pressed against the rear corner and back wall. The force would increase with increasing acceleration, with a corresponding increase on the restoring force of the pendulum resulting in a decrease in the period. This may be easiest to visualize if you imagine β to be 89°.

739. B is correct. If force (the shifting peg) is applied to the system at the same frequency as the resonance frequency, the pendulum will reach its maximum height. Think of pushing someone on a swing.

740. B is correct. Because the system is imperfect, energy is lost at a certain rate; the system is damped. The least damping will occur when the forced oscillations (the shifting peg) match the natural frequency of the pendulum.

741. C is correct. If the forced oscillations are not at the resonance or natural frequency, the pendulum swing irregularly. Again, imagine pushing someone on a swing at intervals that did not match the swing's natural frequency.

742. C is correct. From the equation given for period, we see that the period, and therefore the frequency, are independent of mass. As with any simple harmonic motion, the acceleration at any point is equal to the product of the distance and the square of the frequency ($a = -\omega^2 x$ is true for all simple harmonic motion). Therefore if the force on the board is proportional to the mass, the acceleration, and thus the distance, will remain the same when the mass is increased or decreased. The force on the board at either roller is $F = \mu N$ where N is always proportional to the mass. d is independent of the mass of the board.

743. A is correct. Period is inversely related to frequency. If L is increased by a factor of 4, period increases by a factor of 2, so frequency is decreased by a factor of 2.

744. A is correct. As the center of gravity of the board moves toward one roller, the frictional force due to that roller increases. When the force was opposite the direction of motion, the frictional force pushed the board back to the center. If we reversed the rollers, the frictional force would push the board away from the center and off the rollers altogether.

745. D is correct. If the velocity of the source were added to the wave velocity, the wave fronts would be the same distance apart regardless of source velocity.

746. A is correct. As the source approaches the observer, each successive wave is released closer to the observer. The waves travel at a speed independent of the source speed, so the wave fronts are closer together, creating a greater number of waves per second hitting the observer. The observer perceives a higher frequency.

747. B is correct. The wave velocity is independent of the medium.

748. D is correct. The Doppler effect occurs independently of the wavelength of the wave.

749. C is correct. The wind is equivalent to giving both the source and the receiver a velocity equal in magnitude and in the opposite direction to the wind. Their relative velocity remains the same. In this case, the relative velocity is zero, and there is no Doppler effect.

750. A is correct. **Most problems (probably all problems) on the MCAT concerning the Doppler effect can be solved with the formula $v/c = \Delta f/f_s = \Delta\lambda/\lambda$.** This is an approximation that is good only when the relative velocity v of the source and observer is much less than the velocity of the wave c. This equation cannot account for movement of the wave medium, like wind. For such problems, we must use the full equation: $f_o = f_s[(c \pm v_o)/ (c \pm v_s)]$. In this problem, the observer moves toward the source, increasing the observed frequency. The wind can be replaced by giving both the source and the observer an extra velocity in the opposite direction to the wind. This increases the Doppler effect in this case. The ratio of their velocities plus sound velocity is the amount by which the frequency is increased. If this ratio was 350/340 without the wind, with a 10 m/s wind the ratio becomes 340/330; a greater ratio; a greater increase. (Note: The numbers are hypothetical to illustrate the problem. The velocity of sound has been chosen to be 340 m/s.)

$$v_w$$

$$v_o = 10 \text{ m/s}$$

$$v_w = 10 \text{ m/s}$$

$$v_o$$

$$f_o = f_s\left(\frac{c + v_o}{c + v_s}\right)$$

This situation is like the observer is standing still
and the source is moving toward the observer.

751. D is correct. See question #750. In this case, if the same original ratio from #750 were 350/340, the ratio after considering the wind in the opposite direction would be 360/350; a lower ratio; a lower increase.

752. D is correct. Use the Doppler approximation: $v/c = \Delta f/f_s$. As c increases, the ratio v/c decreases and so does change in frequency due to the Doppler effect.

753. B is correct. Ballot was a stationary observer. He heard a frequency of 440 from the stationary trumpets, and a slightly higher frequency from the trumpets moving toward him. This created a beat frequency.

754. B is correct. Use the Doppler approximation: $v/c = \Delta f/f_s$. As v increases, the ratio v/c increases and so does change in frequency due to the Doppler effect.

755. C is correct. The frequency will decrease, which means the wavelength will increase. Red is on the long wavelength end of the visible spectrum.

756. A is correct. Use the Doppler approximation: $v/c = \Delta f/f_s$. $v/340 = 100/1000$. $v = 34$ m/s. The shift is an increase, so the police car is coming toward the observer.

757. B is correct. Use the Doppler approximation: $v/c = \Delta\lambda/\lambda_s$. $0.1c/c = \Delta\lambda/\lambda_s$. Since the observer moves toward the source, $\Delta\lambda$ decreases. $\lambda_o = \lambda_s - \Delta\lambda = \lambda_s - 0.1\lambda_s = 0.9\lambda_s$

758. A is correct. The source moving toward the observer results in the greatest frequency change. See question #750. When the observer moves toward the source, the frequency changes by a factor of 370/340; when the source moves toward the observer, the frequency changes by a factor of 340/310.

759. A is correct. Use the Doppler approximation: $v/c = \Delta f/f_s$. $v/340 = 2/22$. $v = 680/22$. The car must be moving away so that the frequency goes down.

760. C is correct. The relative velocities of the gas moving away from the earth and the gas moving toward the earth are equal and opposite; therefore the $\Delta\lambda$ must be the same for both but in opposite directions, and the wavelength of light coming from earth must be 500 nm. Now use the Doppler approximation: $v/c = \Delta\lambda/\lambda_s$. $v/(3\times10^8) = 1/500$. This velocity must be divided by 2 because the change in the distance of the path traveled by the light is decreased or increased by a factor twice the velocity of the gas. To visualize this, notice that the box below travels toward the man at 1 m/s. However, the path of light going to the box and back to the man changes from 20 m to 18 m in a second, or 2 m/s. This division by 2 is required here because the source is also the observer, and the wave is making a round trip.

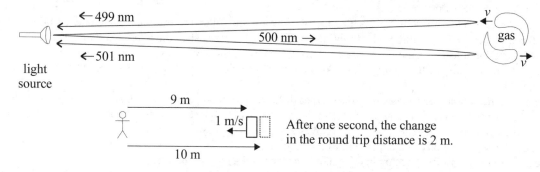

light
source

After one second, the change
in the round trip distance is 2 m.

Lecture 7

761. D is correct. The forces on the ions are electrostatic. They are Newton's third law forces; equal and opposite.

762. D is correct. The force is given by Coulomb's law: $F = kqq/r^2$. When r is doubled, F is decreased by a factor of four.

763. D is correct. The forces on the ions are electrostatic. They are Newton's third law forces; equal and opposite.

764. C is correct. The net charge of the universe is always conserved.

765. B is correct. Typically, charge comes from electrons and protons. Electrons and protons have equal and opposite charges. Electrons are negative and protons are positive.

766. B is correct. $k = Fr^2/(qq)$. F is in newtons, r is in meters, and q is in coulombs.

767. C is correct. The electric field for a point charge can be derived from Coulomb's law. It is the force per unit charge or $E = kq/r^2$. When r is doubled, E is decreased by a factor of four.

768. C is correct. Electrostatic potential energy of a charge within a field created by a point charge can be derived from Coulomb's law. It is given by $U = kqq/r$. When r is doubled, energy is decreased by a factor of 2. The fact that it is a positively charged particle does not change the energy level, but it does change the direction of the energy change. Like charges repel each other, so in this case the energy decreases as the charges separate. If they were opposite charges, the energy would increase as they were separated, but by the same amount.

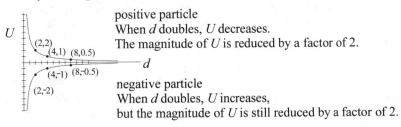

positive particle
When d doubles, U decreases.
The magnitude of U is reduced by a factor of 2.

negative particle
When d doubles, U increases,
but the magnitude of U is still reduced by a factor of 2.

769. B is correct. Coulomb's law ($F = kqq/r^2$) tells us that if the distance from a point charge is doubled, the force will be reduced by four.

770. D is correct. Typically, the electric field strength is given as newtons per coulomb, or volts per meter. (J/m)/C is equivalent to both of these.

771. C is correct. The voltage is the potential energy per unit charge. If we multiply times the charge, we have potential energy. Choice A is incorrect because F changes with the distance d, so a constant force was not applied over the distance d. Choice B is incorrect for the same reason because the electric field due to a point charge is not constant. Choice D has the wrong units.

772. A is correct. Work done per unit charge on a test charge moved from infinite distance to some finite distance through an electric field created by a point charge is one definition of voltage. Choices B and C have the wrong units. Choice D is wrong because the electric field due to a point charge does not remain constant at all distances.

773. B is correct. Only A and B have the correct units. In any electric field, voltage only changes when moving parallel or antiparallel to the electric field lines. Here, the component of the displacement that is in the opposite direction to the field is $d\cos\theta$.

774. B is correct. This is the change in voltage times the charge. See question #773 for change in voltage.

775. C is correct. A positive particle will accelerate in the direction of the lines of force in an electric field.

776. A is correct. The electric field lines are parallel, so the electric field is constant. This means that at all points in the electric field the force on the charge is constant: $F = Eq$.

777. C is correct. A force is required to move the positive charge against the electric field, thus work is done. This energy done on the charge is stored as electrical potential energy.

778. A is correct. A point charge nearby would have diverging electric field lines. A point charge far away would have field lines that were nearly parallel. Electric field lines for both choices C and D are parallel.

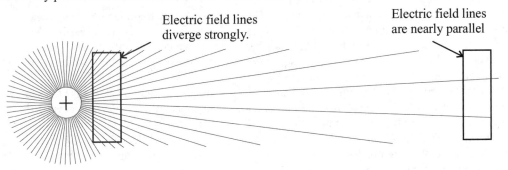

Electric field lines diverge strongly.

Electric field lines are nearly parallel

779. D is correct. There is a constant force Eq on the particle due to the electric field along the electric field lines. The acceleration will be in the direction of the net force as shown.

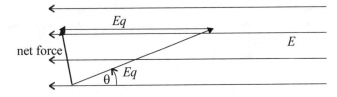

780. B is correct. The field created by a point charge follows Coulomb's law: $F = kqq/r^2$.

781. A is correct. Since the voltage along *d* remains constant, there is no change in electrical potential energy. Since velocity remains constant, there is no change in kinetic energy. No work is done.

782. A is correct. The work done is equal to the change in electrical potential energy. Final energy minus initial energy is $kqq/r - kqq/2r = \frac{1}{2}\,kqq/r$. Whether this work is positive or negative depends upon the signs of q_1 and q_2.

783. D is correct. The magnitude of the force is independent of the signs on the charges. $F = kqq/r^2$.

784. C is correct. Notice that the voltage is a property of the field, and is independent of the charge or sign on q_2. The formula for voltage is: $V = kq/r$. Voltage is inversely proportional to r. As we move against the lines of force (toward positive), voltage increases.

785. D is correct. The formula for electric field is: $E = kq/r^2$.

786. D is correct. The electric potential energy of q_2 can be converted completely into kinetic energy, so we set them equal to each other and solve for *v*: $kqq/r = \frac{1}{2}mv^2$.

787. B is correct. The outside of the neuron is positive with respect to the inside. Electric field lines point from positive to negative.

788. D is correct. Both forces follow an inverse square law, so they change at the same rate. If they are equal at one point, they will be equal at all points.

789. C is correct. The particle accelerates because electrical potential energy is changing to kinetic energy. We imagine the electric field doing work on the particle. The work done on the particle equals the change in electrical potential energy. (Electric potential energy = kqq/r.) From this equation, we see that the particle has four times as much electric potential energy at *r* as at 4*r*, but the energy is negative because the charges are opposite. Thus, the total electric potential energy of the particle has decreased by a factor of 4. (−1 J to −4 J is a decrease in energy by a factor of four. See question #768) From the work energy theorem (Work equals the change in kinetic energy when the only energy change is kinetic. [Since the electric field is doing the work, we don't count its energy as a change in energy for the work energy theorem.]) we see that the electric potential energy lost by the particle is converted to kinetic energy. Thus the particle has four times as much kinetic energy at *r* as at 4*r*. From $K.E. = \frac{1}{2}\,mv^2$ we see that the velocity must double in order to increase kinetic energy by a factor of four.

790. C is correct. The work done is the voltage drop times the charge. The voltage drop is *Ed*, where d is the distance in the opposite direction of the electric field. The electric field *E* is constant, and Y and Z travel the same distance *d*.

791. C is correct. The electric field can push a positively charged particle only in the direction of the electric field. All other motion requires an outside force.

792. B is correct. The particles that finished to the right of their position increased their electric potential energy because they increased their voltage.

793. B is correct. The work is the force times the distance opposite the direction of the electric field: $W = Fd = Eqd = 5\times2\times2 = 20$ J.

794. D is correct. Use the uniform accelerated motion formula: $v^2 = 2ax$. where $a = F/m = Eq/m$. $10^2 = 2\times(10\times10/m)\times2$

795. B is correct. The particle must be attracted to the plate. Since the particle is pulled in a direction opposite to the direction of the electric field, the particle must be negatively charged.

796. D is correct. This is projectile motion due to an electric field. It has similarity to projectile motion near the surface of the earth and similar formulas can be used. If this were projectile motion near the surface of the earth, the formula would be $v = $ sqrt(2*gh*). The velocity would be independent of the mass because the acceleration is the force divided by the mass or *mg/m*, and the mass cancels. Therefore, in the formula $v = $ sqrt(2*gh*), the g represents acceleration, which is *Eq/m* for our electric plate example. The velocity, then, is: $v = $ sqrt[2*Eq/m*)*h*].

797. D is correct. In order to follow the same path on the apparatus shown, objects only need to have the same acceleration. Their acceleration is given by $a = Eq/m$. Since *E* is constant and independent of the object, objects need only have the same mass to charge ratio in order to follow the same path.

798. D is correct. Maximum height is found from the formula $v\sin\theta = $ sqrt(2*hEq/m*). See question #796.

799. D is correct. Since the downward acceleration is *Eq/m*, increasing *m* while decreasing *q* will decrease the downward acceleration, and increase the range. See question #796.

800. C is correct. Since the downward acceleration is *Eq/m*, increasing *m* will decrease the downward acceleration and increase the maximum height. See question #796. This is because the mass of this projectile represents the inertia of the projectile, or its tendency to continue moving upward.

801. D is correct. q_2 is twice as close as q_3 to q_1, so it experiences four times the force according to $F = kqq/r^2$.

802. B is correct. Although q_2 has only half the charge, it is twice as close to q_1, therefore it creates a force twice as great according to $F = kqq/r^2$. Since the charges are all positive, the forces are repulsive and along the lines shown.

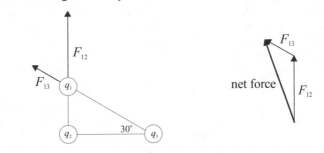

803. A is correct. The electric field inside a charge conductor measures zero.

804. C is correct. The charged sphere behaves as if it were a point charge at its center.

805. B is correct. Any disturbance in an electromagnetic field travels at the speed of light. $d = vt$.

806. A is correct. We can take the electric field generated by each quarter circle and add them as vectors. The field due to the positive section points away, and the field due to the negatively charged section points toward the negatively charged section.

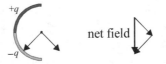

807. C is correct. Electric charge moves through both conductors and resistors; it moves much more easily through conductors.

808. A is correct. An ampere or amp is a coulomb per second, and measures current or moving charge.

809. C is correct. Net charge is the difference between positives and negatives.

810. D is correct. This is charging by induction. The positive charges are repelled off A and on to B by the positively charged rod. When B is removed, it takes the positive charges with it, leaving A negatively charged.

811. A is correct. An amp is a coulomb per second.

812. B is correct. An ohm is a measure of resistance to current.

813. C is correct. Remember that current is the flow of positive charge, and is opposite to the flow of electrons.

814. D is correct. This is Kirchoff's second rule.

815. B is correct. The voltage across the resistor is 16 V. Use Ohm's law: $V = iR$.

816. C is correct. First simplify the circuit. The two resistors are in series, so their resistance adds directly. The effective resistance is 5 Ω. Now use Ohm's law ($V = iR$) to find the current coming from the battery. 6 A comes from the battery. This current has only one path, so it must flow through both resisters. Using Ohm's law again, we have 6 A through 2 Ω gives a voltage drop of 18 volts. Notice the voltage drop over the 3 Ω resister is 3/2 that of the voltage drop over the 2 Ω resistor and 3/5 that of the total voltage. The voltage drop over a resistor in series is always in proportion to the fraction of the resistance it represents in that series.

817. C is correct. These two resisters are in parallel. Simplify the circuit using $1/R_1 + 1/R_2 = 1/R_{\text{eff}}$. The effective resistance is 4/3 Ω. Use Ohm's law to find that the current coming out of the battery is 4.5 A. The current splits at the first node where twice as much current (or 3 A) moves through the resister with half the resistance, and 3 A x 2 Ω = 6 V. An easier way to view this is to know that elements in parallel must experience the same voltage drop. The battery and both resistors are all in parallel. They all experience a voltage drop of 6 V as defined by the battery. (The voltage drop across a battery is always equal to the emf of the battery unless we consider the internal resistance of the battery, which is unlikely to be on the MCAT and would require more information to find.)

818. A is correct. Simplify the circuit:

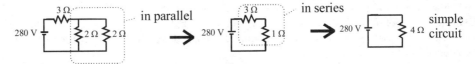

The current coming out of the battery is 70 A. 70 A flow through the 3 Ω resistor creating a voltage drop of 210 V. 70 A flow into the node and split evenly between the 2 Ω resistors. Since the resistance is the same for either path the current splits evenly. If one path had twice the resistance, it would receive half the current. 35 A flow through each 2 Ω resistor creating a voltage drop of 70 V.

819. D is correct. As the capacitor is fully charged, the current becomes zero. Since there is no current through the resister, the voltage across the resistor is zero. This makes the voltage across the capacitor equal to the voltage across the battery. The charge on the capacitor is given by $Q = CV$ where C is the capacitance. (μ indicates microfarads or 10^{-6} farads.)

820. D is correct. The battery, the capacitor, and the resistor are all in parallel, which means that the voltage is the same (10 V as defined by the battery) across each one. The charge on the capacitor is given by $Q = CV$ where C is the capacitance.

821. A is correct. Potential difference is the same thing as voltage. As soon as the capacitor is fully charged, there is no current running through that branch of the circuit. Now, solve the circuit as if the branch with the capacitor on it were not there. The 2 Ω and 3 Ω resistors are in series, so we add them directly. Their effective resistance is 5 Ω which makes the current coming out of the battery 1 A. 1 A flows through the 2 Ω resistor making the voltage drop across the resistor 2 V. The 2 Ω resistor and the capacitor are in parallel, which means the voltage drop across them is the same 2 V. The charge on the capacitor is given by $Q = CV$ where C is the capacitance.

822. D is correct. As soon as the capacitor is fully charged, there is no current running through that branch of the circuit. Thus, the potential across the 1 Ω resistor is zero. Now, solve the circuit as if the branch with the capacitor on it were not there. The 3 Ω and 3 Ω resistors are in series, so we add them directly. Their effective resistance is 6 Ω which makes the current coming out of the battery 2 A. 2 A flow through both 3 Ω resistors making the voltage drop across each resistor 6 V. The second 3 Ω resistor and the capacitor are in series, which means the voltage drop across them is the same 6V. The charge on the capacitor is given by $Q = CV$ where C is the capacitance.

823. B is correct. The initial voltage across the capacitor is 6 V. (See question #822.) When the switch is opened, the battery is on an open loop, and no long generates current. The capacitor begins to discharge. The branch of the circuit with the battery should be ignored because no current can flow through it. Thus, the 3 Ω and 1 Ω resistors are in series with an effective resistance of 4 Ω. The capacitor initially behaves like a 6 V battery producing 1.5 A across the 4 Ω of effective resistance, so 1.5 A flows through the 1 Ω resistor.

824. C is correct. The voltage sources are in parallel, so the voltage across them must be the same. The battery defines the voltage.

825. A is correct. All the resistors are in series, so the effective resistance is the sum of their total resistance; 7 Ω. Using Ohm's law, we have 4 A flowing through each resister.

826. B is correct. Below is a diagram to help you answer questions #826-841. **Don't look at the diagram until you have attempted all the questions.** The branch with the capacitor is ignored, because current only flows through this branch when the capacitor is charging or discharging. The capacitor charges or discharges in a fraction of a second after a switch is opened or closed, or after the battery is switch on or off. Using the diagram shown below and Ohm's law, the current when switch B is open is 5 A.

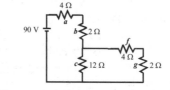

When switch B is open, the circuit looks like this.   When switch A is open and B is closed, the circuit looks like this.

827. A is correct. See question #826. No current runs through any part of the circuit not shown in the diagram above.

828. B is correct. From question #826 we know that the current through the resistor is 5 A. Use $P = i^2R$.

829. B is correct. From question #826 we know that the current through the resistor is 5 A.

830. C is correct. Simplify the circuit shown in the answer for question #826. Resistors f and g are in series making an effective resistance of 6 Ω. This effective resistance is in parallel with resistor c making a new effective resistance of 4 Ω. This new effective resistance is in series with resistors a and b, creating a total resistance of 10 Ω. Use $V = iR$ to find the current coming out of the battery; 9 A. This is the same current flowing through resistor a.

831. B is correct. Use question #830 to find the current coming out of the battery: 9 A. This current splits before flowing into resistor c. Since resistor c has twice the resistance, it receives only half the current as the other path. Resister g receives 6 A.

832. A is correct. See question #831.

833. D is correct. From the answer to question #831 we know that the current through resistor f is 6 A. Use $P = i^2R$.

834. B is correct. From the answer to question #831 we know that the current through resistor f is 6 A. Use $V = iR$.

835. B is correct. We see that the capacitor is in parallel with resistor g. Once the capacitor is fully charge, no current flows through resistor e and we can ignore it. From question #831 we know that 6 A flows through resistor g. This gives a voltage across the resistor g and the voltage across the capacitor as 12 V.

836. D is correct. When both switches have been closed for a long time, we can ignore the branch containing the capacitor because it is fully charged and no current flows through it. d and f are in parallel giving an effective resistance of 2 Ω. This is in series with g giving an effective resistance of 4 Ω. This is in parallel with *c* giving an effective resistance of 3 Ω. This is in series with *a* and *b* giving a total effective resistance of 9 Ω. According to Ohm's law, the current coming out of the battery is 90/9 = 10 A. This is the current going through *a*.

837. C is correct. From question #836 we know that 10 A comes out of the battery and enters the node above resistor *c*. Since *c* has three times the resistance of the effective resistance of the other branch (*d, f*, and *g* as configured), *c* receives one third of the current sent through the other branch. *c* receives 2.5 A and the other branch receives 7.5 A. The 7.5 A is split by *d* and *f* and then reunited a *g*. *d* receives 3.75 A.

838. C is correct. From question #837 we know that the current through *g* is 7.5 A. Ohm's law gives a voltage drop of 15 V across *g*. *g* is in parallel with the capacitor because no current flows through *e* when the capacitor is fully charged. Thus, the voltage drop is the same across *g* and the capacitor.

839. B is correct. From question #838 we know the voltage across the capacitor is 15 V. The energy stored by a capacitor is $U = \frac{1}{2}CV^2$.

840. C is correct. From question #838 we know that the voltage across the capacitor is 15 V. The capacitor will initially behave like a 15 V battery. Current will only flow over resistors *e* and *g* because the rest of the resistors are connected to an open circuit. *e* and *g* are in series, so their effective resistance is 4 Ω. Ohm's law gives the current as 15/4 = 3.75 A.

841. C is correct. This is the same as question # 840. Rather than flowing through *d*, all current will flow from *e* directly to *g* since there is zero resistance between these two resistors.

842. B is correct. The resistors are in parallel, so removing one (or adding one) does not change the voltage across the other. Thus, the current does not change.

843. C is correct. Assume that the circuit has been on for more than a second, so the capacitor is fully charged. Now we ignore the branch of the circuit with the capacitor and solve the circuit. The resistors are in series with an effective resistance of 5 Ω. Using Ohm's law, we find the current to be 1 A. The voltage across the 2 Ω resistor must be 2 V. Since the 2 Ω resistor is in parallel with the capacitor, the voltage across the capacitor is also 2 V. The energy stored in the capacitor is $U = \frac{1}{2}CV^2$.

844. B is correct. In order to answer the next three questions, you must realize that the voltage across the capacitor is a function of the circuit and not the construction of the capacitor. Thus the voltage remains constant as long as only the capacitor changes and the rest of the circuit doesn't change. The voltage across the capacitor is $V = Ed$. The capacitance is given by $C = Q/V$ and $C = A\varepsilon_0/d$. From these equations we can derive that the electric field across the capacitor is $E = Q/A\varepsilon_0$.

845. C is correct. The voltage across the capacitor is a function of the circuit and not the construction of the capacitor. Thus the voltage remains constant as long as only the capacitor changes and the rest of the circuit doesn't change. The voltage across the capacitor is $V = Ed$. The capacitance is given by $C = Q/V$ and $C = A\varepsilon_0/d$. Doubling the area doubles the capacitance. The energy stored in a capacitor is $\frac{1}{2}CV^2$. Thus energy is doubled.

846. A is correct. The voltage across the capacitor is a function of the circuit and not the construction of the capacitor. Thus the voltage remains constant as long as only the capacitor changes and the rest of the circuit doesn't change. The voltage across the capacitor is $V = Ed$. The capacitance is given by $C = Q/V$ and $C = A\varepsilon_0/d$. From these equations we can derive that the electric field across the capacitor is $E = Q/A\varepsilon_0$. Doubling *d* decreases *E* by a factor of 2. Since A is not changed, *Q* is also reduced by a factor of 2. Energy stored in a capacitor is $\frac{1}{2}QV$. Thus, energy is reduced by a factor of 2.

847. D is correct. Capacitors in parallel add directly like resistors in series. 3 + 3 + 3 = 9.

848. B is correct. Capacitors in series add like resistors in parallel. $\frac{1}{3} + \frac{1}{3} + \frac{1}{3} = 1$. C_{eff} is 1.

849. B is correct. Whenever a resistor is added in parallel, it provides an alternate path for the current causing the effective resistance goes down. The voltage is determined by the battery and remains constant. According to Ohm's law, when resistance goes down, currently goes up. $P = iV$, so power increases.

850. C is correct. In a conductor the movement of electrons is similar to gas molecules in air. The velocities vary widely in all directions. When a current is passed through a wire, there is a *drift velocity* of all the free electrons in the opposite direction to the current. Like a slight breeze moving a mass of air molecules, the drift velocity is small compared to the instantaneous velocity of a given electron. Typical drift velocities are on the order of 10^{-3} cm/s.

851. B is correct. You should know this graph for the MCAT. As the voltage across the capacitor builds, the voltage across the resistor decreases, lowering the current and the rate at which charge is distributed to the capacitor. You should also recognize that the graph of a discharging capacitor is the inverse of this.

852. C is correct. The easiest way to remember this graph is to recognize that the area under the curve is the energy stored in the capacitor: $U = \frac{1}{2}QV$. This is the formula for the area of the triangle ($\frac{1}{2}$ base times height) that is created by the straight line.

853. C is correct. For questions #853-856 simply replace the light bulbs with resistors. Anything attached to a circuit that uses up energy, whether is be a toaster, a fan, or a light bulb, is simply a resistor. The greatest current will be found with the lowest total resistance (Ohm's law: $V = iR$). The lowest resistance is when the resistors are placed in parallel. The light bulbs in Z are in parallel.

854. C is correct. See questions #853. The most light is provided by the circuit dissipating the most power. From $P = V^2/R$, we see that the most power is dissipated by minimizing R.

855. B is correct. See questions #853. The least light is provided by the circuit dissipating the least power. From $P = V^2/R$, we see that the least power is dissipated by maximizing R.

856. D is correct. See questions #853. The voltage is defined by the battery.

857. D is correct.

858. B is correct. When the voltage is the greatest, the electric field will be the strongest, and the force Eq on the charge will be the greatest. $F = ma = \Delta v/t$. Thus, the <u>change</u> in velocity of the particle, but not necessarily the velocity, will be the greatest when V is the greatest. The change in velocity is represented by the slope of the graph shown. The slope should be the steepest where V has maximum displacement. A second way to look at this is to recognize that the motion is simple harmonic motion. In simple harmonic motion, energy is shifted between total kinetic and total potential. The potential energy here is electric potential. When V is max, electric potential is max, and kinetic energy is zero (thus velocity is zero). When V is zero, electric potential is zero, and kinetic energy must be maximum (thus velocity is max).

859. D is correct. While the voltage is constant, the acceleration of the particle is constant, so the slope must be a straight line. (see question #858)

860. C is correct. In order for the particle to be moving back and forth in the middle of the plates, we want the maximum velocity to be when the particles in the middle, and the zero velocity to occur when the particle is right next to the plate. From question #859 we see that the particle begins at zero velocity.

861. D is correct. From questions #858 and #859 we know that the particle completes one full cycle or period in T seconds. The area under the curves for these questions represents the distance traveled. The first half is positive, and the second half is negative and the positive and negative distances are equal. The passage says that the particle comes very close to each plate as it moves back and forth.

862. C is correct. From question #861, we know that the particle must be touching one of the plates.

863. D is correct. From question #859 and #861, we know that the particle reaches maximum velocity at exactly midway between the plates. Since the acceleration is constant (question #859), and the particle starts from rest right next to the plate (from the passage), we can use the uniform accelerated motion equation $v^2 = 2ax$ to find the acceleration. Then we can combine $F = ma$, and $F = Eq$ to find the electric field. Finally, from $V = Ed$ we can find the voltage. The final equation is: $V = v^2dm/(2qx)$ where x is 10 m because we want the distance from zero velocity to maximum velocity, and d is 20 m because we want the voltage between the plates.

864. B is correct. We look at #859 and divide the trip into four equal sections. Since acceleration is constant (question #858 and #859) for each section, we can use $v_{avg} = (v_f + v_i)/2$. The magnitude of the average is the same for each of the sections, so the average speed is 10 m/s.

865. C is correct. For simple harmonic motion, $v_{max} = v_{rms}$ x sqrt(2). You should also recognize this (from question #858) as the motion followed by an electron in ac current. To find rms current or voltage for ac current, you use the same equation.

866. D is correct. From question # 858 and #863, we know that the voltage is proportional to the electric field, and thus the force, and thus the acceleration, and thus the maximum velocity of the particle. The time is the same, so a greater maximum velocity indicates a greater average speed, and thus a greater distance traveled. It can be seen by comparing the voltage vs. time graphs in the passage that the average voltage is greater in apparatus B.

867. C is correct. $V_{max} = V_{rms}$ x sqrt(2)

868. C is correct. Magnetism differs from electricity in that a single positive or negative electric charge can be isolated, but magnetic poles (apparently) cannot.

869. C is correct. Definitional

870. D is correct. A stationary, constant electric field does not interact with a stationary, constant magnetic field.

871. D is correct. The force on a charge moving through a magnetic field is proportional to the perpendicular component of the velocity. $F = qvB$ where v is the component of the velocity of the charge that is perpendicular to the magnetic field.

872. B is correct. You should know this for the MCAT.

873. A is correct. We typically think of electric fields as conservative. In other words, mechanical energy is conserved by electrostatic forces. For instance, we move a charged particle against the field, and it gains electric potential energy. This is not true of an electric field induced by a changing magnetic field. These fields are nonconservative and do not produce an electric potential energy.

874. B is correct. $F = qvB$ where v is the component of the velocity of the charge that is perpendicular to the magnetic field.

875. A is correct. The north pole will experience a force equal and opposite to the south pole.

876. A is correct. A current in the wire is a moving charge which will create a magnetic field. If the iron were magnetized, it would have a steady, nonmoving magnetic field which would not interact with nonmoving charge in the wire.

877. B is correct. You should recognize this as a classic ac current generator, so we need a sine wave. The current in the coil has two maximums, one in each direction, each period. These occur when θ is zero because the rotation of the coil moves electrons in the coil at 90° to the *B* field when θ is zero.

878. A is correct. $F = qvB$ where *v* is the component of the velocity of the charge that is perpendicular to the magnetic field. The velocity of the wire is perpendicular to *B* when the θ is zero. If you plugged this into $F = qvB\sin\theta$ than you did not recognize that the θ in this equation is not the same as the one in the diagram.

879. D is correct. From $F = qvB$, we can see that I and III would cause a greater acceleration of the electrons. This makes D the only possible answer. II will increase current because Faraday's law ($\mathscr{E} = -\Delta\Phi_b/t$) says that the induced $\mathscr{E}$ field (and thus the induced current) equals the rate of change in the magnetic flux Φ_b. Magnetic flux is the number of magnetic field vectors piercing through the coil. The SI unit for magnetic flux is the Weber (Wb), which is equal to one tesla/meter². A larger coil will have greater flux and a greater change in flux as it turns. You are unlikely to find flux on the MCAT. However, if you are asked about current induced in a wire, Faraday's law is an easy way to figure out whether or not the current is increasing or decreasing. If the number of lines of flux through a loop increases or decreases in time, there is a current generated in the loop due to the magnetic field. The magnitude of the current is given by the rate of change of the number of field lines.

880. A is correct. Faraday's law ($\mathscr{E} = -\Delta\Phi_b/t$) is the easiest way to visualize the current. (See #879) Since the bar is moving at constant velocity, the area of the loop is increasing at a constant rate, and the flux also increases at a constant rate. From Faraday's law, the current is constant.

881. C is correct. From Ohm's law, increasing the resistance would decrease the current. Choices A, B, and D would increase the rate of change of the magnetic flux (question #879) and according to Faraday's law(question #879), would increase the current.

882. C is correct. Use the right hand rule. If we imagine positive charge in the bar as it moves through the magnetic field, point your fingers of your right hand in the direction of the magnetic field, and your thumb in the direction of the moving charge (the direction of the moving bar). Now, with your hand in this position, push with your palm. This is the direction of the current; up through the bar. This creates a counterclockwise current in the loop.

883. B is correct. Use the right hand rule. Choose a point on the ring; let's say the top of the ring. Now let's move the ring toward the magnet instead of the magnet toward the ring because it is easier to visualize. Since relative movement is what counts in induction, moving the ring instead of the magnet won't change the results. Assume positive charge in the ring at the chosen point. As the ring moves toward the magnet, the charge moves through a magnetic field directed up the page. The fingers of our right hand point up the page, our thumb points in the direction of the moving charge, and we push with our palm. This indicates a current into the page at the top of the ring or a clockwise current. But as we move the ring past the center of the magnet and the magnetic field lines go into the south pole, the direction of the magnetic field reverses and the current reverses.

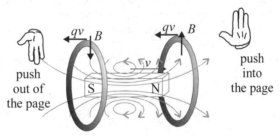

884. B is correct. The current inside the loop generates its own magnetic field. We find this field with right hand rule. Point your right thumb in the direction of the current (See question #883) and grab the ring. The direction in which your fingers wrap around the ring is the direction of the magnetic field. This field works against the field that induces the current in the ring, a phenomenon called Lenz's law.

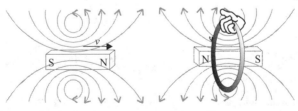

885. C is correct. The force created on the wires is due to their charge moving through a magnetic field. The magnetic field created by a wire has a net force of zero on the wire creating it.

886. A is correct. We can use $F = qvB$ and solve for *B*. *F* is in newtons, *q* in coulombs, and *v* in m/s. An amp (A) is a coulomb per second.

887. B is correct. From a common derivation of the Bio-Savart law ($B = \mu_0 i/2\pi r$ where μ_0 is a constant, i is the current, r is the perpendicular distance from a long straight wire), we know that the magnetic field strength due to a magnetic field created by a long, straight, current-carrying wire is inversely proportional to the distance from the wire. You certainly do not need to know the Bio-Savart law, and probably do not need to know this derivation. However, this is the most likely form that MCAT will use in a passage, and it helps to know the relationship between the current and the magnetic field generated.

888. A is correct. Find the direction of the magnetic field produced by each wire by using right hand rule. Point your right thumb in the direction of the current and grab the wire. The direction in which your fingers wrap around the wire is the direction of the magnetic field. The field generated by wire 1 goes into the page above wire 1, and out of the page beneath wire 1. The field generated by wire 2 goes out of the page above wire 2 and into the page beneath wire 2. Now use the right hand rule a second time to find the force generated on each wire due to the magnetic fields. Remember, the magnetic field produced by wire 1 does not affect wire 1, and the magnetic field produced by wire 2 does not affect wire 2. Point your right thumb in the direction of the current in wire 1, and your fingers in the direction of the magnetic field produced by wire 2. You palm should point upward. The force on wire 1 is upward. Point your right thumb in the direction of the current in wire 2, and your fingers in the direction of the magnetic field produced by wire 1. You palm should point downward. The force on wire 2 is downward.

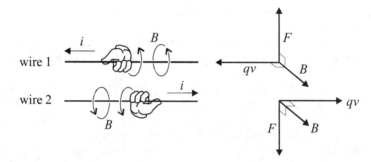

889. A is correct. See question #888.

890. D is correct. Use right hand rule to find the magnetic field (see question #884). Choices A and C create conflicting magnetic fields at the respective points. Choices B and D create only a magnetic field pointing into the page at their respective points. Since magnetic field strength is a vector, the conflicting fields of choice A and C partly cancel, while the fields of choice B and D sum only add. Choice D has more of the wire closer to the point. From question #887 we know that the field strength increases as we approach the wire.

891. D is correct. From the right hand rule (question #884) we know that the magnetic field is generated in the same direction when the currents are in the same direction. From the answer to question #884 we know that the closer the wire is to the point in question, the greater the field strength. The smaller circles are closer and thus generate a stronger electric field. D has the strongest combination of the choices.

892. C is correct. The magnetic field created by the wire will go around the wire. The north pole of the compass magnetic will point against this magnetic field.

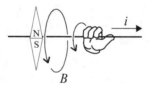

893. A is correct. The electric field portion of the wave is generated in all directions in the plane of the circular path. The magnetic field is always perpendicular to this field.

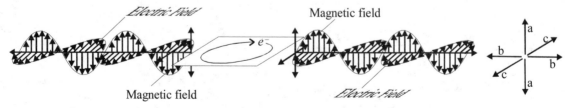

894. C is correct. See question #893. The radiation is generated everywhere along the plane.

Lecture 8

895. A is correct. Memorize this for the MCAT.

896. D is correct. Light has a dual nature: wave and particle.

897. C is correct. In electro-magnetic radiation, a photon traveling in the direction of the *pointing* vector creates an electric and magnetic field perpendicular to each other and perpendicular to the direction of propagation.

898. B is correct. You should probably memorize the wavelength parameters of visible light: 390 nm to 700 nm.

899. B is correct. The highest energy light has the highest frequency and the shortest wavelength. You should know this order from highest to lowest energy: ultraviolet, violet, indigo, blue, green, yellow, orange, red, infrared.

900. C is correct. White light is all the visible colors combined.

901. A is correct. There are three primary colors (blue, red, yellow) from which all other colors can be made. White is produced when all three of the primary colors are mixed. Black is the absence of color.

902. B is correct. We see objects as the color that they reflect.

903. A is correct. An x-ray has higher energy and thus a lower wavelength than visible light. Only choice A works. It is unlikely that you would need to memorize the wavelength of an x-ray, but you should be able to answer a question like this one.

904. B is correct. Choice C and D are wrong because light moves more slowly through any medium than it moves through a vacuum. The formula for the index of refraction is: $n = c/v$. So $1.5 = (3 \times 10^8)/v$.

905. D is correct. Glass has a higher index of refraction than air, so light bends toward the normal when it crosses from air to glass and away when it crosses from glass to air. When light strikes perpendicularly against an interface it does not refract.

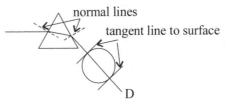

906. B is correct. You should memorize this for the MCAT.

907. C is correct. Use Snell's law: $n_1\sin\theta_1 = n_2\sin\theta_2$. $n_{air} = 1$. $\sin 60^\circ = n\sin 30^\circ$. $n = 0.87/0.5 = 1.7$

908. C is correct. This is the same as question #907 except the light is traveling in the opposite direction. Notice that the direction of light does not change its path.

909. A is correct. A higher index of refraction means that light moves more slowly and bends toward the normal.

910. D is correct. The direction of the light ray cannot be deduced (see question #908). Since the light ray bends away from the normal when passing into the object and toward the normal when passing out of the object, the object has a lower index of refraction than the surrounding medium.

911. C is correct. The light must be refracting away from the normal. When it refracts at an angle of 90°, it's angle of incidence is the critical angle. Angles of incidence greater than the critical angle will result in total internal reflection.

912. C is correct. High frequencies have greater indices of refraction. This results in chromatic dispersion as demonstrated when a prism separates white light into the colors of the rainbow.

913. C is correct. This is the same as question #912.

914. D is correct. The frequency remains constant when a wave crosses from one medium to another.

915. C is correct. The light moves more slowly in glass than air. When the light crosses to the air, the frequency remains the same and the velocity increases. From $v = f\lambda$ we know that the wavelength must increase.

916. A is correct. High frequencies have greater indices of refraction. This results in chromatic dispersion as demonstrated when a prism separates white light into the colors of the rainbow.

917. C is correct. Fermat's principle say that light will take the fastest path between two points. Snell's law gives this path. Use the angles of incidence and refraction for θ, the complements of the angles shown in the diagrams.

$$n_1 = \frac{c}{v_1} \qquad n_1\sin\theta_1 = n_2\sin\theta_2 \qquad \frac{c}{v_1}\sin\theta_1 = \frac{c}{v_2}\sin\theta_2 \qquad \frac{v_1}{v_2} = \frac{\sin\theta_1}{\sin\theta_2}$$

918. B is correct. Use the formula: $n = c/v$. $1.3 = 3 \times 10^8/v$

919. B is correct. The angle of incidence and the angle of reflection will always be the same. Light will bend toward the normal creating a smaller angle of refraction.

920. D is correct. Red light has a wavelength of 700×10^{-9} m. (You should know this for the MCAT.) From $v = f\lambda$, we have: $3 \times 10^8 = f \times 700 \times 10^{-9}$

921. C is correct. Use $E = hf$ where h is Planck's constant and E is the energy of a photon with frequency f.

922. C is correct. When light from the lifeguard enters the pool, it bends toward the normal and may bend enough for the swimmer to see the lifeguard. The reverse must also be true. (see question #908)

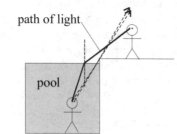

path of light

pool

923. C is correct. The brain assumes that light travels in a straight line, so the brain sees the image marked by the dotted line. (Warning: This is not an image in the sense of a real or virtual image made by mirrors and lenses.)

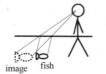

image   fish

924. B is correct. The brain assumes that light travels in a straight line, so the brain sees the image shown. (Warning: This is not an image in the sense of a real or virtual image made by mirrors and lenses.)

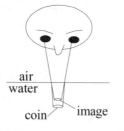

air
water

coin   image

925. C is correct. Diffraction occurs when waves move through an opening that is the size of the wavelength or smaller.

926. D is correct. The intensity of a simple harmonic, mechanical wave is given by $I = \frac{1}{2}\rho\omega^2 A^2 v$ where ρ is the density of the medium, ω is the angular frequency ($\omega = 2\pi f$), A is amplitude, and v is velocity. The intensity is proportional to the energy.

927. C is correct. The energy of a photon is given by: $E = hf$.

928. D is correct. The intensity of a simple harmonic, mechanical wave is given by $I = \frac{1}{2}\rho\omega^2 A^2 v$ where ρ is the density of the medium, ω is the angular frequency ($\omega = 2\pi f$), A is amplitude, and v is velocity. The intensity is proportional to the energy.

929. C is correct. The intensity of a simple harmonic, mechanical wave is given by $I = \frac{1}{2}\rho\omega^2 A^2 v$ where ρ is the density of the medium, ω is the angular frequency ($\omega = 2\pi f$), A is amplitude, and v is velocity. The intensity is proportional to the energy.

930. B is correct. The spreading of light within the same medium is diffraction.

931. C is correct. Reflection does not contradict the effects of a perfectly elastic collision; the angle of reflection would be equal to the angle of incidence in a perfectly elastic collision. Refraction does not seem to follow the rules of particular phenomenon. However, if the each photon were given a little extra momentum when they neared glass because they were attracted to the glass, their trajectories would bend toward the normal just before entering the glass. This would explain refraction.

932. D is correct. Intensity is proportional to energy. When the intensity of light shined upon the metal is increased without changing the frequency, there is no change in the kinetic energy of the ejected electrons. However, if the frequency of light (the energy per each photon) is changed, there is comparable change in the energy of each ejected photon. This indicates that light is formed from particles.

933. A is correct. Only accelerating charges can create electromagnetic waves.

934. A is correct. This is chromatic dispersion. Chromatic dispersion occurs because the index of refraction for shorter wavelengths is greater than that for longer wavelengths in a given medium. This means that longer wavelengths will have a greater angle of refraction when light goes from a medium with a lower of index of refraction to a medium with a higher index of refraction.

935. D is correct. This is chromatic dispersion. Chromatic dispersion occurs because the index of refraction for shorter wavelengths is greater than that for longer wavelengths in a given medium. This means that shorter wavelengths will bend more.

936. C is correct. The light will bend away from the normal when entering the air, and toward the normal when exiting the air. The blue light (higher frequency) will bend more at each interface.

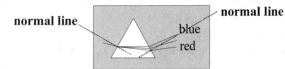

937. B is correct. Beyond a certain radius, the angle of incidence would be so great, that the light would experience total internal reflection. This angle is the critical angle. The critical angle is found by using Snell's law ($n_1\sin\theta_1 = n_2\sin\theta_2$). which in this case is 45°.

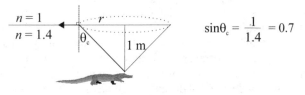

$$\sin\theta_c = \frac{1}{1.4} = 0.7$$

938. A is correct. When the waves arrive at point p, they will be 180° out of phase causing total destructive interference. The number of full wavelengths is irrelevant. Only the fact that they differ by a half wavelength, or 180°, is important.

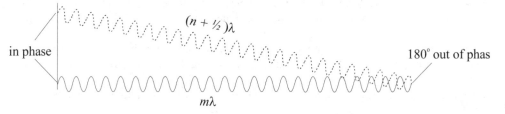

939. D is correct. This is tricky. The amplitude of the waves will double because they experience total constructive interference (see question #938). The intensity is proportional to the square of the amplitude. When the amplitude of a wave is doubled, the intensity is increased by a factor of 4.

940. B is correct. Whenever we add waves, this is interference.

941. A is correct. Only a converging lens (convex lens), and a concave mirror, can make a real inverted image in a single lens system. This is because the object must be behind the lens or mirror, and the focal points on the diverging lens and convex mirror are negative. This means that in the thin lens equation ($1/f = 1/d_i + 1/d_o$), d_i must be negative and smaller than d_o for diverging lenses and convex mirrors.

942. D is correct. If the object comes within the focal distance of a converging lens or a concave mirror, they will make virtual upright images. (See question #941.)

943. C is correct. A negative power indicates a negative focal point and a diverging lens. A diverging lens can only make a virtual image in a one lens system.

944. A is correct. In a plane mirror, the focal point is infinite. Thus, from the thin lens equation ($1/f = 1/d_i + 1/d_o$) we have: $1/d_i = -1/d_o$ The image is always virtual, upright, and the same distance from the mirror as the object.

945. C is correct. Real images are formed behind a converging (convex) lens when the object is outside the focal distance. The lens of the eye is converging with a focal distance of about 2.5 cm. Inverted real images are formed on the retina.

946. D is correct. The radius of curvature is infinite, and the focal point is equal to one half of the radius of curvature.

947. B is correct. The focal point on a convex mirror is on the opposite side to the observer, which is the negative side.

948. B is correct. No matter how far or close the woman stands, her image will form an equal distance from the other side of the mirror. Thus, the mirror will have to extend vertically downward from her eyes to half the vertical distance to her feet, and from her eyes vertically upward to half the vertical distance to the top of her head.

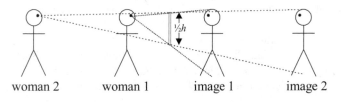

949. C is correct. The magnification is negative so, from $m = -d_i/d_o = h_i/h_o$, the image is inverted. Real, inverted images are made on the observer side of the lens, or behind the lens. From the same equation, we also know that the distance of the image from the lens is the same as the distance of the object from the lens.

950. B is correct. From $m = h_i/h_o$, we know the image is the same size as the object.

951. C is correct. from $m = -d_i/d_o$, we know that $d_i = d_o = 5$ cm. From the thin lens equation ($1/f = 1/d_i + 1/d_o$) we know that $f = 2.5$ cm.

952. C is correct. From question #951, we know the focal distance is 2.5 cm. From $P = 1/f$, we know that the power is 40 diopters. Don't forget to convert to meters. A diopter is m^{-1}.

953. B is correct. $h_i = -3$, $h_o = 6$, $d_o = 10$. From the equation $-d_i/d_o = h_i/h_o$, we have $d_i = 5$. The distance is positive, so the image is behind the lens (on the observer side).

954. A is correct. $h_i = -3$, $h_o = 6$, $d_o = 10$. From the equations $-d_i/d_o = h_i/h_o$, and $1/f = 1/d_i + 1/d_o$, we have $f = 3.3$.

955. D is correct. $h_i = 3$, $h_o = 6$, $d_o = 10$. From the equations $-d_i/d_o = h_i/h_o$, and $1/f = 1/d_i + 1/d_o$, we have $f = -10$.

956. A is correct. $h_i = 3$ or -3, $h_o = 6$, $d_o = 10$. From the equations $-d_i/d_o = h_i/h_o$, we have $d_i = 5$ or -5. The focal distance of a concave mirror is always positive. So, from $1/f = 1/d_i + 1/d_o$, d_i must be positive, and we have $f = 3.3$.

957. A is correct. By definition, all light rays going through the focal point will reflect off the mirror parallel to each other.

958. D is correct. An increase in power indicates a decrease in focal length. From $1/f = 1/d_i + 1/d_o$, we see that d_i must also decrease since d_o remains the same. From $-d_i/d_o = h_i/h_o$ we see that the image must be smaller.

959. B is correct. An increase in power indicates a decrease in focal length. From $1/f = 1/d_i + 1/d_o$, we see that d_o must also decrease since d_i remains the same. From $-d_i/d_o = h_i/h_o$ we see that the image must be larger.

960. D is correct. The negative and positive refer to focal distances. The lens with a negative focal distance is diverging and makes only virtual, upright images; a lens with a positive focal distance is converging and makes either. In the equation: $1/f = 1/d_i + 1/d_o$, d_o must be positive for any single lens system. If we plug in positive one for f and d_o we get d_i = infinity. If we plug in negative one for f and one for d_o we get $d_i = -0.5$. So we know choice C is incorrect. From $-d_i/d_o = h_i/h_o$ and the last example we see that choice B is incorrect. If we plug in 3 for d_o and positive one for f, we see that the image is minified, so choice A is incorrect.

961. D is correct. Fermat's principle states that light will always travel the shortest path in terms of time. Thus, all paths must take the same amount of time. The image forms when the photons from the object converge on the same point at the same time.

962. C is correct. Since the lenses are placed in contact, the power of the two-lens system is equal to the sum of the powers of the individual lenses.

963. A is correct. Rays striking the lens from the pseudo focal point will refract parallel. Rays striking the lens parallel will refract through the focal point. Rays moving through the exact center of the lens will not refract. (This last rule is because the lens is infinitely thin, and thus the name 'thin lens equation'.) You should have also noticed that a converging lens makes a virtual upright image when the object is placed within the focal distance. With lenses, a virtual image is on the same side as the object. Only choice A and D follow this rule.

964. D is correct. Rays coming in parallel will diverge directly from the focal point. Rays directed at the pseudo focal point will refract parallel. Rays moving through the exact center of the lens will not refract. (This last rule is because the lens is infinitely thin, and thus the name 'thin lens equation'.) You should have also noticed that a diverging lens always makes a virtual upright image that is smaller than the object. A virtual image is formed on the object side of a lens. This leaves only choice D.

965. D is correct. Rays striking the lens parallel will refract through the pseudo focal point. Rays striking the center of the lens will not refract. Rays moving through the pseudo focal point will refract parallel. You should also notice that a converging lens will make only a real, inverted image of an object outside the focal distance, which leaves only choices B and D.

966. B is correct. Rays coming from the direction of the focal point will reflect parallel. Rays striking parallel will reflect through the focal point. You should also notice that a concave mirror will make only a virtual upright image of an object that is inside the focal distance.

967. B is correct. Rays striking parallel will reflect directly away from the focal point. Rays aimed at the focal point, will reflect parallel. You should also have noticed that a convex lens makes only smaller, virtual, upright images.

968. C is correct. From the equation: $1/f = 1/d_i + 1/d_o$, we see that if the object and the image distance are the same for both lenses, they would have the same focal distance and the same power. However, the ratio of the distance of the image to the distance of the object could be the same for lenses with different powers. The same ratio would result in the same magnification, so choices A and B are true. Any two diverging lenses will produce an image smaller than the object regardless of power, so D is true.

969. D is correct. For spherical lenses, D is an incorrect statement.

970. A is correct. From the lens makers equation, the only term that will change is n_S. This change makes ($n_L/n_S - 1$) change from (4/1 – 1) to (4/2 – 1), or from 3 to 1. The power (1/f) is reduced proportionally.

971. A is correct. First choose a side on which to place the object. r_1 is convex, so it is positive; r_2 is concave, so it is negative.

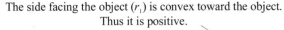
The side facing the object (r_1) is convex toward the object.
Thus it is positive.

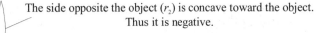
The side opposite the object (r_2) is concave toward the object.
Thus it is negative.

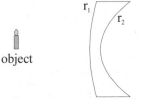
object

972. B is correct. See question #971.

973. D is correct. A thicker center converges, and a thinner center diverges. As shown below, this is a diverging lens with a thin center. A diverging lens has a negative focal length and a negative power. Both r_1 and r_2 are positive, but $1/r_1$ is less than $1/r_2$ making ($1/r_1 - 1/r_2$) negative and the focal length negative. Notice that if the object were placed on the other side of the lens, the lens would still be diverging.

r_1 r_2

object

diverging lens

974. D is correct. This is tricky, but from the equation, we see that ($n_L/n_S - 1$) would become negative, reversing the sign of the focal distance and the action of the lens. See question #936.

975. B is correct. The thickest center converges light the most and has the greatest power. If we use the thin lens equation, we must compare the term ($1/r_1 - 1/r_2$). r is infinite for flat sides. Assume that the magnitude of r is the same for the remaining curves. The side that the object is placed doesn't change the diverging or converging characteristics of the lens. If we place the object on the left of each lens, r_1 is positive for A, B, and D, and r_2 is positive for A and negative for B and C. Plugging in these values to ($1/r_1 - 1/r_2$) gives the largest value and thus the greatest power to B.

976. D is correct. In a two lens system, the image made by the first lens, is the object of the second lens. The object is inside the focal distance of Lens 1, so Lens 1 will make a virtual upright image to the left of Lens 1. This image is the object of Lens 2, and must be outside the focal distance of Lens 2 because Lens 1 is to the left of the focal point of Lens 2 and the image is to the left of Lens 1. Thus, Lens 2 will make a real inverted image to the right of Lens 2.

977. A is correct. The object of Lens 2 is the image made by Lens 1. If the object is behind the lens, the object distance is negative. (Note: This should be compared to the EXAMKRACKERS rule that says: "In a single lens system, the object distance is always positive.")

978. A is correct. The object of Lens 2 is the image made by Lens 1. If the object is behind the lens, the object distance is negative. (Note: This should be compared to the EXAMKRACKERS rule that says: "In a single lens system, the object distance is always positive.") From the thin lens equation ($1/f = 1/d_i + 1/d_o$) we see that the image must be virtual and upright.

979. C is correct. Use the thin lens equation ($1/f = 1/d_i + 1/d_o$) to find the image for the Lens 1. ($1/24 = 1/d_i + 1/6$) The image made by Lens 1 is formed 8 cm to the left of Lens 1. This is 18 cm to the left of Lens 2 making the object distance positive 18 for Lens 2. Now use the thin lens equation again to find the image for Lens 2. ($1/9 = 1/d_i + 1/18$) The image made by Lens 2 is 18 cm to the right of Lens 2.

980. C is correct. $m = -d_i/d_o$. From question #979, the magnification of Lens 1 is 1.33. The magnification of Lens 2 is negative 1. The total magnification is the product of the two magnifications, or −1.33.

981. B is correct. Use the thin lens equation ($1/f = 1/d_i + 1/d_o$) to find the image for the Lens 1. ($1/24 = 1/d_i + 1/6$) The image made by Lens 1 is formed 8 cm to the left of Lens 1. This is 36 cm to the left of Lens 2 making the object distance positive 36 for Lens 2. Now use the thin lens equation again to find the image for Lens 2. ($1/9 = 1/d_i + 1/36$) The image made by Lens 2 is 12 cm to the right of Lens 2.

982. A is correct. $m = -d_i/d_o$. From question #981, the magnification of Lens 1 is 1.33. The magnification of Lens 2 is positive 0.33. The total magnification is the product of the two magnifications, or 0.44. (Notice that magnification is not a property of the lens, but a function of where the object is placed with respect to the lens. Compare questions #982 with #980)

983. A is correct. The pseudo focal point is on the side of the lens opposite to the observer. If the object is between the pseudo focal point and the lens, the image is virtual, upright, and larger than the object. If the object is between one and two focal lengths from the lens, on the opposite side to the observer, the image is real, inverted, and larger than the object.

984. C is correct. A diverging lens makes only virtual, upright images that are smaller than the object.

985. C is correct. A diverging lens makes only virtual, upright images that are smaller than the object.

986. A is correct. From the thin lens equation ($1/f = 1/d_i + 1/d_o$), $d_i = d_o$ when $d_o = 2f$. Also, as the object gets very close to the lens or the mirror, the image also gets very close to the lens or mirror, making it the same size.

987. A is correct. A diverging lens only makes images within one focal length of itself (in a one lens system).

988. A is correct. Use the equation: $-d_i/d_o = h_i/h_o = 2$. So, $-d_i = 2d_o$. Plug this result into the thin lens equation ($1/f = 1/d_i + 1/d_o$). $1/f = -1/2d_o + 1/d_o$. $1/f = 1/2d_o$. $f = 2d_o$

989. B is correct. Use the formula given, and remember to change cm to m. $P = 1/f$. $m_\theta = 0.25(1/f)$.

990. D is correct. Angular magnification gives us the power, not the size ratio of image to object.

991. B is correct. The diverging lens would spread the light before it strikes the eye lens, and the light would refocus on the retina.

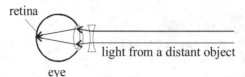

992. C is correct. The converging lens would narrow light before it strikes the eye lens, and the light would refocus on the retina. Both I and II converge light.

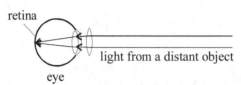

993. A is correct. The object is outside the focal length of the objective lens, so a real inverted image is created. The passage states that the image will be produced just inside the focal distance of the eyepiece. The eye piece creates a virtual upright image of the first image. An upright image of an inverted object is inverted.

994. A is correct. From $P = 1/f$, we know that the focal lengths of the lenses are 1 cm and 0.5 cm. Both focal points are positive. $s = 9.5 - 1 - 0.5 = 8$. Use the equation in the passage to solve for M. Notice from the equation and the lenses that the answer choice must be negative. Thus the answer must be A or C. Answer C is arrived at by not switching cm to m.

995. C is correct. The negative sign on the magnification indicates an upside down image.

996. B is correct. Convert the units to meters and plug into the equation in the passage.

997. B is correct. The bending of light due to a change in the medium is refraction. Light travels more slowly through the air at higher altitudes, which is cooler and more dense. This causes the light to refract downward.

998. B is correct. Light travels more slowly through the air at lower altitudes, which is cooler and denser. This causes the light to refract downward.

999. B is correct. A telescope is used for viewing far away objects. This means that the object is outside the focal distance, and the image made by the objective is a real inverted image. This image falls just inside the focal point of the eyepiece which makes a virtual upright image of the real inverted image. The final image is virtual and inverted. Notice that the magnification is always negative, which indicates an inverted image.

1000. B is correct. From the equation, we see that f_o must be larger than f_e in order to magnify the image.

1001. C is correct. Choice I is called spherical aberration. The lens makers equations and others are approximations for light rays at very small angles. Choice II is called chromatic aberration. Different frequencies refract at different angles. For choice III, the opening of the telescope is much greater than the wavelength of light, and does not create significant diffraction.